Clowns, Fools and

Popular Forms in
Theatre, Fiction and Film

Clowns, Fools and Picaros

Popular Forms in
Theatre, Fiction and Film

Edited by

David Robb

Amsterdam - New York, NY 2007

The paper on which this book is printed meets the requirements of "ISO 9706:1994, Information and documentation - Paper for documents - Requirements for permanence".

ISBN: 978-90-420-2340-6
©Editions Rodopi B.V., Amsterdam - New York, NY 2007
Printed in the Netherlands

Contents

Introduction   1
David Robb

1.   Where the Antic Sits   9
Robert Cheesmond

2.   Modern Tragicomedy and the Fool   25
Faye Ran

3.   The Postmodern Theatre Clown   37
Ashley Tobias

4.   Nietzsche and the Praise of Masks   57
Rüdiger Görner

5.   Clowning Around at the Limits of Representation: 71
On Fools, Fetishes and Bruce Naumann's *Clown
Torture*
Maxim Leonid Weintraub

6.   An American Circus: the Lynch Victim as Clown   87
Barbara Lewis

7.   The Court Jester in Nigerian Drama   101
Kayode Gboyega Kofoworola

8.   "Fratello Arlecchino": Clowns, Kings, and Bombs   115
in Bali
Ron Jenkins

9.   Scaramouche: The Mask and the Millenium   127
Stephen Knapper

10.   The Cinema of Masks: *Commedia dell'Arte* and   147
Jean Renoir's *The Golden Coach*
Des O'Rawe

11.   From Nestroy to Wenzel & Mensching: 163
      Carnivalesque Revolutionaries in the German-
      Speaking Theatrical Tradition
      David Robb

12.   Karlos Koun, Karaghiozis and *The Birds*:   179
      Aristophanes as Popular Theatre
      Marina Kotzamani

13.   The Clown as Social Critic: Kerouac's Vision   195
      Stephen Llano

14.   Picaresque Narratology: *Lazarillo de Tormes* and   211
      Edgar Hilsenrath's *Der Nazi und der Friseur*
      Bernhard Malkmus

      Notes on Contributors   231

Introduction

David Robb

By its very nature the clown, as represented in art, is an interdisciplinary phenomenon. In which ever artform it appears – fiction, drama, film, photography or fine art – this figure carries with it the symbolic association of its usage in popular culture – ritual festivities, street theatre, circus – and interacts with that artform. Literature, drama and art continually change, forging and reflecting new consciousness; the figure of the clown mutates too, but it is always there – as far as any society *needs* or allows it to be there – providing the foil for the shortcomings of dominant discourse or the absurdities of human behaviour.

The clown, like its extended family of fools, jesters, picaros and tricksters, has a variety of functions all focussed around its status and image of being "other." The clown's illusiveness, hybridity or transmutability may form a critical counterpart to rigid social homogeneity or ideological dogma; its mask may serve as a projection of a society's illusions or repressed utopian longings; or it may function as an ironic celebration of the "other" that is feared, denied and substituted by falsehoods. The clown may even serve as an image of the "other" that society hates and wishes to banish. The clown is a tool, an artificial device. Its mask, whatever form it takes – white face, red nose, grotesque features of any kind – is essentially a blank space on which anything can be projected. Author and audience conspire mutually in this projection, be it of longing, loss, love, sadness, fear, loathing or hostility. It can be a grotesque reflection of a commonly experienced contradiction, disorder, lack or void. The clown aesthetically resolves that contradiction and fills that void.

In this way the clown continually inhabits a world on the boundary between perceived opposites: structure and non-structure, reality and dream, tragedy and comedy, reason and madness. As the embodiment of contradiction itself it is perhaps then not such a contradiction-in-terms (as some may assume) to take this popular figure of anarchy, spontaneity and laughter and subject him to the rigours of academic analysis. From 4-6 September 2003 scholars and practitioners from four continents converged on the conference "Clowns, Fools and Picaros – Popular Forms in Literature, Drama and Film" at the Queen's University of Belfast. In a creative and often exhilarating atmosphere the thirty papers, fourteen of which have been specially selected for this volume, explored traditions of the clown over a variety of historical periods and cultural contexts from East Asia to Africa, Europe to North America, from Antiquity up to postmodern times.

Many articles have been written about clown figures in drama and literary studies. Of interest to this editor were, to name but a few, Richard Sheppard's article on German literature from Mikhail Bakhtin's carnival perspective,[1] Rudolf Münz's studies on Austrian Harlequins,[2] Joel Schechter's analysis of Brecht's clowns,[3] and the considerable exisiting research on Karl Valentin and Charlie Chaplin. The challenge was now, it seemed, to bring such varied investigations together at an international conference to ascertain commonalities, overlaps and differences, and, perhaps above all, to examine the role of the clown in our cultures today. This introduction will attempt to pull the threads together that connect the following chapters, which represent the latest research on the figure of the clown and its extended family.

Several of the chapters explore the relationship of the clown, fool or picaro to postmodernity. The aforementioned "blank space" represented by the clown's mask enables an arbitrariness of signification which questions assumptions about signification in general. For **Bernhard Malkmus** the picaro assumes any role he likes for his own survival; he is a "hollow man" living in "the evanescence of social structures." In his limitless transformations the picaro exposes the illusion of social role and status: these are merely adopted by people or ascribed by society in a process whereby individuality is "depersonalised." **Max Weintraub** is also concerned with signification. He argues that the clown traditionally operated in "the gaps of representation" of the circus event precisely to create an "illusion of representation's seamlessness." This illusion is shattered (and simultaneously exposed) in Bruce Nauman's postmodern video installation *Clown Torture*, which tortures the audience as opposed to humouring it. In this way Nauman's clown reveals "the machinery of representation's own masquerade." Here Weintraub sees the postmodern clown as a descendent of the socially critical jester who with his puns and nonsense-speak exposed "the arbitrary nature of symbolic conventions [...] while simultaneously staging for us as his audience our own equally contingent existence within these conventions." Nauman's clown exposes this precisely by preventing the illusion; tension cannot be resolved by laughter because the clown's torture is intolerable for the audience. Weintraub declares: "[W]e encounter ourselves *at the site of* representation's inadequacy" and refers to Nauman's comment: "No thing and no mask can cover the lack, alas."

The fact that contemporary western culture appears fixated on covering up this precise lack points to a potential crisis for the figure of the clown in post-modern times. **Robert Cheesmond** explores this in his essay "Where the Antic Sits," in which he states that the "grand narrative" of the day is "simply too terrible, *too* 'grand,' to be dealt with by such a simple figure as the clown." The individual has become too allmighty. Failure, death, sickness have become too taboo. If people cannot face up to the deficits, lacks and voids, and feel these have to be erased, filled or smoothed over, there can be no role for the popular clown. Thus, as **Ashley Tobias** states in his chapter, the postmodern clown fragments, subverts and inverts, but can only do so from a position of marginality.

But are we not merely covering up these deficits with our new, arguably more refined masks of today? **Rüdiger Görner**, in his essay "Nietzsche and the Praise of Masks," claims we employ ever more clowns and magicians to divert ourselves from our roles as "the sorcerer's apprentices of progress in civilisation." Dependent on clowns, our own masks grow accordingly "at the expense of the faces they once pretended to protect."

Several writers in the volume implicitly or explictly challenge the ambivalent, carnivalesque model as a tool for analysing fools in the modern period. Bakhtin emphasised the utopian, comical aspect of the fool's mask in carnivalesque literature of the Middle Ages and Renaissance. But already in the Romantic period he observed a more sinister development whereby madness, for example, loses its comical ambivalence and is depicted as sickness. Modern and postmodern portrayals of clowns in this volume likewise point to more negative characteristics of the mask, some indeed distinctly dystopian in nature. Görner acknowledges the traditional view of masks as "images of opposites", for example, freedom and servitude in the court jester. But he emphasises the compulsory aspect of wearing masks as a means of survival and finds instances in twentieth century literature (such as the Jewish inmates of a concentration camp who are forced to act as court jesters in Dagan's *Die Hofnarren)* where the humour is annihilated and the mask of captivity becomes the deformed identity of the people themselves. **Faye Ran**, too, observes more complex and "deliberate" traits in the fools and madmen of modernity and postmodernity. These can reflect twentieth century conditions of neurosis, displacement and self-division as in the alienated figure of Gregor Samsa in Kafka's *Metamorphosis*, who wakes up and finds he has transformed into a bug, or the townspeople who have mutated into rhinoceri in Ionesco's *Rhinoceros*. Ashley Tobias also talks of a break from clown tradition with the "clowns of defeat" in the modern, dark tragi-comedies of the Theatre of the Absurd.

It could be argued that the carnivalesque ceases to function in its traditional way in situations where "the wholeness of the world's comic aspect," as Bakhtin would say, has been destroyed.[4] **Stephen Knapper**, for example, describes Justin Butcher's play *Scaramouche Jones*, in which a clown makes children laugh who are awaiting execution in a concentration camp. The victims are temporarily elevated, but unlike in carnival, the oppressors are not brought down to earth. Knapper calls this a direct invertion of Bakhtin's concept of grotesque realism. There is a further inversion of the carnivalesque principle in the dystopian image of the corpses in the mass graves, whose "contorted faces and twisted limbs" have been covered in white lime, thus appearing as clowns. This has echoes of **Barbara Lewis's** essay on the image of a black American lynch victim who had his face painted white like a clown. Here, too, the clown has undoubtedly lost its utopian, ambivalent aspect; it can no longer subvert, but rather is purely a sacrifice of dominant cultural behaviour; an expression of containment of the "other" that is deemed frightening or inferior.

Ron Jenkins, however, sees in contemporary Balinese clowning the continuance of the tradition of the ambivalent-orientated clown who can look into and laugh at himself. This is apparent in "Topeng" chronicle plays performed as a response to the terrorist bombings of 2002 in Bali. Instead of demonising the attackers, as American culture did in the aftermath of 9/11, the clowns look to Balinese past history for constructive responses to tragedy. Thus includes addressing their shortcomings which may have contributed to the disaster. In this respect Jenkins talks of historical, personal and even fictional memory as "an essential component in the art of the clown," a description reminiscent of the narrative perspective of the picaresque figure Oskar Matzerath in Grass's *The Tin Drum*,

The survival – however relative this may be – of the figure of the clown in modern societies is surely an expression of such cultural memory. The clown has always been amongst other things a symbol of contrariness, and was instrumentalised as such in modern literature and art from the late nineteenth century onwards after a spell of relative obscurity during the Enlightenment, in which the clown's lack of reason was deemed inappropriate. Many of the chapters of this volume deal with precisely this: the reappropriation of the traditional clown or fool figure as a remnant of popular, festive ritual and practice in twentieth century culture.

Jenkins, for example, finds striking commonalities between Dario Fo, "the archetypal Harlequin" of the twentieth century, and the traditional clowns of Bali. This is evident in the unity of opposites which the clown reveals, whereby good and evil, death and life, heaven and hell are shown to be necessarilly inter-related. This is central to the Balinese tradition, but also highly reminiscent of the carnival culture, as described by Bakhtin, which was at the roots of *commedia dell'arte*. Another example is apparent in **Kayode Gboyega Kofoworola's** chapter on the role of the court jester in Nigeria. Here we again encounter the "two-world condition" recognisable from the European clown tradition, for example, the upside-down use of objects by the yan kama or in the depictions of the Wawan Sarki similar to the satyrs of Greek theatre dressed as half-men and half-goats with a phallus in front, a traditional corporeol symbol of the cycle of life and death, as is the yan kama's obsession with food, which mirrors variations of the Harlequin and Scaramouche figures of *commedia dell'arte*. Such dualism is also seen in the function of the Nigerian court jesters as priest-like intermediaries between

God and man. And with the figure of Ogun, Kofu draws a parallel with the gods in Greek tragedy who embody both creativity and destruction and possess the ability to unite both human human and supernatural realms in their persons.

Faye Ran looks at the various clown typologies that are the antecedents of twentieth century tragicomic fools. While ascertaining the aforementioned complexities and deviations in modern developments of the fool, she concludes that it is precisely his archetypal tragicomic contradiction that lends itself so well to expressing "the ambivalent self-constructs of the modern individual." The formal relevance of traditional clown aesthetics to modernist artistic approaches is encapsulated by **Des O'Rawe**. In his essay on "The Cinema of Masks" he emphasises the inspiration which filmmakers like Eisenstein and particularly Renoir found in the masks, typology and artifice of the Italian *commedia dell'arte*. Traditionally the donning of masks has focussed attention on the theme of appearance, illusion and deception (such as in comic mistaken identities), such an approach revealing, as O'Rawe states, "a truth about the appearance of truth." It was precisely this non-naturalistic artifice which such filmmakers wished to construct. It mirrored the tradition of theatre that depicted the "theatricality" of life; the artificial constructs of culture and society itself. An example of the latter is provided by Johann Nestroy's *Freedom Comes to Krähwinkel*, a precurser of modernist political comedy, which I refer to in my essay. In its parody of the 1848 revolutionary mob in Vienna "playing" out the illusion of being rebels, it represents theatre depicting such "theatricalisations" of public life.

This brings us on to the possibilities of the clown in political theatre. My essay "From Nestroy to Wenzel & Mensching: Carnivalesque Revolutionaries" concerns the survival of remnants of the *commedia* tradition in German speaking theatre from Austrian *Volkstheater* up to contemporary political clowns revue. In this respect it has parallels with **Marina Kotzamani's** examination of the survival of popular forms from Antiquity in modern popular political Greek theatre. In it she compares the grotesque figure Kargaghiozis from early twentieth century Greek puppet theatre with the character of Pistherairos in Karalos Koun's 1959 production of Aristophanes' *Birds*. Remnants of rituals and festive imagery abound such as the humour, sensuality and indeed sexual ambiguity of "the people" symbolised by the birds. But despite the revolutionary undertones a comic ambivalence reigns, an identifiable motif in modern comic political theatre and film (for example in Chaplin's *The Great Dictator*). Indeed in this there is a marked similarity to Nestroy's *Freedom Comes to Krähwinkel*. Like the clownesque rebel figure Ultra, Pistherairos is ambivalently depicted: his heroic affinity for the oppressed is matched by his ability to parody himself; like Ultra, he uses the traditional trait of nonsense-speak and a quick wit to mock officialdom and subvert power relations. But in both plays the cycle comes round; Pistherairos ends up as an authoritarian ruler himself, while the one-time revolutionary Ultra seeks the hand of a lady in marriage.

Kotzamani's essay touches on the question of the relationship between laughter and censorship, a theme that Bakhtin writes about in *Rabelais and his World* where he is concerned with a universal non-direct, parodic laughter that has been honed over the ages in altercations with authority.[5] This is well documented in this volume: Jenkins sees it in the skill of the clown Sugama at the Balinese Ministry of Religious Affairs, and Kofu encounters it in the non-personalised humour of the jester in the Nigerian royal courts. But there is evidently no recipe for a laughter that is guaranteed to escape censorship. Although, as Kotzamani states, the people's victories over authority are presented as "play," *Birds* was nonetheless banned by the right-wing government of Greece in 1959. There is clearly a revolutionary (however transient) moment in such theatrical descendents of the carnival, which can be perceived as threatening by authorities depending on the severity of the political circumstances of a performance. A parallel can be seen with *Freedom Comes to Krähwinkel*, which could only be performed in Vienna during the short period of the 1848 Revolution during which censorship was uplifted. Similarly the parody of GDR authority in Wenzel and Mensching's 1989 production *Letztes aus der Da Da eR* was deemed as containable up until the dying days of the GDR. On October 7, 1989 against the background of rioting in Berlin the revue was banned in Hoyerswerda by the secret police and the duo briefly imprisoned.

Despite the many deviations from the traditional model in the twentieth century, the attraction of the clown for many continues to lie in its comedy and the challenge to authority which it personifies. Jenkins talks about the traditional dialogic function of the clown "to re-establish an equilibrium in the face of power, which is immobile and static." **Stephen Llano** in his essay describes this function in the clown figures of the novels of Jack Kerouac. The "dialogic heteroglossia" (Bakhtin) of characters such as Dean Moriarty in *On the Road* challenge the dominant hierarchy through language; they unmask life's lies by deliberately misunderstanding and parodying the language of others. Bernard Malkmus, in developing a theory of the grotesque, relates to Jean Paul's notion of humour as "the inverted sublime" based on the idea (reminiscent of Karl Valentin) that "humorous contempt for life enables humans to overcome their 'mechanical determinism.'" And Ashley Tobias finds traditional irony and comical hybrides in the boundary crossing of the postmodern clowns Lindsay Kemp and Charles Ludlam.

The themes briefly surveyed above (and many more besides) are dealt with in length in the following chapters. These show a great deal of skill, commitment and love for the subject. It was a great boost that the Rodopi interdisciplinary series "At the Interface/ Probing the Boundaries" declared a willingness to publish a book of our findings. It was already in the process of publishing *The Clown Doctor Chronicles* by Caroline Simonds and Bernie Warren, a book about the use of clownery and laughter in the treatment of hospitalised children. This and our book on the clown in literature, drama and film have a basic aspect in common in that they present the clown in contexts with which he is not always immediately associated.

It is hoped that this volume, the editing of which has been a most rewarding experience, will stimulate further discussion on the theme of clowns. I would like to thank Karin Hirdina who gave the spark to this project when she employed me to teach a course on Forms of the Clownesque at the Aesthetics Department at the Humboldt University in Berlin from 1997-98. I am also indebted to Des O'Rawe, David Grant, Melissa Sihra, Moray McGowan, Matthias Uecker, Colin Walker, David Johnston and Jill Farquhar for their support.

[1] Richard Sheppard, "Upstairs-Downstairs – Some Reflections on German Literature in the Light of Bakhtin's Theory of Carnival," in *New Ways in Germanistik*, ed. Richard Sheppard (Providence, Oxford and Munich: Berg, 1990), 278-315.
[2] Rudolf Münz, *Das "andere" Theater: Studien ueber ein deutschsprachiges teatro dell'arte der Lessingzeit* (Berlin: Henschel Verlag, 1979).
[3] Joel Schechter, "Brecht's Clowns: Man is Man and after," in *The Cambridge Companion to Brecht*, ed. Peter Thomson and Glendyr Sacks (Cambridge: CUP, 1994), 68-78.
[4] Mikhail Bakhtin, *Rabelais and his World* (Bloomington: University of Indiana Press, 1984), 12.
[5] Bakhtin, *Rabelais*, 268-269.

Where The Antic Sits

Robert Cheesmond

1.   Introduction

> *"...for within the hollow crown*
> *That rounds the mortal temples of the king*
> *Keeps Death his court; and there the antic sits,*
> *Scoffing his state, and grinning at his pomp"*

In Richard's lugubrious musing upon his own situation and the wider condition of the body politic the "antic" begins as court jester to Death, but clearly widens his remit as the speech progresses to Richard, sovereignty in general., and the English crown in particular. I do not suggest that "clown" and "jester" are interchangeable terms. However, I think we may apply the problematic term "clown" here, to the extent that the figure of the clown/jester *fulfilled, or was conceived to fulfil, ,a therapeutic/antagonistic purpose in the regulation and moderation of individual or establishment aspirations, and collective –"societal"- assumptions and governances, deploying laughter as a principal strategy.* At least, at certain times and places in history. (The italics are intended to denote a formula which will be repeated.)

There are also some shortcuts I take in what follows in consideration of "carnival," and the "carnivalesque." Whether carnival, in the form of the Saturnalia, or the medieval Feast of the Ass/Boy Bishop/Fools, has ever been genuinely subversive or regenerative, or whether that was wishful thinking on the part of Bakhtin carrying in his train a whole raft of late twentieth century academics, is a question I pose, but do not answer. An answer I do suggest, along with others, without here posing the question, is that the English Pantomime may fairly be regarded, in some of its aspects at least, as a vestige of the European carnival tradition.[1] I will return to Pantomime in due course.

Having, not so long ago, found myself leading a series of seminars on the topic of "The Sacred Clown" with a group which included a visiting American student who was half Hopi, I am aware of many dangers in superficial cultural comparisons. Nevertheless, I here accept the use of the term "clown" to apply to performance traditions from two culture-groups which I know only through the ethnographic studies I have used as sources.

To refer back to my earlier formula, both of the examples I will use feature a *more-or-less grotesque personage adopting a therapeutic/ antagonistic position toward dominant beliefs and practices, and using humour, however, nearly approaching threat*[2], *as a strategy.*

2.   Transgressive Clowning

In 1976 Ranjini and Gananath Obeyesekere published an account of
a Sri Lankan tradition of ritual clowning. That term is theirs, their title being:
Comic Ritual Dramas in Sri Lanka, included in the omnibus series of TDR,
Psychological Release.[3] They offer a description of *Hatabambura* as:

> a long white beard trailing down to his naked belly, a set of
> large false teeth made of mother-of-pearl with two tusks
> protruding at the ends, a large "false" nose, and a pair of
> bulging eyes [wonderfully suggesting] the gross carnality
> and lasciviousness of Hatabambura – a senex-amans type
> demon.

This is of course a familiar figure to Europeans, and literati in
general, in the Pantalone from the *commedia dell'arte*, principal wellspring
of Pantomime. The first ritual described is a comic "shaving":

> The ritual commences with two *kapuralas* [priest/actors]
> entering the arena to the beat of drums [...] They dance in
> the arena, shouting, clutching at their stomachs. Their
> dancing bells jingle. They then start to introduce themselves
> in song. The songs are not so much sung as shouted and
> laced with peals of raucous laughter.

> Oh Hatabambura, holder of a warrant from the gods
> Deflect the evil influences away from us.
> The stone raft of the god is his abode,
> To banish *dos*[misfortune, troubles] the Bambura enters the
> arena

> [two more stanzas are given]

> After more dancing and horseplay one *kapurala* leaves the
> arena. An attendant places a chair in mid-arena and sits on
> it.
> Hatabambura dances around the chair for a few minutes and
> then he gets to work on the seated attendant. He dances up
> to him, throws a white cloth over the man in much the same
> way as a barber does, then steps back in a dance to survey
> his work, sharpens a razor (a strip of banana bark) and in
> superb comic mime makes soap suds with a brush (another
> piece of fashioned banana bark) and brushes soap on the
> man's face. He steps back, surveys his work, dances for a

while in the arena, snatches a piece of decorative banana
bark from one of the altars (constructed in the arena for the
gods), sharpens his razor once again, and begins to shave
his victim from the face down to the armpits. He then
shaves the chest and stops at the stomach. Next he shaves
his victim (the attendant playing the role seems acutely
uncomfortable) from the feet upwards [...]

This is perhaps enough to convey the flavour of the performance,
though there is considerably more. The ritual concludes:

[...] he hauls the man out of his chair, embraces him and
dances with him in the arena, much to the embarrassment of
his victim. What is impressive is that all the while he
performs sodomous and homosexual pranks on his victim.
While shaving, he faces his "victim" and thrusts his body
backwards and forwards. While oiling the head, he
performs a sodomous mime. He attempts to fool around
with the genitals of the victim. The sodomous and
homosexual content of the ritual is deliberate and
unmistakeable.

Another ritual described, "The Shooting of the Gun," consists of
masturbation imagery, ejaculation, orgasm and mimed imitations of
intercourse. Obeyesekeres terms it: "obscenity piled on obscenity."
These performance tropes are of similar length and structure, and
employ props, costumes and performance styles very close, to the comic
tropes of the European circus clown. The important differences are the
extremely transgressive nature of the humorous content, and the fact that the
performers are religious functionaries – we might call them priests – and that
the whole performance is located in the *Gammaduva* rituals mainly focused
upon the goddess Pattini – as close to the concept of a "mother" goddess as
makes no matter for the present purpose.
The context is serious, and sacred, however ribald the humour, and
the comedy functions also as a therapy and an exorcism for key collective
and individual problems and anxieties, including castration anxiety, fear of
impotence, and so on.
The Obeyesekeres offer an explanation why some of these common
concerns apply – or applied (their account was written in 1976) – in the
cultural context of rural Sri Lanka. For my present purpose I am content to
establish that we have here an example of *extremely transgressive clowning
within a religious context, and with a recognised and acknowledged highly*

serious purpose, that being both exorcism of spiritual anxieties, and therapy for psychological ones.

In those respects my other "other" example corresponds with the Sri Lankan one. The US Office of Indian Affairs circular no. 1665, April 26, 1921 as quoted in Jenkins and Wapp (1976) contained the following:

> The sun-dance, and all other similar dances and so-called religious ceremonies are considered "Indian Offences" under existing regulations, and corrective penalties are provided. I regard such restriction as applicable to any (religious) dance which involves […] the reckless giving away of property [...] frequent or prolonged periods of celebration [...] in fact any disorderly or plainly excessive performance that promotes superstitious cruelty, licentiousness, idleness, danger to health, and shiftless indifference to family welfare.

Jenkins and Wapp continue:

> [...] Clowns were among the principal architects of the "licentiousness" The Office of Indian Affairs was determined to eliminate, and in many cases these performances were destroyed successfully. A particular event targeted was a Hopi clown performance in which simulated copulation took place on a sacred shrine [...] Clowns such as these or the Plains "heyoka" served to remind the people that it is not the tricks of the shaman, sacred paraphernalia, or ritual observances of the people that are the repositories of power; by showing the "wrong way," the clown suggests the "right way" [...] [4]

Making due allowance for individual differences across the vast spectrum of native American cultures, transgressive clowning traditions are found everywhere:

> The Cherokee Booger Dance is an example of collective clowning which apparently predates white contact but was altered after contact to make Europeans and other non-Indians the object of satire. In that event a company of masked men ("boogers," representing non-Indians) boisterously enters an ongoing night dance party, falling on the floor, farting, hitting spectators, trying to grab the women, acting insane, and in this way improvising their

imitations. When asked their identities and where they come from they fart and give vague, nonsensical answers. When asked what they want, they say "Girls," lunge at the women and try to start fights. The Indians tell the Boogers they are peaceable and do not want to start fights.

Again the Boogers are asked their names. One by one, each man announces his name by way of a song, the words of which consist of the name repeated four times. Names of the Boogers Frank Speck witnessed in 1935 were "German" (the leader), Black (man), Black Buttocks, Frenchman, Big Testicles, Sooty Anus, Rusty Anus, Burster (penis), "Making Pudenda Swell." The dance that accompanies each song is as grotesque as the name.[5]

Among the south-western peoples, Hopi, Zuni, Mayo, Yaqui, there are strong traditions of transgressive clowning, within cultural contexts which otherwise valorise sexual propriety and modesty, particularly female modesty. Writing much earlier than Jenkins and Wapp and not so long after the dates of the bulletins of the Bureau of Indian Affairs, Parsons and Beale suggest:

> In general the clowns have a punitive and policing function in ceremonial matters and through their license in speech and song a somewhat similar function in domestic matters, ridicule being a strong weapon among the Pueblos [...] As scouts or war dance assistants the clowns have war functions. In short, through their police power, their magical power and their license in conduct, all fear-inspiring characters, social regulation is an outstanding function of the clown groups [...] Last and not least, today, certainly, the clowns amuse the people; they clown in our modern sense of the word. They attract more attention and arouse more interest than any other public performers. Dances and dramatisations are often held in a pueblo with few lookers-on, but almost everybody comes out to watch the clowns. Their practical jokes or "horseplay" and their "personalities" and indecencies violate all ordinary rules of conduct in communities where casual bodily contacts are uncommon, where people are timid about gossiping, and where sexual expression in public is very restrained. [6]

Two questions arise. Firstly, as Western society strives for its Utopia in the elimination (at least in theory) of conditions which are the cause of anxieties and inequities – the general trend which we term "political correctness," and which itself generates its own raft of such anxieties – is there a continuing place for the transgressive humour of the clown?

David Robb has discussed an example of how adoption of the mask of the clown might serve to facilitate serious, and conscious, political purpose.[7] The other outstanding example in Europe for the last decades has been Dario Fo. I would argue, however, that Fo operates at the level of middle-class intellectual culture rather than at what we might call a "popular" level. At that "popular" level, I look for, but have not found, a significant functioning tradition of "transgressive" clowning in developed (Western) culture. (I will consider whether I am right in this in due course).

Secondly, if there are no clowns to make them into fun, and the Utopia has not yet arrived in which they are eliminated, what do we do with those anxieties, neuroses, and deep-seated problems which it is part of the clown's function to express and exorcise? These are not going to go away.

For example, we have learned, or at least we strive, to disregard the difference imposed by impaired physical ability; to minimise its consequences through "access" policies, equal opportunities employment legislation, consciousness-raising programmes, and so on. We have not, however, made the condition of physical impairment *desirable*. (I exclude here such mythic "exchange of power" tropes as Odin's surrender of an eye). Speaking as a parent, I have both said, and have many times heard "that they be born healthy" as an aspiration for our children, indicating that our deepest fear is that they may not be.

In the absence of a popular, public clowning tradition, humour exorcising these fears is relegated to the playground, to bar-room, racist, sexist jokes, or to that particular type of stand-up comedy in which the comedian adopts a very different political stance from that of the clown, and whose humour therefore is not enfranchised to be "incorrect."

3.   Circus and Pantomime

The circus company *Archaos* took the Edinburgh Festival by storm in 1989, and then embarked on a highly controversial but at first successful tour of Britain, until the momentum of mythology surrounding them, that to join you had to have sex with every member of the company, that people cut their chins off juggling chainsaws, and so on, served to unite the British press and establishment in banning their performances in towns such as Bristol. This must have been a factor, though not the only one, in their eventual bankruptcy and collapse. They were, in effect, run out of town for their transgressive behaviour.

My favourite among their tropes, featured in their marketed video *Metal Clown*, has an act in which two beautiful acrobats, one male, one female, perform, nearly naked, a highly erotic acrobatic-dance to soaring and beautiful music. It is without doubt one of the most beautiful and sexy acts I've ever seen. I defy any spectator, of any sexual persuasion, not to feel, mixed with the aesthetic approval and admiration of skill to which we would all admit, some level of sexual arousal, to which we might not.

The clowns know that. Around and below the two performers, at floor level, they gather, dirty faced, clad like beetles in raincoats and corrugated iron plates, leering and simulating masturbation; telling, perhaps, a little too much truth for the good people of Bristol.

At another moment, a female clown "executes" a male, using a chainsaw to cut off his head, which rolls along the floor. With the most grotesquely lascivious expression on her face, she seizes the head, brandishes it for all to see, and then thrusts the face between her legs in frenzied simulation of cunnilingus.

Nothing in the history of Pantomime has ever approached quite that level of sexual transgression – after all, we tell ourselves, "it's for the children" – yet illustrations from the Regency period of Pantomime feature the "dismemberment" of a dandy, a beheading, or Grimaldi's red-hot poker routine. More recently, in the early 1990s, a Pantomime production was touring with the title *Snow White and the Seven Real Dwarves*. Lyn Gardner wrote in *The Guardian* (of the season at Epsom):

> The insertion of "real" into the title is a calculated marketing ploy to see off those lesser productions [...] who use children instead of small people. There is a national shortage of small people with acting skills at this time of the year [...] Political Correctness has not yet spread to the nether regions of Surrey. So far there has only been one complaint at the box office about the exploitation of people with growth deficiency syndrome. The Epsom Seven have no time for this kind of right-on cant. They don't see why they should be denied the right to make a living like everyone else. Pop, a grandfather from Watford, enjoys the seasonal break from his job as a sheet-metal worker while for full-time showbiz pros like Rusty – a man about whom it was once said "never before in the field of human entertainment has so much been given to so many by so little" – it's six weeks top-of-the-bill work. "I'm hardly going to complain about being called a dwarf. I'm 4ft 2ins. I am a dwarf," he says.

If "political correctness" has the worthy aim of ensuring that everyone is entitled to equal respect, is it not the function of the clown to remind us that we are also all entitled to equal *dis*respect?[8]

What, then, is the relationship between the clown and the Holy Fool? Clearly, the particular position of the clown as disempowered, and therefore, paradoxically, supremely empowered, permits and imposes the role of truth-sayer at the deepest level.[9] In this sense, the real or feigned affliction of madness in Shakespeare's King Lear, Hamlet, and Titus Andronicus serves a similar function. All three "become their own clown(s)" in order to express and confront horrors, fears, anxieties too overwhelming for a rational response.[10]

The "madness" of Pantomime lies in its deliberate confusions and ambiguities which equate to the "silliness" which is a required characteristic of the clown. The question remains, however: does the English Pantomime, serve, or has it ever served, an authentic (transgressive) clowning function within its native cultural context? (England, notwithstanding Pantomime's Italian origins).

Certainly, at least at key points in its history, the Pantomime was the truest expression of the popular in English entertainment (I have elsewhere considered it as such in our own time).[11] A key feature of Pantomime, however, in spite of its reputation as a repository of hallowed theatrical tradition, has always been its mutability in response to popular taste.

Pantomime history may, albeit simplistically, be divided into chunks. One – not quite the first – of these is the period during the eighteenth century when John Rich established it as the dominant popular form. Significantly Rich was a Harlequin, performing as an acrobatic trickster-dancer with many of the magical, shamanic attributes of the trickster-clown, and the little dramas in which he performed were love-denied stories in which he and Columbine would be first thwarted by, and then would triumph over, the comic pairing of Pantalone and an accomplice, rival suitor to Columbine, who eventually became, most commonly, Clown.

My argument is that, although the humour of these early pantomimes partook in many respects of what David Robb (supra) termed the "clownesque," and although there are aspects of all of our friends, jester, fool, trickster and so on, throughout the period, the authentic ("popular?" "carnival"?) humour of the clown, paralleled by the growth in the relative importance of the character, developed toward the end of the century, as did the increased focus on questions surrounding "self," "identity" and so on, and the political and economic upheavals characterised by the two Revolutions – the French Revolution and the Industrial revolution.

After the death of Rich, a kind of hiatus led in 1805/6 to the triumphant emergence of Joe Grimaldi, as Clown, more or less as England entered upon the Regency, which, socially, artistically, and politically, was a troubled time. Historians agree on the real possibility that Britain might have experienced its own revolution. It did experience riots consequent upon the unemployment and privation caused by the development of capital and industrial technology, coinciding with notions of liberty and political equality; and this was the time, until his retirement in 1828, when Grimaldi bestrode the stages of London as a gluttonous, lustful, thieving, anarchic pantomime clown, stealing food, chasing women and mocking authority, bringing the European clowning tradition as close as it has ever come to the aggressive/transgressive humour of the sacred clowns of the culture groups I have cited as examples.

Grimaldi, in the days when circus as we know it was barely a gleam in the eye of Philip Astley, imposed the garishly costumed, *grotesquely war painted* (I choose both words carefully) persona upon the rather effete, silken-costumed Pedrolino, a minor character of the *commedia* (Pierrot in the French). With his pockets always stuffed with stolen sausages, live animal produce, and his defiance of the "peelers" – the newly invented police force, Grimaldi struck a resounding chord with the mass audiences cramming the theatres in rapidly-expanding industrial London, and his imitators filled the theatres Royal in all the great conurbations peopled by workers who had deserted the land to provide the labour necessary to support the "drive for power" (Jacob Bronowski's coinage as chapter heading in *The Ascent of Man*).[12]

Illustrations showing the proliferation of dismemberments, beheadings, cudgellings and so on, date from this time, at which, paradoxically, Shakespeare's *Titus Andronicus* was regarded as unstageable. Those murders and amputations were "serious." Clown turned them into fun.

The popular theatre everywhere was dominated by the Pantomime, and the Pantomime was dominated by the clown. This could not last. As Richard Schechner has pointed out, with reference to the French Revolution, the carnival with no end leads to the terror.

Or, as Umberto Eco put it "An everlasting carnival does not work."

Or, as Angela Carter puts it "You can't keep it up, you know. No-one ever could."

As the Regency gave way politically and socially to the imposed stability and order of the Victorian age, voices were raised on all sides protesting at the lessons taught by Clown to the people, and in particular the children who were more and more seen as the target audience of the Pantomime. Writers such as Palgrave Simpson, in the pages of *The Theatre*, and even pantomime writers such as E. L. Blanchard, and J. R. R. Planche, began to call for order, some sort of aesthetic organisation, to what had become a feast of excess; and, above all, for curtailment of the amorality, the licentiousness, of the figure of clown (they didn't like Punch either). To offer Simpson as exemplar:

> Yet what is to be said? Are not all the clown's enormities
> considered merely very fine jokes, which everybody ought

to admire and applaud? Was not the "jolly old clown" applauded and admired when he taught these cruel tricks, and set these dangerous examples? and isn't he "such a good fellow!" Why, everybody laughed at him, and said so. And why should naturally cruel and mischievous urchins be blamed for what was hailed with delight in the glorious prototype?

He concludes:

[...] the character of the Clown, utterly sundered from his former odious antecedents, and existing only as a peculiar type by himself, which audiences are compelled to accept as now seen, without any previous enlightenment, is to my mind one of the most detestable beings ever set before a numerous, and especially a juvenile audience, as an object of admiration [...][13]

This article elicited an enthusiastic response later the same year from Jeremiah Wiencke: "Indeed, the harlequinade may be likened, without much exaggeration, to a non-poisonous snake, and the preceding part to a viper."[14]

The influx of music hall stars bringing their "blue" humour and Augustus Harris with his notoriously underdressed female choruses were targets for similar obloquy. They may be regarded by some as a kind of rearguard anxious to revive the fun, but there is a sense toward the end of the nineteenth century, borne out by the events of the early twentieth, that new socio-political concerns imposed a change in the pattern of knockabout comedy. Anxieties became more focused, particularly in the area of gender politics, with the emergence of the New Woman, economically independent and threatening, legislation such as the Married Women's Property Act, and the movement for Women's Suffrage. Not surprisingly, with hindsight, the Clown finally gives way in Pantomime to a new dominating figure – a clown of a different sort – the cross-dressed Dame.[15]

Significantly, however, the later twentieth century saw something of a repeat pattern. Traditional pantomime came to be seen as the repository of so many "politically incorrect" manifestations – the dwarfs in *Snow White*, Man Friday in *Robinson Crusoe*, that it again became a target. Its chief enemies were – and are – the feminist movement, identifying both Principal Boy and Dame as expressions of misogynistic fantasy, and equal opportunities consciousness-raising groups who do not want children to laugh at dwarfs.

So, to repeat my question: collectively, we have effectively done away with *Archaos*. And if now even so feeble a simulacrum of rebellion as the watered-down pantomime is not to be allowed to express the truth of our darker inner anxieties and fears, what do we do?

Where does our antic sit?

This question is of course based upon my earlier remark concerning the lack I perceive of a truly popular transgressive clowning tradition in our Western developed culture. This may well be the most debatable part of my argument, and there will no doubt be voices raised to suggest that Jim Carrey, Michael Crawford, Rowan Atkinson, John Cleese, Peter Sellers as Clouseau, Jacques Tati, Chaplin, Keaton and a host of others belong in that tradition.

This may be resolved, I think, in two ways. One of these is that many of these I would define as deployers of the "clownesque"; the second I find in the Jungian analysis suggested by Ann and Barry Ulanov (1987) positing the clown as the expression of anima, the feminine principle within male consciousness:

> The clown figure embodies a different [from the Witch] set of primordial emotions, all the feelings that are outlawed by the fixed conventions of masculine identity and the society that fixes them in place. The clown plays fool to the hero, the effeminate one to the manly, the unsettled maudlin one to the composed leading man [...] Is he strong enough to escape all the wreckage he causes, or a victim whose slightest plan must disintegrate? [...] He bodies forth the archetype of feeling defended against, a feeling that is then discovered or aroused in others by the clown but always masked in himself. Thus he depicts the dissociated or rejected female element in a man's personality that is really part of his masculinity. [16]

It occurred to me in reading this work that I had myself already identified (1994) the figure of the "feminised man" (Buttons, Wishee-Washee) as part of the central matrix of characters in contemporary pantomime. [17] Clearly, this manifestation of the clown flourishes in Western culture at many levels, and through a variety of media. On the whole, however, the comedy of these figures is at the opposite end of the (gender-related) spectrum to the machete-wielding Sri Lankan priest-clown, or the excrement-eating, girl-grabbing Cherokee Booger. Theirs is a burlesque of exaggerated masculinity and aggressiveness.

The very plurality of Western comic figures is crucial here. The "traditional" clowning traditions cited flourish – or flourished – within cultural contexts small enough to have retained a homogeneity of culture and belief. There was, in other words, the possibility still of some sort of "grand narrative" which the clown helps to stabilise and define by his (or her) humorous oppositional stance. As the "grand narratives" fragment in the pluralism of post-modern culture, so, too, have the clowns undergone their own diaspora – the Sri Lankan example provides a near-perfect model here.

I have some fears, but these are speculative and wide open for debate. One is that the "grand narratives" of contemporary experience: the growth of global corporate capitalism; the fanatical ideological conflict between East and West, Christian (atheist) and Muslim, valorised as the "war on terror," the desperate battle against environmental decline; the obscenity of world hunger; the third-world AIDS crisis; near-global concern at paedophilia, are all simply too terrible, *too* "grand," to be dealt with by so simple a figure as clown. There are some things you do not touch, as the makers of the TV programme *Brass Eye* discovered when they addressed, not paedophilia itself, but public attitudes to it.

Coda: **A Right Laugh- (and some wrong ones).**

I have a friend, a Hull woman whom I have known for about twelve years, and who would not be offended to be called working class. She's not much of a theatregoer, though she took her children to the Pantomime when they were young enough; she's never heard of Dario Fo. Sometimes she goes to "dressing up" parties, where she and her mates will wear "naughtier" (i.e. more "transgressive") clothes than they would otherwise be seen in public. Tarts and Vicars, and so on. They do this in a much less serious spirit, taking themselves less seriously than (one is led to understand), say, members of fetish clubs doing a more extreme version of the same thing. The Ann Summers party is another example of women (who, as Joseph Campbell points out in *The Masks of God* have retained, much more than men, the primal sense of "play") indulging in a little fun at the expense of their own sense of "propriety."

Describing one of these events to me, my friend (who, knowing I work in a Drama Department, had borrowed a wig from me) concluded: "We had a right laugh."

When I discussed this paper with a group of students – predominantly female – they immediately offered as an example their own participation in "Skooldaze." This is a weekly event at a local club at which women and men, mostly students, dress up in fetishised – i.e. sexualised – school uniforms (some of them as teachers) and play out St. Trinians fantasies in a spirit of sexually-charged-but-innocent fun redolent of the ambivalent humour of Pantomime. Alternatively one could argue it has more in common with the sexual role play in Britney Spears' rather more disturbing "Hit Me One More Time" video.

However cautious an attitude one might adopt to such goings-on, I note a contrast here with what used to take place, and for all I know still does, every Wednesday afternoon in the Student Union bar at Hull University.

Members of the victorious-or- not rugby club could be found standing on tables and dropping their trousers to the sweetly intoned melodies of "Four and Twenty Virgins" or "Hi zigga zumba."

Get 'em down, you Zulu warrior.

The notion of the Cherokee Boogers as a masculine, but collectively sanctioned, war society becomes more credible set against this non-institutionalised display of aggressive foolishness.

Finally, British newspapers and television news reports over a period of weeks in October/ November 2003 were full of accounts of various forms of vandalism with fireworks – rockets fired into open windows of moving cars, lids blown off post boxes, and so on. The majority of these incidents appeared to have no particular objective – they were not strategies for robbery, or organised political violence. They were pointless, and genuinely destructive, transgression. The pyrotechnic equivalents, perhaps, of the machetes which so disturbed Howard Jacobson, but wielded, not by priests in a controlled context of ritual performance, but by, it would seem, aimless young people who have, or acknowledge, no priests. Neither, I would suggest, do they have clowns, and so they "clown around" themselves.

I know of no particular interview from which to quote, but the syndrome is common enough for one to be able to guess at a possible reply, were someone to ask: "why did you do that?"

It was for a laugh.

Notes

[1] For the most entertaining exposition of this point of which I am aware, see Angela Carter's "In Pantoland", *The Guardian*, 24 December 1991, 4

[2] Attending a Sri Lankan performance for the television series *Seriously Funny,* Howard Jacobson experienced genuine terror at being the focus of attention of priest/clowns wielding machetes, which they then used to hack to pieces the "scenery" surrounding the event. The video clip included in the programme shows them to be, or to appear to be, threatening indeed.

[3] Ranjini and Gananath Obeyesekere, "Psychological Release: Comic Ritual Dramas in Sri Lanka," *The Drama Review* (1976), 8-9.

[4] Linda Walsh Jenkins and Ed Wapp Jr., "Native American Performance," *The Drama Review*, 20 (1976): 5-12.

[5] Elsie Clews Parsons and Ralph L. Beals, "The Sacred Clowns of the Pueblo and Mayo-Yaqui Indians", *American Anthropologis*, 36 (1934): 491-514.

[6] Ibid.

[7] See this volume, 161.

[8] I owe this conceit to a former student, Jane Thomas. If you're reading this, thank you Jane.

[9] See E. T. Kirby, "The Shamanistic Origins of Popular Entertainments," *The Drama Review*, 18 (1974): 5-15.

[10] See D. J. Palmer, "The Unspeakable in Pursuit of the Uneatable: language and action in *Titus Andronicus*," *Critical Quarterly* 14 (1972), 320-39.

[11] Robert Cheesmond, "Oh No It Isn't!: Toward a Functionalist (re)Definition of Pantomime", in *Popular Theatres*, ed. Ros Merkin (Liverpool: John Moores University Press, 1994), 230-231.

[12] Jacob Bronowski, *The Ascent of Man* (London: British Broadcasting Corporation:1973)

[13] Palgrave Simpson, "Stage and Street Popular Types, *The Theatre*, 1 August (1881): 230-231.

[14] Jeremiah Wiencke, *The Theatre*, 1 October 1881, 203-206. The attitude and writing are rather reminiscent of the bulletins of the Bureau of Indian Affairs.

[15] For a Freudian analysis of the function of Pantomime in the exorcism of deep-seated collective anxieties, the classic text is David Mayer, "The Sexuality of Pantomime," *Theatre Quarterly*, 4 (1974): 55-64. That text does not deal much with the clown, but with the cross-dressed figures of Principal Boy and Dame. For a more in-depth account of the Clown-dominated Pantomime of the Regency period, see his *Harlequin in His Element* (Cambridge, Massachusetts: Harvard University Press, 1969).

[16] Ann Belford Ulanov and Barry Ulanov, *The Witch and the Clown* (Wilmette, Illinois: Chiron Publications, 1987), 9-9.

[17] Cheesmond, *op cit*

Bibliography

Ashley, Kathleen M. "An anthropological approach to the cycle drama – The Shepherds as Sacred Clowns." *Fifteenth Century Studies* 13, 213 (1988): 123-135.

Beck, Peggy V. "In the company of laughter," *Parabola: The Magazine of Myth and Tradition* 11, 3 (1986): 18-25.

Charles, Lucille Hoerr. "The Clown's Function." *Journal of American Folklore* 58 (1945): 25-34.

Cheesmond, Robert. "Oh No It Isn't!: Toward a Functionalist (re)Definition of Pantomime." In *PopularTheatres?*, edited by Ros Merkin, 220-239. Liverpool: John Moores University Press, 1994.

Epskamp, Kees P. "The Political exploitation of the clown figure in Asia."

Humor: International journal of humour research 6, 3 (1993): 271-84.

Fellini, Federico. "Why Clowns?" *Fellini on Fellini*. Delacorte Press, New York, 1976, 115-139.

Fisher, R L and Fisher, S. "The Comic's Quest for Goodness." *Western Folklore* 43, 1 (1984): 71-79.

Jenkins, Linda Walsh and Wapp, Ed Jr. "Native American Performance." *The Drama Review* 20, 2 (1976): 5-12.

Handelmann, D. and Kapferer,B. "Symbolic Types, Mediation and the Transformation of Ritual Context: Sinhalese Demons and Tewa Clowns." *Semiotica* 30 (1980): 41-47.

—. "The Ritual Clown, Attributes and Affinities." *Anthropos* 76 (1981): 321-371.

Heseltine, Patricia. "Ritual as frame for the folk humour of the trickster, the fool and the clown." *Tamkang Review* Spring 13, 3 (1983): 209-226.

Hieb, Louis A. "Meaning and Mismeaning:Toward an Understanding of the Ritual Clown." In *New Perspectives on the Pueblos*, edited by A. Ortiz, 163-195. Albuquerque: University of New Mexico Press, 1972.

Honigman, John J. " An Interpretation of the Socio-Psychological Functions of the Ritual Clown." *Character and Personality* 10 (1942): 220-226.

Kirby, E.T. "The Shamanistic Origins of Popular Entertainments." *The Drama Review* 18, 1 (1974): 5-15.

Levine, J. "Regression in Primitive Clowning." *Psychoanalytic Quarterly* 30 (1961): 72-83.

Lewis, Thomas H. "Traditional and Contemporary Ritual Clowns of the Crow." *Anthropos* 77 (1982): 892-895.

Makarius, L. "Ritual Clowns and Symbolic Behaviour." *Diogenes* 69 (1970): 44-73.

Mayer, David. *Harlequin in His Element*. Cambridge, Massachussets: Harvard University Press, 1969.

—. "The Sexuality of Pantomime." *Theatre Quarterly* 4, 13 (1974): 55-64.

Mitchell, E (ed). *Clowning as Critical Practice: Performance humour in the South Pacific*. University Pittsburgh Press 1992.

Myers, C. M (ed). *Holy Laughter*. Seabury Press, New York, 1969.

Obeyesekere, Ranjini and Gananath. "Psychological Release: Comic Ritual Dramas in Sri Lanka." *The Drama Review* 20, 1 (1976): 5-20.

Opler, M. E. "The Sacred Clowns of the Chiricahua and Mescalero Indians." *El Palacio* 44, 10-12 (1938): 75-79.

Palmer, D.J. "The Unspeakable in Pursuit of the Uneatable:language and action in *Titus Andronicus.*" *Critical Quarterly* 14 (1972): 320-39.

Parsons, Elsie Clews and Beals, Ralph L. "The Sacred Clowns of the Pueblo and Mayo-Yaqui Indians." *American Anthropologist* 36, 4 (1934): 491-514.

Steward, J H. "The Ceremonial Buffoon of the American Indian." *Papers of the Michigan Academy of Science, Art And Letters* 14 (1930): 187-20.

Swain, Barbara. *Fools and Folly During the Middle Ages and the Renaissance.* New York: Columbia University Press, 1932.

Ulanov, A. B. and Ulanov B. *The Witch and the Clown: Two Archetypes of Human Sexuality.* Wilmette Illinois: Chiron Publications, 1987.

Welsford, E. *The Fool: his social and literary history.* London: Faber, first published 1935, re-published 1968.

Willson-Disher, M. *Clowns and Pantomimes.* London: Constable & Co., 1925.

Modern Tragicomedy and the Fool

Faye Ran

The tragicomic mode of literary discourse has become more prominent in the twentieth and twenty-first centuries than at any other time in Western literary history. Modern tragicomedy consists of four defining categories: an inconclusive double perspective, one lacking resolution, reconciliation or reconstitution; contradictory or ambivalent mood and effect; a problematic and often protean protagonist; and the incorporation of destabilising and non-naturalistic literary modes or strategies such as surrealism, absurdity, fantasy and the grotesque.

The dualistic nature of tragicomic creation, perception and reflection has led to a whole new sense of character – a new type of protagonist or hero. These new protagonists reject the notion of reality as a closed system with finite possibilities. Theirs is a prismatic reflection of the rational and irrational, the mundane and the transcendental, the normative and the anomalous. The ubiquitous presence of the fool in tragicomedy exemplifies our modern penchant for dialectical subversiveness and multifaceted indeterminacy. In twentieth and twenty-first century tragicomic drama, film and literature, writers, dramatists and filmmakers invariable choose antinomian protagonists – descendents and amalgams of fools, clowns and madmen to embody their explorations of the universal and tragicomic encounter of self and society. In discussing the fool as an archetype, we will come to a deeper understanding of the role of the fool in popular culture, the way in which historical anti-types have become modern and postmodern prototypes, and why the presence of a fool character in modern literature immediately locates us in the realm of the tragicomic.

There is a proverb: "God loves fools; otherwise why would he have made so many?" Fool figures run the gamut from idiot-saints to sage-fools, to inspired and uninspired madmen; devilish rogues and bedevilled jesters, half-wits and whole wits; tricksters, clowns, conjurers, butts and buffers, to the surprised and seemingly rational persons which we think we are. (Aren't we?) Indeed, fool figures are persistently evident in world drama, literature and most recently film. Fools and fool variants may be regarded as pivotal to the comprehension of twentieth century tragicomedies because, as protagonists, fools embody opposing principles and values. The fool in twentieth century drama, film and literature is emblematic of rebellion, protean passions and problematic perceptions which thematically dovetail into a tragicomic perspective of the human condition and existential malaise. The fool's philosophic "modernity" should not, however, obscure the fact that fool behaviours are based on antecedent traditions and patterns of subversion.

No definite "terminus a quo" has been established in the history of the fool figure. The fool may have originally been a village idiot, a natural fool to whom magical powers were attributed, a prophetic madman, a biological anomaly, like the first known court fool, a pygmy in the court of Dadkeri-Assi, a Pharaoh of the Fifth Dynasty, or an iconoclastic pariah. Yet, despite successive transformations in person, custom and context, fool characters are readily identifiable by their iconoclastic presence, a presence which Enid Welsford, in *The Fool, His Social and Literary History*, has aptly described as one which "dissolves events, evades issues and throws doubt on the finality of fact."[1]

The derivation of the word "fool" is the Latin "follis," meaning a pair of bellows expelling empty air; extended to persons, it implies insubstantial thought, and applied to phenomena casts doubt on the "finality" and even the "reality" of fact. Perhaps the prevalence of the fool may be accounted for through its definition as a type of person who is both ridiculous and inferior, one who represents the failure, and consequences of failure, of the individual who does not internalise or function according to given social values and standards:

> [...] fool making is a continual social process; it is safe to say that every group must have a fool [...] the fool represents values which are rejected by the group; causes that are lost, incompetence, failure and fiasco. So that, in a sense, fool-making might be called a process of history.[2]

Often portrayals of fool figures include detailed descriptions of physical uniqueness or deformity and psychic or behavioural deviation. Fools, in all contexts and varieties, are viewed as characters who inevitably "violate the human image" and come to a "modus vivendi with society by making a show of that violation."[3] Fools have often been singled out for their contrary behaviours. For example, among the American Plains Indians we find ceremonial buffoons and clown shamans chosen to provide entertainment, revelation, or both. Contrary behaviours also took the form of scatological clowning, satiric policing and mock war-games. Modern fools, unlike the Cheyenne contraries, rarely revert to normal behaviour, altruistic, or otherwise. They remain conspicuously devoted to their anti-heroic behaviour.

Although the origins and developments of the fool have been comprehensively studied[4] and described, it nonetheless remains appropriate in the course of our discussion to cull and summarise the characteristics of the fool, whenever and in whatever generic context he or she appears. A composite picture of the fool figure as an archetypal constellation will then emerge. The fool's archetypal configuration consists of the following five aspects:

Firstly, an idiosyncratic appearance and behaviour: the fool will manifest some anatomical deformation or anti-natural appearance, often in combination with aberrant psychological or cognitive functioning.

Secondly, a maladaptation: as a result of an unusual and often aberrant appearance and behaviour, the fool's adaptation may take the form of non-conformity (deliberate or not), subversiveness or rebelliousness, incompetence or deficiency. The fool will contradict, oppose or distort normative systems and ideologies. His/her conduct will evince the exact reverse of behaviour commensurate with social expectation and custom.

Thirdly, his/her function as a target and source of humour and laughter: the fool is considered a comic character in so far as he/she inevitably elicits laughter and mirth, or derision and ridicule. The fool him/herself may engage in mimicry, mockery, humorous banter, obscenity, impersonation, etc. His/her "foolishness" will consist of humour inducing or eliciting behaviours.

Fourthly, his/her marginality: the fool, whether by custom, nature or function, is traditionally a social misfit or pariah.

Fifthly, duality: folly and non-folly and order and disorder are always simultaneously implied in the person and behaviour of the fool. This duality operates as negative example, an object lesson or symbol. When we judge a fool to be inappropriate, we are, *ipso facto*, acknowledging normative standards and effectively criticising subversive or deviant behaviour. People may respond with laughter, yet harbour feelings of repulsion, pity or fear. Thus, in addition to his anomalous personality, the duality of the fool is also evinced by his/her marginal position, his/her simultaneous power and powerlessness, and the ambivalent reactions he or she evoke.

Although the fool may function in many ways, for instance, as a satirist, jester or clown, he or she will also undoubtedly serve as a catalyst for comic catharsis. Fools embody a universal need for periodic self-abandon, laughter and rebellion. In fact, fool figures, by their very presence, signal a conditionality – circumstances in which values will be tested, pitted against their opposites and reassessed for their validity and usefulness. Fools can be expected to reverse relationships between those dominant and those subservient. The court fool of the Renaissance, for example, gained recognition for acknowledged defeats which were socially acceptable as entertainment. While deprived of ordinary rights and responsibilities, the fool was placed in "the paradoxical position of virtual outlawry combined with utter dependence on the support of the social group to which he belongs."[5]

A fool's infirmity or deviance could be rationalised as inspiration, madness or clairvoyance. The possession of any striking deformity would be regarded as an evil omen or as a safeguard against malignant influences. Mixed motives and mixed reactions, an indulgence either humane or sadistic, could account for the fascination and curiosity which succoured fool types. Consider too, the paradoxical nature of "foolery" and "foolishness." Those assigned the status of the fool are no longer restricted or inhibited by custom, propriety or convention. The fool is free from moral strictures and ethical proscriptions. Yet, "to be made a fool" is a fall from grace; imperfections are exposed, credibility denied, and social approval withheld.

Fools have always been allocated to one of two categories – the "natural," and the "artificial" or "deliberate." Leslie Fiedler devotes an entire book, *Freaks*, to the study of "natural" fools. Among the unusual array of nature's mutations, Fielder discusses the *monstre par defaut*, (e.g. missing some essential features), the *monstre par exces* (possessing an extraneous appendage such as a third eye or tail), and the *monstre double*, (a hybrid being, like a hermaphrodite). Nature's freaks are those creatures which test, frustrate and confound the time-honoured boundaries between "male and female, sexed and sexless, animal and human, large and small, self and others."[6] Consequently, they are permitted free reign in "commuting" between illusion and reality, fantasy and fact.

"Artificial" fools are often Everyman types, (later to include an Every-woman), who will, due to circumstance or psychological predisposition, deliberately choose the "stance" of a fool. A role-playing fool, while maintaining his or her conspicuous impersonation, may, at any given moment, revert back to an original self. In some cases, reversion may take the form of being unmasked or exposed. Examples of characters who "play the fool" include Andreyev's masochistic clown in *He Who Gets Slapped,* Shakespeare's blustering Falstaff, Cervantes' chivalric Don Quixote and Dostoevsky's brazen buffoon, the father in *The Brothers Karamazov*. An "artificial" fool may also be a "fool-actor," or a professional who counterfeits folly for entertainment or personal gain. For example, Jacques in William Shakespeare's *As You Like It* is desirous of being dubbed a fool in order that he might practice folly. Jacques would most readily act the fool: "O that I were a fool/ I am ambitious for a motley coat," if, by his foolery, the world could be cured of its many ills, and he, perhaps, of his own "humorous sadness" (VI; 1 17):

> Invest me in my motley, give me leave
> To speak my mind and I will through and through
> Cleanse the foul body of th' infected world,
> If they patiently receive my medicine.[7]

The twentieth century fool, however, will be a hybrid creature, an involuntary and very deliberate fool. *The Tin Drum,* (1959), by Gunter Grass is an excellent example of a modern novel whose central protagonist is a "natural" fool – a priapean, lunatic, drum-playing dwarf, a *monstre par defaut* named Oscar, whose voice can shatter glass – and an "artificial" fool who allows himself to be committed to a lunatic asylum for a murder he did not commit, hence, a deliberate fool. Oscar describes his life as a picaresque parody of a "percussive" Pied Piper who leads people nowhere.

Both natural and deliberate fools behave capriciously, eccentrically, provocatively, and sometimes more rationally than one might care to admit. Deliberate or artificial fools are those individuals who avail themselves of a constructed or crafted persona with the help of costume, mask or make-up. In fact, the very word "mask" is derived from the Arabic, *maskharat*, meaning "clown." Masks have the power to attract or repel, submerge the authentic identity of the actor or invest the wearer with special power and privilege. As such, masks and make-up have been strongly been associated with fool and clown characters from the face masks worn of Balinese clowns, Kawakiutl fool dancers, members of the Iroquois False Face Society and *commedia dell'arte* characters to the make-up of the Roman mimes, American blackface minstrels and white moon-faced French Pierrots.

The *commedia dell'arte*, a form of improvised spectacle theatre played by professional actors in *commedia* companies, became known as the "Comedy of Masks."[8] *Commedia* portrayed a chaotic world, but a world capable of moral reconstruction, a world of merriment and happy endings where good triumphed over evil. The majority of performers wore masks to establish stock characters, i.e. fixed character types. The word "type," derived from the Latin *typus,* meaning image or model, implies familiar visual, conceptual or structural forms. The masquerade element, its physical and emotional transvestitism, accorded actors the power and privilege of their adopted roles. In the twentieth century, actors both discerned and added an additional vantage. They realised the power and potential of disguise in permitting an "inside take" and hence, a "double take." It is a double take in the psychological sense that it allows the self to contradict itself, to become another self, or be two selves simultaneously. Two prime examples of this include Billy Wilder's famous gender masquerade film *Some Like it Hot*, 1959, and Sydney Pollack's film *Tootsie*, 1982, starring Dustin Hoffmann. In *Some Like it Hot*, actors Jack Lemmon and Tony Curtis play two heterosexual musicians who, in order to escape from Chicago mobsters, join an all girls' band – as girls. Curtis falls in love with Marilyn Monroe and plays a triple role (musician disguised as a girl, disguised as a playboy millionaire). Curtis essentially remains true to his original self, while Lemmon, proceeds to "live" his role. He begins to look foolish when he takes his wig off, and much to his own surprise, feels uncomfortable resuming his original persona. When clown millionaire Joe E. Brown proposes marriage, Lemmon regretfully laments: "I'm a guy, I'm a guy. I wish I was dead." In the film, *Tootsie,* Dustin Hoffman, a real life actor, plays an actor playing an actress. Much to his surprise and chagrin, the actor's actor discovers that he is more successful and popular as a woman than as a man. In the end, however, the character reverts to his primary role, having discovered that "being a woman" has ultimately made him a better man.

Humour itself is often judged by the efficacy of its "mask," that is, the efficacy of a disguise to mask hostile and aggressive impulses. A disguise "fails" when a joke fails to elicit laughter. It becomes obvious that strong feelings of resentment, bitterness, scorn or contempt are actually present. There are even socially sanctioned "everyday life" opportunities to engage in disguise, duplicity and trickery. In the United States and the United Kingdom, April first, "April Fool's Day," has been specially designated as a "fool holiday." Practical jokes, aggressive pranks and playful duplicities are permitted. Any and all persons may be tricked or "fooled."

Comic "unmasking" may take the form of tragicomic or jocular self-exposure, such as may be found in Francois Truffaut's confessional comedy, *Day for Night* (1973), where Truffaut plays himself – a harried director embroiled in the behind-the-scenes chaos of making a film; or in John Barth's book, *Lost in the Funhouse* (1969), where the author describes his own creative processes – his processes of feeling, thinking, remembering and writing. Foolery is often dualistic as regards the nature of the created fool and the author who may "disguise" or present himself as a fool character, or as regards a character who is depicted as a fool-creator, that is, as a fictive author of fool characters.

R. J. Broadbent, in his book, *A History of Pantomime*, presents a useful typology of fools and clowns in the Middle Ages. He makes a significant distinction between the fool figure who was considered a mere idiot or witty hireling retained to entertain his masters as a pet companion, and the clown figure, a more complex, polymorphic character. Broadbent sorted fools and clowns into nine categories:

1. The general domestic fool, termed often but improperly clown; described by Puttenham as a "buffoune or counterfeet foole."
2. The clown, who was a mere country booby, or a witty rustic.
3. The female fool, who was generally an idiot.
4. The city or corporation fool, an assistant in public entertainments.
5. The tavern fool, retained to amuse customers.
6. The fool of the ancient mysteries and moralities, otherwise known as "the Vice."
7. The fool in the old dumb shows, often alluded to by Shakespeare.
8. The fool in the Whitsun ales and Morris dance.
9. The mountebank's fool, or Merry Andrew.[9]

There are three broads categories into which we may now sort these clown and fool types: firstly, hired fools, comparable to twentieth century stand-up comedians and comic actor/celebrities; secondly, performers known for their humorous dramatic roles, or their enactment of a specific comic character, such as Pierre Gringoire's Mere Sotte, Joseph Grimaldi's "Joey" clown; and Chaplin's little tramp character; and thirdly, "natural" fools, systematised according to physical or mental aberrations. However, there remains embedded in Broadbent's codification without precise mention, a fourth category based on the perennial appearance of a familiar character that displays a combination of characteristics from several different "types" – the diabolic or scoundrel fool, a trickster type who is not a devil or vice figure.

In the twentieth century, it is more likely that the fool as devil or vice figure will appear as a trickster or rogue rather than as a genuinely demonic malefactor. Isaac Bashevis Singer's short story "The Last Demon" begins with the humorous frustration of a miscreant demon: "I, a demon, bear witness that there are no more demons left. Why demons, when man himself is a demon. Why persuade evil to someone who is already convinced."[10] Human moral conduct has deteriorated to such a degree that "people want to sin beyond their capacities. They martyr themselves for the most trivial of sins."[11] The whining, self-pitying demon ironically feels isolated and useless for "reasons contrary to reason" – the polymorphous perversities of mankind have usurped his uniqueness. Our demon will witness the destruction of Poland, the Jews and the European Jewish community and find himself in world of horror beyond "devilish" comprehension. In a world without good and evil demons, *ipso facto*, vanish. Singer has subtly invoked the holocaust, an evil beyond evil, an unequalled, indescribable and all encompassing annihilation of morality. In an absurd and unpardonably cruel world, a world filled with ineffable atrocities there can be no holy fools, no laughing fools, no vixen fools. All that remains is prodigious chaos and dissolution. When Man usurps the demonic, Man becomes the demonic.

Feeling "foolish" or fear of being one creates an entire literature of fool characters who try to avoid foolishness only to become more foolish in doing so. The tragicomic, ineffectual and self-victimising protagonist of the twentieth century is the excessively self-aware fool who combines Freudian complexes with Kafkaesque insecurities. In both Italo Svevo's the *Confessions of Zeno* (1923) and Philip Roth's *Portnoy's Complaint* (1969), we see tragicomic paroxysms of rationalism run amok. In *The Confessions of Zeno,* the central character suffers from what Dante, in *The Inferno,* termed the reprobate sin of "*vilta*" – i.e. cowardly irresoluteness and pusillanimity. Zeno fails to satisfy his own expectations as well as those of his significant others, tragicomically spending his life compulsively rationalising infidelities and justifying his lack of determination and will power. Philip Roth's most famous and noteworthy tragicomic fool figure, Portnoy, is an angst-ridden trickster-like figure *kvetching* his way through Roth's wry Borscht Belt styled *Bildungsroman.* Guilt serves as the novel's prime comic catalyst, neurotic outpourings as its rhetoric. Portnoy's quest for the Self becomes confused with the quest for "a perfect lay." The heroic combines with the pornographic stand-up which merges into psychoanalytic babble as the self-conscious tragicomic fool seeks catharsis and redemption via folly and failure.

Although female fools share many of the male-fool categories and behaviours, they also add special dual-natured variants of their own: the virgin, old maid, sorceress, bawd, matchmaker, femme fatale, scheming or domineering wife, overbearing mother or mother-in-law, nurse, gossip, trollop, dizzy damsel, widow, feminist, and failed fashionista. Among the most celebrated examples are Chaucer's Wife of Bath who celebrates her sexuality and the fact that she has outlived five husbands; Rabelais' Gargamelle who gives birth, after an eleven month gestation period through her ear, to the giant, Gargantua; Shakespeare's bawdy, busybody Nurse in *Romeo and Juliet;* and Sheridan's bumbling and loquacious Mrs. Malaprop in *The Rivals* and in the twentieth century, the innocent and simple Gelsomina in *La Strada,* the hallucinating Juliet in *Juliet of the Spirits,* and the famed *Chic-Lit* anti-heroine, Bridget Jones. Courtship and marriage, betrayal and divorce have always provided comedians and tragedians with ample fool material.

Tommaso Landolfi's short story "Gogol's Wife" (1963), is a post-humanist tragicomic love story, a combination real-life and comic book reminiscence in which actual voices, (i.e. the author's), become fused or suffused into fictive character voices. The author in fact becomes a character-author. He masquerades as the first person narrator, a biographer, who has before him the difficult task of exposing some problematic information about his "good friend" Gogol (ironically and significantly, a "real" author, known for his comic-grotesque stories and dramas). We are told that Gogol's so-called "wife" is actually a flesh coloured rubber dummy who can be blown up at will. She may be blown up so as to appear thin and androgynous, or well endowed and sensual.

"Gogol" is portrayed as a fool character representing the real author-creator, Gogol, in the same way that the biographer is a fool character representing his real creator, Landolfi. Landolfi caricatures the actual Gogol who, in reality, was impotent with women. Lanolin creates a fantasy of "Gogol's fantasy," i.e. a Gogol able to create a "suitable" wife. As Caracus, the "dummy" wife, begins to have a life of her own, independent of her creator's desires and intentions, the story also begins to have a life of its own – it is a "living" fiction.

The actual Nikolai Gogol, in his story "The Nose" (1836), wrote about a character named Major Kovalev, who lost his nose and consequently, his self-esteem. (Many critics have identified the loss of the "nose" as a Freudian symbol for Gogol's own supposed sexual impotence.) In the real Gogol's story, the Nose goes on to become "real." It impersonates a State Councillor, complete with uniform, sword and cockaded hat, causing his owner untold distress before returning to its proper place – i.e., on Kovalev's face.

Both Caracus and the Nose are examples of the double as incomplete self. The fool is the tragicomic individual who has lost, hidden or denied a vital aspect of his or her own being. When the emblematic double acts on its own behalf, either by abandoning, tormenting or rejecting the original or creator self, it is essentially an act of self-betrayal. For example, Landolfi's "Gogol" creates a shrewish wife, an object of love-hate, who betrays him. She not only dares to "age," she also turns into a bitter, querulous creature given to sexual infidelities and religious excess. On the eve of their silver anniversary, the fictive Gogol explodes Caracus, sending her parts flying through the air, tragicomically "exploding" the myth of their marriage. The various role transformations, substitutions and projections become part of the twentieth century fool's dual characterisation and dual perspective.

In the twentieth century, the joke will often be on the joker. A prime example is Joseph Heller's *Catch 22* and its militaristic fool-world where madness and sanity are interchangeable. Heller's mock-hero, fighter-pilot Captain Yossarian determines to live forever or die trying. The contradictory lunacies of warfare and patriotism are demonstrated in this new combinate – the rogue-victim fool caught in military bureaucracies.

> There was only one catch and that was Catch 22 which specified that a concern for one's safety in the face of dangers that were real and immediate was the process of a rational mind. Orr was crazy and could be grounded. All he had to do was ask; and as soon as he did, he would no longer be crazy and would have to fly more missions, Orr would be crazy to fly more missions and sane if he didn't, but if he was sane, he had to fly them. If he flew them he was crazy and didn't have to; but if he didn't want to, he was sane and had to. Yossarian was moved very deeply by the absolute simplicity of this clause, of Catch 22, and let out a respectful whistle. [12]

The sane/insane distinction, like the fool/non-fool distinction is a preoccupation with identity, with one's self image and adaptation to the world. In the self division of the mad-fool, boundaries are displaced and transversed. Only the individual himself can reconcile and integrate the opposing or warring aspects of his agonised self.

Fool figures are often, in fact, "madmen" beginning with tricksters, shamans, and village idiots and coming full circle with twentieth century "Everyman-in-analysis" types such as Woody Allen or Saul Bellow's Herzog, Faulkner's family of fools in *As I Lay Dying,* Beckett's crazed self-analytic grotesques, and Harold Pinter's tragicomic minimal-mads. Fools are psychically "possessed." They are closely affiliated with the surreal and the grotesque because of their ability to refuse the given and "de-realise it."

Both "natural" and "deliberate" or "artificial" fools evince elements of contradiction, duality and self-division. They may appear in a variety of forms, as a partial, incomplete or split self, to a schizoid, double, severed or twin self. A dispositional schism within the fool's own self may occur as a result of metamorphic substitution, self-conscious regression, mystical transformation or masochistic displacement. In Franz Kafka's story "The Metamorphosis" (1912) the central protagonist's self is trapped within a second self, looking out. Gregor Samsa wakes up one morning, inexplicably transformed into a large repugnant bug. Not only is Samsa separated from his former life, but from the "humanness" of life, from meaningful participation in normal, human social life. The fool now "is" his disguise.

An example of aggregate metaphoric substitution and transformation occurs in Ionesco's *Rhinoceros* (1959), a play set in a provincial town, where all the townspeople are mystically mutated into rhinoceri – monstrous, brutish and aggressive pachyderms. The epidemic infection not only transforms the individual, but also imbues the individual with an irresistible urge for complete transformation. Only Berenger, a humanist, remains steadfast in his refusal to transmutate. However, even Berenger, in spite of his condemnation of conformity, expresses regret, he feels isolated and marginal, because of his inability to transmute into a rhino[13], a tragicomic statement of the antithetical attractions of conformism and defiance, surrender and rebellion.

Whereas traditional fools played "mirthful games with their contemporaries' assumptions about reality" and happily violate and subvert norms and normative expectations, modern fools seek values, norms and meanings. They may turn them upside down and inside out like traditional fools, but they do so in an attempt to flee from folly, or escape the role of the fool.

Thus, any author or creator who chooses the problematic presence of the fool figure elects the anti-type as prototype and inevitably demonstrates the ideological and behavioural condition of modern man/woman as a tragicomedy in which moral dilemmas are manifest, but never resolved. The fool figure, as both agent and object of laughter and ridicule, becomes an archetypal representative of modern man as social agent and dupe. The incongruous and contradictory synthesis of tragedy and comedy manifested by the fool directly mirrors the ambivalent self-constructs of the modern individual, his/her problematic sense of self and problematic interaction with society. The fool will use his or her dialectical nature to create a "poetics of contradiction," deflating ideological pretensions, subverting tradition and exposing the limitations of social convention.

Fool figures will always remains in the vanguard, showing us the way – the right way and the wrong way. They will, however, never tell us which is which. Therein lies the potential for tragedy, comedy, and more often than not, tragicomedy.

Notes

[1] Enid Welsford, *The Fool, His Social and Literary History* (New York: Doubleday, 1961), 324.

[2] Orin Klapp, "The Fool as a Social Type," *The Pleasures of Sociology*. ed. L. Coser (New York: Mentor, 1980), 248.

[3] William Willeford, *The Fool and His Scepter* (Illinois: Northwestern UP, 1969), 13.

[4] Welsford, and Willeford.

[5] Welseford, 56.

[6] Leslie Fiedler, *Freaks* (New York: Simon & Schuster, 1977), 24.

[7] William Shakespeare, *As You Like It* (New York: Washington Square Books, 1963), II, 7, lines 42-60.

[8] *Commedia* was also known by other names: improvised comedy, *Commedia Improvisa*, comedy by subject *Commedia a Sogetto* and as off-the-cuff comedy *Commedia a Braccia*.

[9] R. J. Broadbent, *A History of Pantomime* (New York: Citadel Press, 1901), 38.

[10] Isaac Bashevis Singer, "The Last Demon" in *The Collected Stories of I.B. Singer* (New York: Farrar, Straus & Giroux, 1982), 179.

[11] Ibid, 180.

[12] Joseph Heller, *Catch 22* (New York: Dell, 1962), 47.

[13] Anton Zijderveld, *Reality in a Looking-Glass* (London: Routledge & Kegan Paul,1982), 11.

Bibliography

Broadbent, R. J. *A History of Pantomime.* New York: Citadel Press, 1901.

Fiedler, Leslie. *Freaks.* New York: Simon & Schuster, 1977.

Heller, Joseph. *Catch 22.* New York: Dell, 1962.

Klapp, Orin. "The Fool as a Social Type." In *The Pleasures of Sociology*, edited by L. Coser, 248-256. New York: Mentor, 1980.

Shakespeare, William. *As You Like It.* Edited by L.B. Wright. New York: Washington Square Books, 1963.

Singer, Issac B. "The Last Demon." In *The Collected Stories of I.B. Singer*, 179-187. New York: Farrar, Straus & Giroux, 1982.

Welsford, Enid. *The Fool, His Social and Literary History.* New York:

Doubleday, l961.

Willeford, William. *The Fool and His Scepter*. Illinois: Northwestern UP, 1969.

Zijderveld, Anton. *Reality in a Looking-Glass*. London: Routledge & Kegan Paul, 1982.

The Postmodern Theatre Clown

Ashley Tobias

During the postmodern era the status of the clown underwent significant change as the figure shifted from social, artistic and academic marginality to centre-stage. Indeed, the clown became integrally enmeshed with the perceptions, attitudes and operations of the phenomenon known as postmodernism. Inexplicably, the clown type I term the "postmodern theatre clown" has been virtually overlooked by academic research.[1] In this paper, I initially outline the fundamental approach to be followed when seeking to define the postmodern theatre clown. Subsequently, I demonstrate the approach by focusing on two outstanding exemplars of the type and illustrate by referring to specific scenes from their performances and texts.

The term "clown," when used generically, refers to a very extensive group of figures going back in time to the most primitive of tribal existence but equally at home in contemporary, technologically advanced societies. A fond figure of imaginative fiction, a pivotal participant in social ritual, or a very real person in the realm of historical fact, clowns reside in many worlds, often straddling the boundaries of fact, fiction, ritual, art and reality. This group is comprised of many and varied types known as: fool, court-jester, buffoon, theatre clown, mime-clown, silent film clown, *alazon, eiron, bomolochos, commedia dell'arte* clown, street clown, circus clown and ritual clown. In addition to these terms used to label the specific types, clowns are also referred to as: comedians, comics, drolls, farceurs, humorists, Harlequins, jokers, mimes, mummers, pranksters, tricksters, wags and wits. Often there is neither absolute consensus on the exact referents of the various neither terms nor full agreement on their precise usage. They are, therefore, frequently used loosely or freely interchanged.[2]

Given the vast variety and differentiation of all those entities generically referred to as clowns, there is, as Lowell Swortzell informs us, no simple answer to that seemingly simple question "What is a clown?"[3] For example, the most common and basic perception of the clown is that he is a comic figure who induces laughter.[4] This is, in most instances, true and is, therefore, commonly presumed to be an axiomatic and defining feature of the clown. However, serious study of the figure reveals that even this basic assumption is not entirely indisputable. Kenneth Little, for instance, informs us that contemporary clowns are frequently "poetic" and "reflective," and their performance not necessarily "funny" but designed to stimulate meaningful contemplation.[5]

Since it is impossible to provide a succinct definition of the clown, I focus on certain characteristics, attributes and affinities considered to be universal to all clown types.[6] Those that prove to be particularly pertinent to the delineation of the post-modern theatre clown are marginality, critical practice, vitality, sexuality, the crossing of boundary, and order-chaos-reorder.

The clown often assumes a marginal position in relation to society. He is an outsider who perceives, understands and acts in a manner very different from the "normal order of things."[7] According to Mikhail Bakhtin, the clown represents the *other* in this world and from the perspective of his social marginality sees the "underside and falseness of every situation."[8] He, therefore, engages in what William Mitchell terms "critical practice": both "critical" of accepted social norms and values, and initiating change at "critical" phases during social development.[9] The energy required for the clown's critical practice may be seen to derive from his inherent vitality. The clown, according to Susanne Langer, is the personification of a vital spirit, an *elan vital*, and his indomitable will to live finds expression in his versatility, resilience and capacity to survive.[10] Another striking manifestation of the clown's vitality is his sexuality, which is often excessive, uninhibited and licentious. In this form it is seen to be symbolic of life itself in that it represents fecund biological proliferation. The clown's sexuality, however, may take on other more ambiguous forms: clowns may be androgynous, appear as male-female pairs or engage in cross-dressing.[11] The clown's unrestrained vitality and his inability, or unwillingness, to behave in accordance with the normal order of things, results in him transgressing all manner of clearly defined boundaries. In doing so he invariably brings into incongruous fusion disparate elements, which are conventionally kept apart by such boundaries. The clown's crossing of boundary implies both transgression and hybrid fusion, and as such is an expression not only of his anarchic spirit but of his association with the principles of order-chaos-reorder. By irreverently crossing boundaries, the clown destabilises those boundaries and reduces to chaos the order they establish and maintain.[12] Through his transgressive actions, the basic assumptions, hierarchies and values of the established order that are upheld by the various boundaries are questioned, reassessed and subverted. Consequent to his boundary crossings the clown, as Richard Pearce points out, generates new order and new values.[13]

I distinguish between three broad categories to organise the clown types: traditional, modern and postmodern clowns. Traditional clowns, in the broadest sense, are all those types in whom the universal characteristics of the clown are most unequivocally manifest. Included in this category, for example, are ancient clown types such as the ritual clown, the fool and the court jester. However, also included are more recent types such as the *commedia dell'arte*, circus clowns and even the comic personae of the great, silent film clowns, Charlie Chaplin and Buster Keaton. These latter figures, if considered chronologically may erroneously be labelled modern clowns but they are essentially traditional clowns in whom the basic universal characteristics are manifest in the most conventional of forms.[14]

The modern clowns are those that I term "clowns of defeat."[15] These modern clowns are the central protagonists in the modern, dark tragicomedies of the Theatre of the Absurd. They are very different to the traditional clown and represent a break from the clown tradition by radically inverting the universal clown characteristics. Trapped in a hostile and purposeless universe, these figures become painfully aware of their anti-heroic stature. They are the helpless victims of a grand cosmic prank but unable to "take arms against a sea of troubles," as there is no absolute force against which to struggle, nor gain to be achieved through rational endeavour. These are clowns defeated both from within and without. Their bodies, psyche, memory, emotion, desire, motivation and language are all in a state of ever increasing, grotesque degeneration. Consequent to this physical and mental atrophy, they have neither the will nor the physical capacity to procreate nor overcome adversity. Death is an enticement but they lack the strength of will and, ironically, the vitality to make the decisive move. So they succumb to the despair and anxiety of the known and unknown. They are impotent clowns who have despaired of despair itself. The clown as social outsider takes on new meaning in the dark comedies: not only are they outside society but rootless in an Absurdist Void. Their critical practice is negated, as they have no society to censor and can initiate no change at critical moments in social development. These clowns of defeat find themselves trapped in dramatic structures of stasis.

Prior to defining the third category, the postmodern clown, and specifically the postmodern theatre clown type, we must examine the concept "postmodern." As in the case of the clown, concise definition of the postmodern is extremely problematic. The very notion of a postmodern "era," i.e. a specific time period, is in itself controversial. First, there is no consensus as to the boundaries of the time period being referred to.[16] Moreover, there are certain authoritative critics, such as Umberto Eco, who insist that the postmodern is "not [...] to be chronologically defined" but is rather, a "metahistorical" or "ideal category," or a "way of operating" that may be identified in any number of historical periods.[17] Basing myself on the authoritative theoreticians of the postmodern, Charles Jencks and Margaret Rose, I refer to that period extending from the early 1960s to the late 1990s as the postmodern era.[18]

When we attempt to determine what precisely it is that the postmodern encompasses and ascertain the exact manner in which it operates, we encounter a fundamental difficulty. The very success of the term, as Dick Hebdige notes, has resulted in it being "stretched in all directions across different debates, different disciplines, and discursive boundaries, as different factions seek to make it their own, using it to designate a plethora of incommensurable objects, tendencies, emergencies."[19] Therefore, writing about the postmodern in the general, all-encompassing terms of a *zeitgeist*, leads to confusion and amorphous discussion. One can only appreciate the perceptions, attitudes, characteristics, styles and the manner in which the postmodern operates by entering into the detail of the various discourses that make-up the complexity that is the postmodern. I focus on the discourse in four areas specifically relevant to my discussion of the postmodern theatre clown: the crossing of boundary, comedy, gender and text.

The crossing of boundary is used, as in the case of the clown, to indicate both "transgression" and "hybridisation of disparate elements." It is fundamental to the postmodern and is manifest in all discourses, in all fields and, indeed, *between* all fields, the postmodern being essentially interdisciplinary in nature.[20] These boundary crossings have deconstructional and decanonisational implications. Ihab Hassan maintains that "fragmentation" and "decanonisation" are definitive features of the postmodern, which according to Jean-Francoise Lyotard, "wages war on totality," questions the "grand narratives" underlying modern scientific knowledge, and thereby delegitimises the "master-codes" that underpin modern Western society.[21] These anarchic aspects of the postmodern, however, bring about change, renewal and revitalisation. As the old established authorities are undermined and overturned, previously marginal, oppressed or counter-cultural groups assert their norms, values, opinions and behaviours. As the cultural canon with its distinct generic categories and hierarchies gives way, new forms come into being through the iconoclastic eclecticism of postmodernism, which fuses elements from all styles and cultural codes from all periods, past and present.[22] Boundary crossing is also fundamental to, and implicit in, all that is postmodern in the other three areas on which I focus.

In the area of comedy, I identify three forms of the genre. Traditional comedy, known as New Comedy, is that 2500 year-old form based upon the comic characters and plot structure of Greek New Comedy.[23] Modern comedy, represented by the tragi-comedies of the Theatre of the Absurd, fuses tragedy and comedy in a dark comic vision that reflects the despair and *angst* of the human condition as experienced towards the middle of the twentieth century.[24]

Postmodern comedy is that form of the genre proposed by the Russian semiotician Mikhail Bakhtin, who derives his contemporary theory of comedy from the Medieval and Renaissance phenomenon of carnival.[25] Carnivalesque comedy has for some time now been recognised as being paradigmatic of postmodernism itself.[26] Ihab Hassan, literary critic and prominent theoretician of the post-modern, regards "carnivalisation" as a defining feature of postmodernism. He elucidates this by stating that "what Bakhtin calls [...] carnival [...] might stand for postmodernism itself, or at least for its ludic and subversive elements that promise renewal." Hassan maintains that the carnivalesque "riotously embraces" the fundamental elements that define the postmodern, "indeterminacy, fragmentation, decanonisation, selflessness, irony, hybridisation." It is a form of the genre which, he claims, conveys the "comic [ethos] of postmodernism" as it is the "feast of becoming, change and renewal" with a "peculiar logic of the 'inside out' [...] 'turnabout' [...] parodies, travesties, humiliations, profanations, comic crownings and uncrowning." Conceived as a "polyphony" or "heteroglossia," carnival implies "the gay relativity of things, perspectivism and performance, participation in the wild disorder of life, and the immanence of laughter."[27] It is in the grotesque imagery, bawdy language, overt sexuality and scatological activity of carnivalesque comedy that postmodern boundary crossings are profusely manifest. This carnivalesque postmodern comedy is a robust form that restores and reinvigorates the subversive dimension of the genre that, I maintain, has been attenuated in traditional comedy and completely lost in modern comedy.

Boundary crossings also feature prominently in the treatment of gender. The postmodern has brought gender issues into the foreground and the discourse has taken on the form of a radical inquiry into the nature of gender identity and sexual preference.[28] The certainties of the biological foundations of gender and sexuality have been seriously questioned and discarded. Gender identity is perceived as a social construct and sexual behaviour as a matter of choice.[29] These issues, once considered to be dictated by, and solidly rooted in, ontological reality are in the postmodern conceived of as learnt behaviours established and perpetuated, in no small part, through the signs of gender in performance.[30] In the postmodern, conventional and accepted notions of gender and sexuality are deconstructed and new possibilities reconstructed, suggested and acted out. One of the dominant ways in which this is accomplished is through the crossing of the gender divide using techniques such as cross-dressing, creating ambivalent fe/male entities, making ambiguous the signs of gender in performance.

We encounter boundary crossing once again when we study the various forms of what are known as postmodern texts. These are texts created by playing "sophisticated games" with existent texts.[31] Most prevalent amongst these "*play*giaristic" games are post-modern parody, intertextuality, appropriation, pastiche, and playful or ironic citation.[32] These techniques re/create "new" texts by crossing the established boundaries between the various media, generic categories and cultural hierarchies. High, low, mass and pop culture merge as "new" texts emerge in the form of prolific pastiche citations of materials reworked, or quoted *verbatim*, from sources as disparate as high literary or dramatic canon, TV soap-operas, Hollywood B-Movies, Sci-Fi paperbacks, comic books and even recipe books.[33] According to the authoritative literary critic John Barth, these postmodern techniques for re/creating texts revitalise the "exhausted" literary canon, which, towards the end of the modern era, was in a "terminal phase in which all creative impetus is spent."[34]

We begin to understand the clown's shift in status when we recognise that there is an intrinsic link and a considerable intersection between the universal characteristics of the clown and the perceptions, attitudes and operations of the postmodern. Both phenomena are immanently anarchic, deconstructional and decanonisational. Both challenge, subvert and invert established order, long-standing hierarchies, accepted values and normative behaviour by transgressing, confusing and dissipating seemingly immutable boundaries of many different kinds, in many different fields. Also, both phenomena ultimately renew, reinvigorate and revitalise as they bring into being new forms through their iconoclastic and eclectic fusion of incongruous and normally disparate elements. The postmodern is a "critical" period in human social development; things such as the cultural canon, generic categorisation, gender identity and sexual preference are not only reassessed but also undergo radical change. It is therefore not surprising that the figure of the clown as critic, harbinger and initiator of change has shifted from his traditional position on the periphery to centre stage. He has been embraced together with those other marginal or counter-cultural groups, who vigorously assert their voices and step in to fill the void as the old authorities topple and disappear.

The intrinsic affinity between the clown and the postmodern, however, does not mean that every clown is automatically so. One of the significant findings of my research is that the postmodern theatre clown does not represent a radical departure from, but a radical reconfiguration of the traditional clown. The postmodern theatre clown embodies the universal characteristics that have always been part of the clown but he manifests these in a manner that is distinctly postmodern. For example, the clown's universal characteristics come into play in all forms of comedy but post-modern clowns are those who tend to create and perform in postmodern comedies.[35] The clown's sexuality finds a convenient and appropriate arena in the postmodern where issues of gender and sexuality have been brought to the fore and are dealt with explicitly. However, simply engaging in overt, uninhibited sexual behaviour does not indicate that he is postmodern as most traditional clowns do this in some form or other. The clown must actively be involved in the radical inquiry into the nature of gender identity and sexual behaviour before he can be considered a postmodern clown. He must be part of the process whereby conventional notions of gender and sexuality are deconstructed and alternatives reconstructed. The same kind of specificity is required in the area of text. There is a long and well-established tradition of clowns who have found their domain in the written dramatic texts of great playwrights. In the case of the postmodern clown, however, his dramatic texts are postmodern texts re/created through the *"play*giaristic" techniques which play sophisticated games with existent texts. We can only determine what exactly is meant by a postmodern theatre clown by studying specific clowns in order to establish whether, and in what manner, they intermesh with that which is postmodern in the four specific areas: the crossing of boundary, comedy, gender and text.

Two case studies provide a comprehensive understanding of the fundamental parameters that constitute a post-modern theatre clown: Lindsay Kemp (ex-UK) and the late Charles Ludlam (USA).[36] I initially selected these two as they comply with four important factors. First, they are clowns: they are comic figures who induce laughter; they can be closely aligned with specific clown types; and they exhibit all the universal clown characteristics. Consequently, both are labelled clowns and refer to themselves as such. Second, they lived and performed in that time period referred to as the postmodern era. Third, both are theatre clowns i.e. to say that though they did perform in other media, their most significant contribution to contemporary clowning was made on the theatre stage. Finally, both are prolific creators of their own performance texts. This enabled me to establish that there is something distinctly postmodern in the type of comic performances they created as vehicles for themselves.

Kemp and Ludlam tend to conceive and create their comedy within the postmodern paradigm of the genre. For example, performances such as Kemp's *Flowers: A Pantomime for Jean Genet* and *Dream*; Ludlam's *Conquest of the Universe / When Queens Collide, Turds in Hell* and *Salammbo*, exhibit all the definitive features of Bakhtin's carnivalesque comedy.[37] They are counter-cultural performances that subvert the accepted norms and values of establishment society by inverting its icons and grotesquely crossing the boundaries of its language and generic hierarchies. The immutable, the accepted, the official, the ideal, the sanctioned, the sacred and the defined are degraded and buried only to be revived and renewed according to the peculiar logic of carnival: "inside out," "turnabout," shifts from "top to bottom, from front to rear," "parodies [...] travesties, humiliations, profanations, comic crownings and uncrownings." These performances truly reflect the carnivalesque process of "becoming," "change," and "renewal." The laughter is that of carnival: "universal" and "ambivalent." All are subject and object of the laugh, which both denies, mocks and degrades but is, at the same time, gay, triumphant, reviving and renewing. Their comedies are both a humiliation and a celebration. The imagery of these performances is also that of carnival: sensuous, spectacular, "grotesque," "grandiose, exaggerated, immeasurable," intermeshing with the world through themes of fertility and abundance." This imagery predominantly highlights the activities of the "material bodily principle," focuses especially on the "lower" bodily zones and profusely portrays the ingestion of food, defecation and copulation. The counter-cultural nature of these postmodern comedies of these two postmodern clowns reinstates the clown to his traditional status as critical practitioner.[38]

One scene of many that serves to illustrate the carnivalesque nature of their comedies is to be found in Lindsay Kemp's *Dream*. This scene is Kemp's innovative and bawdy post-modern parody of Shakespeare's original degradation of Titania. Shakespeare himself, it must be noted, originally created a carnival grotesque when his Puck fuses onto Bottom's shoulders the head of an ass. Shakespeare's image is appropriate because Bottom is an "ass of a man" and exhibits both the stupidity and vitality that the highly sexed ass connotes. Kemp's version of Bottom as a hybrid, carnival grotesque takes Shakespeare's grotesque image into the darker realms of carnival's "lower body strata" and human sexuality. Kemp's Puck conjures up a monstrous, grotesque Bottom, who emerges like a medieval vice figure amidst plumes of smoke and flashing lights from a downstage trap door. Kemp's Bottom ascends from a world below. He is completely naked and his body is smeared with either mud or excrement. Both substances imply an ambivalent carnival degradation and fertility. His groin is covered with a thick furry mass of hair and has attached a long, dangling, exposed penis. Kemp exchanges Shakespeare's asses head with a huge spongy horn and a shaggy main of unkempt hair. Kemp's grotesque Bottom is not an "asses head" but a "dick-head." He is both grotesquely sexual and grotesquely stupid. Bottom is transformed in carnival fashion into an ambiguous, grotesque figure of man as mythical unicorn and phallus. Bottom as clown, the lowliest of men, assumes a degraded and grotesque form, as demonic, primal, instinctual, sexual man and beast.

As this grotesque being rises up from below, the ethereal Titania, Queen of the fairies, is suspended in mid-air as she sleeps on the swing in her bower. She awakens and is drawn irresistibly to the man/beast by the power of the love potion that Puck sprinkled over her sleeping eyes. As she descends to Bottom, the elevated is brought low and the base and lowly elevated. The two meet and fuse. Confronting the grotesque Bottom, Titania goes down on her knees and begins to perform oral sex. He flips her over on her back, bringing her down even further. He spreads her legs and penetrates her with his phallic horn. Then, turning her over enters her from behind. These are the grotesque bodies of carnival exceeding their own limits and fusing in bawdy acts of fornication. This ribald sexuality explicitly performed as dance to the primal rhythm of drums and an electronic sound score is, at once, erotic, pornographic and comic. As the fairy Queen and the man/beast engage in base sexual play, Puck rises up on the Bower swing, laughing as he mischievously observes the degradation of Titania. The scene epitomises the grotesque of carnival and its inversions. The ethereal Queen is degraded as she cavorts with the lowliest of beings. Bottom is transformed into a grotesque image of man/beast/instinct. The lowly, laughing jester literally rises up as instigator and lord of the carnival turnabout. This moment of grotesque carnival fusion and inversion, however, ultimately facilitates the reconciliation between Oberon and Titania. The humiliation of Titania and the grotesque transformation of Bottom are in accordance with the ambivalent principle of degradation in the carnivalesque. Both are degraded but the action ultimately brings about reconciliation and harmony in the Athenian and fairy worlds. It must be noted, that despite the conclusion of this specific episode, *Dream*, unlike Shakespeare's play, does not ultimately return to a reconciled and harmonious form of the old and previous order – that would definitely not be postmodern. Kemp's performance, culminating in a final cross-dressed and homoerotic tableau, presents us with the possibilities of new gender identities and alternative sexual choice. These represent the "boundary crossings" of the postmodern, those "transgressions" and "hybridisations of disparate elements," which are the "anarchic aspects" of the postmodern that "bring about change, renewal and revitalisation."[39]

Both Kemp and Ludlam give postmodern expression to the clown's characteristic marginality, sexuality and vitality by actively participating in the radical inquiry into the nature of gender identity and human sexuality, which characterises the postmodern. Without exception, all their performances consistently and vigorously deconstruct and reconstruct conventional notions of human sexuality and gender by making ambiguous the signs of gender in performance through cross-dressing, and by staging alternatives such as androgyne and explicit homoeroticism.

Kemp makes significant use of cross-dressing but the androgyne is particularly meaningful for him both in performance and in his own life. As a creative artist, Kemp views himself as occupying the "privileged position of being divinely androgynous." He recognises in androgyny a way to "free people" by "breaking down barriers between [...] the sexes" and highlighting the fact that "there is not so much difference between a man and a woman."[40] When casting himself to play androgynous roles, such as Divine in *Flowers*, Salome and Onnagata in the performances of the same name, Kemp is very much representing his own personal sexual identity: "I *am* inside, the most beautiful woman."[41]

A perfect illustration of the androgynous Kempian drag performance is his portrayal of Divine, the central protagonist in *Flowers*. Divine is what Senelick would describe as the quintessential androgyne, whose "masculine body is not effaced but coexists with its femininity."[42] This ambiguous fe/male identity is affirmed in a scene in which Divine prepares for bed with Darling. Divine disrobes to reveal a jock strap clad body. It is anatomically male, as it has no breasts but rather a barrel-chest and narrow hips. Yet, through some almost mystical means, Kemp creates the illusion of an "ideal" female body, which is graceful, sensuous, soft and curvaceous. The illusion is evidence of Kemp's acting skill. The figure manifests his ability to project and physicalise an inner, imaginative reality. It is also a carnival inversion, for, by disrobing, Kemp reveals a male body that, paradoxically, affirms an inner female spirit. There is a certain sense of the carnival grotesque in this image: a pathetic, aging drag queen performs a travesty of an erotic striptease. The scene could have been ludicrous but there is poignancy, gentility and authenticity. Ironically, the truth revealed allows the plausibility of illusion: this image of a "man who is essentially a woman" confirms the possibility of androgyny.

Ludlam has very definite views on sexuality and gender, and expresses them in no uncertain terms: "the greatest and most restrictive bond on one's identity is sex. It is fixed biologically or bio*ill*ogically at birth. Anatomy is destiny."[43] As a postmodern theatre clown, Ludlam proudly asserts his gay otherness by proclaiming that "sex is *all* preference."[44] He also states that "we have to acknowledge our sexuality, but we also have to laugh at it and put it in its proper place."[45]

The device of drag is, according to Ludlam, "supercharged with theatricality" and his stage career was launched through drag.[46] In 1966, he appeared as Norma Desmond in John Vaccaro's production of *Screen Test* for the Play-House of the Ridiculous. The role was his drag version of the fading silent-movie idol in Billy Wilder's *Sunset Boulevard*. Sporting a "black wig that had once belonged to Salvador Dali and a brown silk beaded dress," Ludlam took the stage by storm. What was intended as a "30 minutes curtain raiser" soon evolved into a full two hour virtuoso performance.[47] The role of Norma Desmond was the first time that Ludlam had appeared in drag. It was a creation of intuitive brilliance and according to Ludlam, Norma "kind of sprang from Zeus totally formed." Ludlam recalls that this first experience of acting in drag gave him a new freedom and changed his entire approach to acting.[48]

Ludlam prides himself on having "pioneered the idea that female impersonation could be serious acting." Drag as "serious acting" does not mean, however, that in assuming female roles Ludlam ceases to be a comic actor. Despite moments of serious pathos, his drag performances are always comic. Laughter is intrinsic to Ludlam's drag performance because he deliberately highlights the comic incongruity of a man dressed as a woman. For Ludlam, "serious" cross-dressing means that the actor does "real acting" in drag. He considers drag a legitimate acting technique and a serious approach to the creation of persona.[49] Ludlam's performance as Galas, in the play of the same name, is an example of the kind of drag roles that he describes as "serious." Ludlam was fascinated by the opera singer, Maria Callas, whom he regarded as a "genius who revolutionised her art form." He, therefore, set about creating a role, which he hoped would "prove that female impersonation could be taken seriously as art in Western theatre."[50]

One can surmise that the involvement of Kemp and Ludlam in the issues of gender and sexuality derives from their personal commitment to the gay counter-culture, which, until the mid-1960s had been a marginal social phenomenon, but became increasingly assertive as the postmodern era moved on. Both Kemp and Ludlam are gay but being gay, it must be noted, is not in itself an essential parameter of the postmodern theatre clown. What is postmodern is being actively involved in the gender discourse and contributing to the process whereby conventional gender identity and human sexuality are reappraised and transformed. Any clown, male, female, gay or "straight" can participate in such activity.

Moving on to the area of text, we discover that Kemp and Ludlam play sophisticated games with existent texts and traditional textual structures. They create postmodern performance and dramatic texts by employing all the techniques made available by *play*giaristic postmodern strategies. They transform high dramatic and literary canons through the technique of postmodern parody and re/create "new," "original" texts through profuse and playful citation. Kemp's *Flowers: A Pantomime for Jean Genet* is his free, creative, movement interpretation of Jean Genet's poetic *Notre Dame Des Fleurs*. Kemp's *Dream* is Shakespeare's *A Midsummer Night's Dream* virtually without words, the Bard's text transcodified into a rich, visual movement collage. His *Alice* freely fuses episodes from both of Lewis Carroll's literary texts, *Alice in Wonderland* and *Through the Looking-Glass*. Kemp's *The Big Parade*[51] is a pastiche performance citing a wide range of famous scenes from the Hollywood silent movie era. Ludlam's *Camille*,[52] based upon Alexandre Dumas' *Lady aux Camellias* and Verdi's *La Traviata*, pays homage to these classic texts, as is the manner of postmodern parody, rather than merely satirising them. Ludlam's *Conquest of the Universe* is a reworking of Christopher Marlowe's Jacobean tragedy *Tamburlaine the Great*, transformed and recontextualised within the popular style of the Sci-Fi comic-book genre. His *Turds in Hell* is liberally sprinkled with citations appropriated from: Dante, Coleridge, Shakespeare, cookbook recipes and untranslated Spanish texts. Kemp and Ludlam's postmodern texts demonstrate how the clown's characteristic crossing of boundary and his affinity with order-chaos-reorder take on a distinctly postmodern form in the iconoclastic and eclectic fusion of disparate elements in the postmodern texts of the postmodern theatre clowns. These postmodern texts, which reinvigorate and revive textual originality, are a distinctly postmodern manifestation of the clown's characteristic vitality.

Ludlam's *Le Bourgeois Avant-Garde: A Comedy Ballet After Moliere* (1983), for example, is, as the title and subtitle clearly indicate, an appropriation of Moliere's comedy-ballet, *Le Bourgeois Gentilhomme*.[53] For as Ludlam claims *Le Bourgeois Avant-Garde* is "my Moliere!"[54]

Ludlam retains the basic plot, almost all the characters, much of the action and many of the episodes in Moliere's text, but transforms them into his own satiric postmodern parody. His central comic protagonist, Mr. Foufas, known as "Friendly Foufas of the Friendly Foufas Food Stores," represents the American *nouveau riche*. He, like Moliere's naive, bourgeois Monsieur Jourdain, aspires with vigorous determination to become a "man of culture." To this end Foufas surrounds himself with a group of pretentious, hypocritical, avant-garde artists, who exploit his gullibility and milk him for his newly made wealth. They represent Ludlam's updated post-modern parody of Moliere's Masters of Philosophy, Dance, Music and Fencing. Through these figures, Ludlam satirises the pretensions of the contemporary, American avant-garde art scene: music, literature, the plastic arts, dance, theoretical discourse and rhetoric, sexual and marital practice, and, of course, performance. Ludlam transforms Moliere's play through to express his personal artistic vision and life philosophy. He satirises an avant-garde, which had become, according to Ludlam, "more conservative than its audience."[55]

In conclusion, Kemp and Ludlam are fine exemplars of the postmodern theatre clown type and through them it is possible to establish the fundamental parameters of that which constitutes the type. They provide a comprehensive paradigm, which can be the basis for the future study of additional clowns, who may also fit into the same category.

Notes

[1] In my doctoral dissertation I sought to redress this academic oversight by delineating the parameters of what constitutes a postmodern theatre clown and outlining the link between this apparently "new" clown type and certain specific discourses, central to the era in which he operated. Ashley Tobias, "The Post-modern Clown" (Doctoral Dissertation Tel Aviv University, 2001).
[2] William E Mitchell, "Introduction," in *Clowning as Critical Practice: Performance Humour in the South Pacific* (Pittsburgh: University of Pittsburgh Press, 1992), 18-9, 32.
[3] Lowell Swortzell, *Here Come the Clowns* (New York: Viking Press, 1978), 4.
[4] Clowns are, and always have been, both male and female. For the sake of simplicity, I refer to the clown using the male pronoun *he* and the male possessive article *his*. This does imply an objectionable gender exclusion but

given the limitations of the signs of gender rooted in our language, there no alternative.

[5] Kenneth W. Little, "Pitu's Doubt: Entrée Clown Self-Fashioning in the Circus Tradition," *The Drama Review* 30. 4, T-112 (Winter 1986): 55-6.

[6] William Willeford, *The Fool and His Sceptre.* 1969 (Evanston: Northwestern University Press, 1980).

[7] Ibid, 26-7

[8] Mikhail Bakhtin, *The Dialogic Imagination,* trans. Caryl Emerson and Michael Holoquist, ed. Michael Holoquist (Austin: University of Texas Press, 1981), 159-161.

[9] Mitchell, vii

[10] Susanne Langer, "The Comic Rhythm," 1953, in *Comedy: Meaning and Form*, ed. R. W. Corrigan (Pennsylvania: Chandler Publishing Co., 1965), 133-5.

[11] Willeford 1969, 11-2, 85-6, 170, 179, 183, 186.

[12] Ibid, 108.

[13] Richard Pearce, *Stages of the Clown* (Carbonsdale: Southern Illinois University Press, 1970), 102.

[14] Ashley Tobias, "The Clown Triumphant" in "A Spectrum of Clowns: From Triumph to Defeat" (Masters Thesis, Jerusalem University, 1986), 23-61.

[15] Ashley Tobias, "The Defeated Clowns," in ibid, 133-180.

[16] Charles Jencks, "The Post-modern Agenda," 1991, in *The Post-Modern Reader*, ed. Charles Jencks (London: Academy Editions, 1992), 16-7.

[17] Umberto Eco, "Postscript to *The Name of the Rose,"* 1983, in *The Post-Modern Reader* ed. Charles Jencks (London: Academy Editions, 1992), 73-75.

[18] Jencks 1992, 17.

[19] Dick Hebdige, *Hiding the Light: on Images and Things* (New York: Routledge, 1988), 181.

[20] Ihab Hassan, "Pluralism in Postmodern Perspective," 1986 in *The Postmodern Turn: Essays in Postmodern Theory and Culture* (Columbus, Ohio: Ohio State University Press, 1987), 168-170. Linda Hutcheon, *The Politics of Postmodernism* (New York: Routledge, 1989), 5, 18-19.

[21] Hassan 1986, 168-170. Jean-François Lyotard, *The Post Modern Condition: A Report on Knowledge,* 1979, trans. G. Bennington and B. Massumi, *Theory and History of Literature*, 10, (Minneapolis: University of Minnesota Press, 1984), 37. Jean-François Lyotard, "Answering the Question: What is Postmodernism?" 1982, in *The Post Modern Condition: A Report on Knowledge.* trans. Regis Durand. *Theory and History of Literature,* 10, (Minneapolis: University of Minnesota Press, 1984), 72, 82.

[22] Hutcheon, 5, 18-9. Jencks 1992, 23.

[23] T.G.A. Nelson, *Comedy: An Introduction to Comedy in Literature, Drama, and Cinema* (Oxford: Oxford University Press, 1990), 19. Norththrop Frye, "Mythos of Spring: Comedy," in *Anatomy of Criticism* (New Jersey: Princeton University Press, 1973), 163-176.

[24] R.W.Corrigan, "Comedy and the Comic Spirit" in *Comedy: Meaning and Form*, ed. R.W.Corrigan (Pennsylvania: Chandler Publishing Co., 1965), Wylie Sypher, *Comedy* (New York: Doubleday Ander Books, 1956), 193-7.

[25] Mikhail Bakhtin, *Rabelais and His World*, trans. Helene Iswolsky (Cambridge, Massachusetts: M.I.T. Press, 1968) 1-57.

[26] John Docker, *Postmodernism and Popular Culture* (Cambridge: Cambridge University Press, 1994), 169-170. Peter Stallybrass and Allon White, *The Politics and Poetics of Transgression* (London: Methuen, 1986), 6-7.

[27] Hassan, 198.

[28] Lawrence Senelick, "Changing Sex in Public: Female Impersonation as Performance," *Theater* 20. 2 (Spring/Summer 1989): 6.

[29] Judith Butler, "Performative Acts and Gender Constitution: An Essay in Phenomenology and Feminist Theory," 1987, in *Performing Feminisms: Feminist Critical Theory and Theater,* ed. Sue-Ellen Case (Baltimore: John Hopkins University Press, 1990), 270, 279. Lawrence Senelick, "Introduction" in *Gender in Performance*, ed. Lawrence Senelick (Hanover and London: University Press of New England, 1992), ix.

[30] Judith Lynne Hanna, "Tradition, Challenge,and the Backlash: Gender Education through Dance," in *Gender in Performance,* ed. Laurence Senelick (Hanover: University Press of New England, 1992), 223.

[31] Manfred Pfister,"How Postmodern is Intertextuality?" in *Intertextuality,* ed. Heinrich F. Plett (Berlin: Walter Gruyter, 1991), 208, 214.

[32] The term *"play*giaristic" was coined by Raymond Federman cited in Hassan, 170. Hutcheon, 93-4.

[33] Frederic Jameson, "The Cultural Logic of Late Capitalism," 1984, in *Postmodernism, or the Cultural Logic of Late Capitalism* (Durham: Duke University Press, 1991), 2-3.

[34] Pfister 1991, 208.

[35] The exception, as I note above, are the modern "clowns of defeat" who perform in modern tragi-comedies of the Theater of the Absurd.

[36] For a detailed discussion of Kemp and Ludlam as clowns see Tobias 2001, 11-13.

[37] Lindsay Kemp, *Flowers: a Pantomime for Jean Genet,* based on *Our Lady of the Flowers* by Jean Genet, adapted and directed by Lindsay Kemp, with Lindsay Kemp and Company, Milan (Rome: White Lights, Video Creation and Production, n.d) videorecording. Lindsay Kemp, *Dream,* based on *A*

Midsummer Night's Dream by William Shakespeare, adapted by Lindsay Kemp, directed by Lindsay Kemp and David Haughton, with Lindsay Kemp and Company, Teatro Olimpico, Rome (Rome: White Lights, Video Creation and Production, 1989) videorecording. Charles Ludlam, *Conquest of the Universe/When Queens Collide: A Tragedy,* 1967, in *The Complete Plays of Charles Ludlam* 25-48; Charles Ludlam, *Salammbo: An Erotic Tragedy,* 1985, ibid, 845-876; Charles Ludlam, *Turds in Hell,* 1969, ibid, 49-82.

[38] Bakhtin 1968, 7-12, 19.

[39] For the discussion of postmodern boundary crossings, see page 4 article.

[40] Carol Mann, "Lindsay Kemp, Nonstop," *International Herald Tribune,* 19-20 September 1981, 8W.

[41] Steve Grant, "Dance of the Seven Veils," *Time Out,* London, n.m.1977,15.

[42] Lawrence Senelick, "Changing Sex in Public: Female Impersonation as Performance," *Theater* 20. 2 (Spring/Summer 1989): 10.

[43] Charles Ludlam, "A Monograph and a Premature Memoir: Why I Use Female Impersonators in My Plays," in *Ridiculous Theatre: Scourge of Human Folly; The Essays and Opinions of Charles Ludlam,* ed. Steven Samuels (New York: Theatre Communications Group, 1992), 151-2

[44] Charles Ludlam, "Opinions" in in *Ridiculous Theatre: Scourge of Human Folly; The Essays and Opinions of Charles Ludlam,* ed. Steven Samuels (New York: Theatre Communications Group, 1992), 238.

[45] Ibid, 238.

[46] Charles Ludlam "Confessions of A Farceur," in *Ridiculous Theatre: Scourge of Human Folly; The Essays and Opinions of Charles Ludlam,* ed. Steven Samuels (New York: Theatre Communications Group, 1992), 21.

[47] José Osvald Rosado-Perez, *Gilding the Lily: Charles Ludlam and the Ridiculous Theatrical Company, 1967-1987* Diss. New York University (Ann Arbor, Michigan: UMI Dissertation Services,1993), 8

[48] Isaac, Dan. "Charles Ludlam/Norma Desmond/Laurette Bedlam - and Interview with Charles Ludlam." *The Drama Review* 13. 1, T-41 (Fall 1968): 116. Charles Ludlam "Confessions of A Farceur," 137-8.

[49] Charles Ludlam "Confessions of A Farceur," 40

[50] Ibid, 117-8

[51] Lindsay Kemp, *The Big Parade,* devised, designed and directed by Lindsay Kemp, with Lindsay Kemp and Company, Teatro San Carlo, Naples (Rome: White Lights, Video Creation and Production, 1993), videorecording.

[52] Charles Ludlam, *Camille: A Travesty on La Dame aux Camelias,* 1973, in *The Complete Plays of Charles Ludlam* (New York: Harper and Row, 1989), 221-253.

[53] Charles Ludlam, *Le Bourgeois Avant-Garde: A Comedy Ballet After Moliere,* 1983, in *The Complete Plays of Charles Ludlam* (New York: Harper and Row, 1989), 697-730.
[54] Charles Ludlam "Confessions of A Farceur," 116
[55] Ibid.

Bibliography

Bakhtin, Michael. *The Dialogic Imagination.* Trans. Caryl Emerson and
    Michael Holoquist, edited by Michael Holoquist. Austin: University
    of Texas
    Press, 1981.
— . *Rabelais and His World,* translated by Helene Iswolsky. Cambridge,
    Massachusetts: M.I.T. Press, 1968.
Butler, Judith. "Performative Acts and Gender Constitution: An Essay in
    Phenomenology and Feminist Theory," 1987. In *Performing
    Feminisms: Feminist Critical Theory and Theater,* edited by Sue-
    Ellen Case, 270-282. Baltimore: John Hopkins University Press,
    1990.
Corrigan, R.W. "Comedy and the Comic Spirit." In *Comedy: Meaning and
    Form,* edited by R.W. Corrigan, 1-11. Pennsylvania: Chandler
    Publishing Company, 1965.
Docker, John. *Postmodernism and Popular Culture.* Cambridge: Cambridge
    University Press, 1994.
Eco, Umberto. "Postscript to *The Name of the Rose,*" 1983. In *The Post-
    Modern Reader,* edited by Charles Jencks, 73-75. London: Academy
    Editions, 1992.
Frye, Norththrop. "Mythos of Spring: Comedy." In *Anatomy of Criticism,*
    158-186. New Jersey: Princeton University Press, 1973.
Grant, Steve "Dance of the Seven Veils," *Time Out,* London, n.m.1977,15.
Hanna, Judith Lynne. "Tradition, Challenge,and the Backlash: Gender
    Education through Dance." In *Gender in Performance,* edited by
    Laurence Senelick, 223-238. Hanover: University Press of New
    England, 1992.
Hassan, Ihab. "Pluralism in Postmodern Perspective," 1986. In *The
    Postmodern Turn: Essays in Postmodern Theory and Culture,* 167-
    187. Columbus, Ohio: Ohio State University Press, 1987.
Hebdige, Dick. *Hiding the Light: on Images and Things.* New York:
    Routledge, 1988.
Hutcheon, Linda. *The Politics of Postmodernism.* New York: Routledge,

1989.

Isaac, Dan. "Charles Ludlam/Norma Desmond/Laurette Bedlam - and
Interview with Charles Ludlam." *The Drama Review* 13. 1, T-41
(Fall 1968): 116.

Jameson, Frederic. "The Cultural Logic of Late Capitalism," 1984. In
Postmodernism, or the Cultural Logic of Late Capitalism, 1-54.
Durham: Duke University Press, 1991.

Jencks, Charles."The Postmodern Agenda," 1991. In *The Post-Modern
Reader*, edited by Charles Jencks, 10-39. London: Academy
Editions, 1992.

Kemp, Lindsay *The Big Parade,* devised, designed and directed by
Lindsay Kemp, with Lindsay Kemp and Company, Teatro San
Carlo, Naples. Rome: White Lights, Video Creation and Production,
1993. Videorecording.

—. *Dream*, based on *A Midsummer Night's Dream* by William
Shakespeare, adapted by Lindsay Kemp, directed by Lindsay Kemp
and David Haughton, with Lindsay Kemp and Company, Teatro
Olimpico, Rome. Rome: White Lights, Video Creation and
Production, 1989. Videorecording.

— . *Flowers: a Pantomime for Jean Genet,* based on *Our Lady of the
Flowers* by Jean Genet, adapted and directed by Lindsay Kemp,
with Lindsay Kemp and Company, Milan. Rome: White Lights,
Video Creation and Production, n.d. Videorecording.

Langer, Susanne."The Comic Rhythm," 1953. In *Comedy: Meaning and
Form*, edited by R. W. Corrigan, 133-5. Pennsylvania: Chandler
Publishing Co., 1965.

Little, Kenneth W."Pitu's Doubt: Entrée Clown Self-Fashioning in the Circus
Tradition." *The Drama Review* 30. 4, T-112 (Winter 1986): 55-6.

Ludlam, Charles. *Le Bourgeois Avant-Garde: A Comedy Ballet After
Moliere,* 1983. In *The Complete Plays of Charles Ludlam*, edited by
Steven Samuels and Everett Quinton, 697-730. New York: Harper
and Row, 1989.

—. *Camille: A Travesty on La Dame aux Camelias*, 1973. Ibid, 221-253.

—. "Confessions of A Farceur." In *Ridiculous Theatre: Scourge of Human
Folly; The Essays and Opinions of Charles Ludlam*, edited by
Steven Samuels, 1-142 . New York: Theatre Communications
Group, 1992.

— . *Conquest of the Universe/When Queens Collide: A Tragedy,* 1967. In
The Complete Plays of Charles Ludlam, edited by Steven Samuels
and Everett Quinton, 25-48. New York: Harper & Row, 1989.

—. "A Monograph and a Premature Memoir: Why I Use Female

Impersonators in My Plays." In *Ridiculous Theatre: Scourge of Human Folly; The Essays and Opinions of Charles Ludlam*, edited by Steven Samuels, 151-153. New York: Theatre Communications Group, 1992.

—. "Opinions." Ibid, 173-260.

—. *Salammbo: An Erotic Tragedy,* 1985. In *The Complete Plays of Charles Ludlam*, edited by Steven Samuels and Everett Quinton, 845-876. New York: Harper & Row, 1989.

—. *Turds in Hell,* 1969. Ibid, 49-82.

Lyotard, Jean-François. "Answering the Question: What is Postmodernism?" 1982. *The Post Modern Condition: A Report on Knowledge*, translated by Regis Durand, 70-82. *Theory and History of Literature* 10 (1984) Minneapolis: University of Minnesota Press.

—. "*The Post Modern Condition: A Report on Knowledge,*" 1979, translated by G. Bennington and B. Massumi. *Theory and History of Literature* 10 (1984) Minneapolis: University of Minnesota Press.

Mann, Carol. "Lindsay Kemp, Nonstop." *International Herald Tribune,* 19-20 September 1981, 8W.

Mitchell,William E. "Introduction." In *Clowning as Critical Practice: Performance Humour in the South Pacific*, 18-9, 32. Pittsburgh: University of Pittsburgh Press, 1992.

Nelson, T.G. A. *Comedy: An Introduction to Comedy in Literature, Drama, and Cinema.* Oxford: Oxford University Press, 1990.

Pearce, Richard. *Stages of the Clown.* Carbonsdale: Southern Illinois University Press, 1970.

Pfister, Manfred. "How Postmodern is Intertextuality?" In *Intertextuality*, edited by Heinrich F. Plett, 207-224. Berlin: Walter Gruyter, 1991.

Rosado-Perez, José Osvald. *Gilding the Lily: Charles Ludlam and the Ridiculous Theatrical Company, 1967-1987.* Dissertation, New York University. Ann Arbor, Michigan: UMI Dissertation Services,1993.

Senelick, Lawrence. "Changing Sex in Public: Female Impersonation as Performance." *Theater* 20. 2 (Spring/Summer 1989): 6-11.

—. "Introduction." In *Gender in Performance*, edited by Lawrence Senelick, xi-xx. Hanover and London: University Press of New England, 1992.

Stallybrass, Peter and White, Allon. *The Politics and Poetics of Transgression.* London: Methuen, 1986.

Swortzell, Lowell. *Here Come the Clowns.* New York: Viking Press, 1978.

Sypher, Wylie. *Comedy.* New York: Doubleday Ander Books, 1956.

Tobias, Ashley. "The Clown Triumphant." In *A Spectrum of Clowns: From Triumph to Defeat*. Masters Thesis, 23-61. Jerusalem University, 1986.

—. *The Postmodern Clown*. Doctoral Dissertation. Tel Aviv University, 2001.

Willeford, William. *The Fool and His Sceptre*, 1969. Evanston: Northwestern University Press, 1980.

Nietzsche and the Praise of Masks

Rüdiger Görner

1. Introducing the Artifical Nature of Masks

Is language but a mask of thought? Are masks stories that froze before someone had the chance to tell them? Who can unlock the expression captured by the mask and turn it into an element of the narrative? Or are we to take masks at their face value?

The interplay of masking and unmasking, let alone the unexpected dropping of masks, constitute the defining moments in the history of stage drama regardless its specific cultural tradition. In the hollowness of the mask resound comedy and tragedy, the occult and the profane on the Greek, Japanese and Elizabethan stage alike. The mask as the name for an object and a procession-like dance represents transfigurations of realities into illusions which lure the spectator into a world of fantasy.

Masks are to attract attention and to deter evil spirits; but they also seem to function as thing-like images of Man's so-called second nature. The creation of masks requires a high degree of expertise from the artisan. What is nowadays called, somewhat profanely, "make-up artist" used to carry the title of "masker" in English, *le mouleur* in French and *Maskenbildner* in German. Who and what was the masker? An artisan and/or manipulator of identity? Part of his job description was the manufacturing of death masks as representations of the unspeakable.

One of the main episodes in Rainer Maria Rilke's experimental novel *The Notes of Malte Laurids Brigge* consists of a young Dane in Paris passing the establishment of such a "mouleur" where he finds two masks hanging next to the entrance. It is the death mask of a drowned young woman and a replica of the famous one of Beethoven. The narrator describes the face of Beethoven as an object that resembled a knot of tightly contracted senses so much so that he likens it to an image of relentless self-intensification from which music seemed to evaporate. The woman's mask had captured the beauty of her deceptive smile that looked as if it knew something that others could not know.[1]

Masks in general are to cause fright, even shock; masks create a sense of alienation and distance. Undermining any sense of familiarity, they indicate deceit, deception but also absence of development. Masks can amuse and appal, bedevil and dismay. They are relicts of rituals and distortions of nature. Masks are exaggerated human features, often revealing their proximity to those of animals. Masks can cover anything – from the satanic to the grotesque and clownish. Perhaps the most shocking dimension of all is their claim to be true thus to be giving an authentic representation of what humans are "really" like behind the façade of their so-called normality. In that, they would appear ironic since masks would bring into the open what lies behind people's faces. This, however, required a certain degree of audacity on part of the bearer of masks if he/she saw it as an emblem of self-revelation.

But masks serve other purposes, too. They are to deter evil spirits or, in other words, they provide a means of self protection. We seem to be in need of masks in order to survive. The building up of an appropriate mask can be an important element of psychotherapy for someone who feels pathologically vulnerable. To put it crudely: Who ever has lost his/her face needs to replace it with a good supply of masks for all occasions and circumstances. Knowing thyself therefore includes knowing thy masks and the moment when you need them. This question is even more acute in cases of people who identify themselves so much with their respective 'masks' that they become their bearers' second identity. In analogy to Yeats's famous phrase we might then ask: Who can tell the persona from the mask?

In his essay on *The Truth of Masks* (1891), which was partly designed to discuss the necessity of using costumes in stage productions, Oscar Wilde came to the somewhat staggering conclusion that "the truths of metaphysics are the truths of masks."[2] This essay was written at a time when Wilde had long mislaid his Irish accent and adopted the mask of impeccable Englishness – to paraphrase one of Seamus Heaney's points on Wilde in his 1992/93 Oxford Lectures *The Redress of Poetry*.[3]

Wilde's essay is as one would expect an homage to deception written in praise of costume and appearance as the only aspects of truth that are attainable through the senses. *The Truth of Masks* suggests a close connection with the English Elizabethan masque, which combined the various forms of art to express mythological and allegorical subjects in the form of colourful pageantry. A late resonance of this use of the arts is Harrison Birtwistle's opera *The Mask of Orpheus* (1986) which remained strikingly faithful to the original myth and avoided much reinterpretation. But the question must be asked what it is that the simple or elaborately decorated face-mask or a pageant masque conceals. Is it, to put it paradoxically, the truth of deception or rather the truth that Man cannot but deceive others and himself because he cannot bear the truth about the reality of life?

2.   Nietzsche's Advocacy of Masks

This question brings us closer to Nietzsche and his fundamental concern in *The Birth of Tragedy*. Nietzsche's point was that all main characters on the Greek stage, such as Prometheus and Oedipus, were but masks of Dionysus. Through these masks, Nietzsche argued, he was present in every theatre performance. Dionysus's masked presence on stage created a strong sense of mystery. Nietzsche suggested that this spell-bound effect of masks was, however, broken with the arrival of the Socratic imperative:

"Know thyself." Against the backdrop of Socratic enlightenment the mask was disgraced and seen as a mere hindrance to self-recognition. Masks turned into relics of a mythological past and thus, for the time being, into redundant utensils.

Nietzsche's initial intellectual programme included the unmasking of his own time but, ironically, he was prepared to unmask himself only up to a point. But which was this very point? In *The Gay Science* (1882) Nietzsche argued that we need to rediscover and recapture the delights in masks. He acknowledges the folkloristic aspects of the mask which he experienced particularly in Basle during the carnival seasons. He speaks of the good conscience that we should have when wearing masks; for they connect us with our primordial desires.[4] Intimately connected with Nietzsche's reappraisal of the mask is his recognition of the actor as the main protagonist of his time and the times to come. The actor's ability to camouflage, his or her art of mimicry and, in general, the mimetic disposition of their artistic skills turns in *The Gay Science* into Nietzsche's prime object of study. He realizes that the great artist, even the genius, ultimately derives from the fool and clown. Somewhere in even the most sublime of artists lurks the Harlequin. In Nietzsche's case this argument ends with a twist into theatrical misogyny: the female figures as the ultimate ever seductive actor.

This said there is yet another dimension to Nietzsche's advocacy of masks and acting in *The Gay Science*; for he suggests that Jews have been forced to act and to camouflage their identity given the scale of hostility they had been confronted with all over Europe (KSA 3, 608). Without saying it Nietzsche seemed to regard all attempts of Jews to assimilate into their Christian contexts as a case of severe acting. If we followed Nietzsche's argument in *The Gay Science* we would have to refer to Jewish assimilation and emancipation as prime examples of masking identities and integral parts of Jewish survival tactics over the centuries.

However, the question of masks and masking oneself did not disappear after *The Gay Science*. If anything it became ever more urgent and intensive. Was it that Nietzsche began to see himself increasingly as a jester at the court of the *Weltgeist*? Was it the re-encounter with Venice in spring 1885, this city on stage with every house and piazza as a potential backdrop for a theatre performance, that inspired Nietzsche to focus his mind again on the meaning of masks? It was at that time when Nietzsche, with the crucial help of his friend Köselitz, read the proofs of the fourth and final part of *Thus spoke Zarathustra* with its striking section "Der Zauberer," the old magician, Nietzsche's answer to Prospero, whom Zarathustra confronts and forces to abandon the rest of his fading magical powers. This magician finally concedes that he is tired of himself and his casting of futile spells. Zarathustra regards this confession as the only aspect in the magician's character that he feels he can respect.

3.   Unmasking Zarathustra

Zarathustra has made the magician, generally seen to be a reincarnation of Richard Wagner, drop his mask. But are we sure that Zarathustra is not wearing a mask himself? It was in Venice in May 1885 that Nietzsche wrote to his friend Franz Overbeck in Basle: " [...] at times I am not sure whether I am the sphinx that asks questions or the famous Oedipus who is been asked[...]."[5] The question of identity had become acute for Nietzsche and with it the clarity about the function of masks. In a letter to his sister around the same time Nietzsche emphasized that Zarathustra's views were not identical with his own; although he calls him his son[6] but later refers to him as his hide-out like Schopenhauer and Wagner. Hiding behind the mask of Zarathustra and others had developed into his *condition de vivre*. In a sense, Nietzsche's style of writing and the way in which he combined analytical with poetic language was almost predestined to be distorted by interpreters. He was evidently conscious of the fact that his very language and use of words amounted to a colourful array of strikingly, if not exotically, looking and sounding thoughts.[7] That is to say, his language, too, possessed mask-like qualities. Nietzsche argued that what he had written up to now (1885) was a mere "foreground" to his innermost thoughts camouflaging their dangerousness. To exaggerate the point for sake of argument: Nietzsche entertained a certain intellectual clownery in order to veil his "real" intellectual disposition. But like with so many clowns he found it increasingly hard to tell which of his images was the genuine one.

This is at least some of the context in which Nietzsche's most famous pronouncement on masks in the second part of *Beyond Good and Evil* needs to be interpreted. In what must be one of the truly self-revealing passages in this "prelude to a philosophy of the future" Nietzsche stated:

> Everything profound loves the mask [...] Should not nothing less than the *opposite* be the proper disguise under which the shame of a god goes abroad? [...] a hidden man, who instinctively uses speech for silence and concealment and is inexhaustible in evading communication, *wants* a mask of him to roam the heads and hearts of his friends in his stead, and he makes sure that it does so; and supposing he does not want it, he will one day come to see that a mask is there in spite of that – and that is a good thing. Every profound spirit needs a mask: more, around every profound spirit a mask is continually growing, thanks to the constantly false, that is to say shallow interpretation of every word he speaks, every step he takes, every sign of life he gives. [8]

The morale of this passage is: masks are inevitable, or to be precise, masks are images of opposites and, generally speaking, the logical product of misunderstandings. Consequently, masks emerge from communication which involves the constant misinterpretation of profound thoughts.

It is, at first sight perhaps, somewhat surprising that Nietzsche did not deplore this state of communication. On the contrary, he seemed to have rejoiced in it at times. His own experience told him to live with this scale of misunderstanding and allow the mask to continue to grow around him. Some fifty years later George Orwell was to offer an alternative image. Speaking of the character of the average colonialist the future author of *Nineteen-Eighty-Four* wrote in one of his poignant early essays: "He wears a mask, and his face grows to fit it."[9] The difference between these two references to the mask as a quasi intellectual and artistic instrument is, however, a principle one. Whilst Nietzsche stressed that the mask is alive and could change in character Orwell underlined the static quality of masks that offers a specific shape of identity which we endeavour to match. Both, however, realized that the identity of the mask had become more important than the identity of its bearer.

4.   Deformed Identities

In a world of masks the surreal prevails. The more Nietzsche emphasized the presence of masks in life the more acutely aware he became of the absurd conditions and manifestations of life.[10] Nietzsche's insistence on masks becoming the real face was part of anti-Platonic strategy; since for Plato the philosopher's task was to discover what lay behind the (actor's) mask. This Platonic argument still mattered to Voltaire who saw in the myths and popular legends surrounding the so-called "man with the iron mask," allegedly the twin brother of Ludwig XIV's, a deplorable symbol of the counter-enlightenment.

But the man in the iron mask, to whom Alexandre Dumas was to give novelistic hero status, symbolised, too, a sinister counter-figure to the court jester. The iron mask was evidently designed not to grow but to extinguish the identity of this ominous figure and outcast for good. This mask epitomised the negation of freedom whilst the court jester[11] through his buffoonery, enacted an element of liberty as Friedrich Hebbel observed in a letter of 1838 in which he reflected on what he regarded as the dark ages of absolutism.[12] This argument, however, did not take into account the personal tragedy of those who acted as court jesters as exemplified by Gundling, who entertained his brutish master King Friedrich Wilhelm I of Prussia constantly pushed to the point of humiliation and despair. In his novel on the King called *Der Vater* (1937) Jochen Klepper was the first author to have drawn attention to Gundling's fate, which could also come straight from a

Shakespeare play.[13] What Klepper makes the reader witness is the disintegration of an individual – from scholar to fool.

An even darker side of the court jester's existence was told in a novel of our time. The Israeli writer and diplomat Avigdor Dagan describes in his story *Die Hofnarren* (1990) the struggle for survival in a concentration camp in which a commander forced four of his favourite prisoners to act as his "court jesters" as the price for their survival. The narrator, one of the commander's victims, speaks of himself and his fellow-survivors as men who emerged from this traumatic experience as psychologically deformed individuals. With his chilling parable Dagan seems to confirm Nietzsche's point about the Jews and their enforced use of masks.

The question of deformed identity, albeit in an obviously different context, was already at the heart of Nietzsche's concern with masks. He associated an entire pathology with the use of masks. According to Nietzsche even noble-mindedness can be a matter of wearing the right mask as he stated in the aforementioned letter to his composer-friend Heinrich Köselitz of July 1885. But it was in the final manuscript that Nietzsche had prepared for print, his *Dionysos-Dithyramben*, where his expression of ecstatic praise of deception gained its ultimate form:

> Only fool! Only poet!
> Only speaking colourfully
> speaking through fools' masks
> climbing around on deceiving bridges of words
> on rainbows of lies
> meandering, creeping about
> between false skies
> *only* fool! *only* poet! […]
> Is this the – punter of truth? […] [14]

The poet as jester fooling with words and lustfully betraying truth – was this Nietzsche's dithyrambic expression of ultimate release and final showdown with the Platonic tradition that rejected all masks? Or is this a form of final self-criticism. After all he saw himself as the chief analyst of décadence but seemed to have realized, at least at times, that he himself had fallen victim to the luring of décadence.

5.   The Mask Called Richard Wagner

This ambivalence is, of course, reflected in his attitude towards the one who was in his eyes the actor of actors, deceiver of deceivers and ultimate confidence man in the arts – Richard Wagner. Nietzsche's most notorious attack on the composer written in the form of an extended letter from Turino under the polemic title *Der Fall Wagner* (1888) is a relentless attempt to unmask the magician in music. For him what Wagner stood for was "the arrival of the actor in music" and composition. Nietzsche's point is that Wagner had acted the composer pretending that he was capable of creating unsurpassable depth in music. Bayreuth had turned into the court of an impostor with all the musicians, singers and conductors behaving like Wagner's, the great charlatan's, court jesters. From early on Nietzsche realized Wagner's intention to turn him, the young professor, into one of his court jesters, too, who would have been responsible for promulgating and interpreting Wagner's artistic mission.

This said the way in which Nietzsche analyses Wagner's mask-like appearance in the history of music suggests that he thought of this conception of art to have had a certain inevitability. The question implied in Nietzsche's approach to Wagner is whether music can and, perhaps at times, must turn into an acoustic mask and resounding travesty of truth. However, Nietzsche had stated as one of the reasons why he examined Wagner's conception of art so painstakingly that music "should not turn into an art of lying."[15] Yet, at the same time, music lends itself to just that. Even the supposedly innocent music of his friend Peter Gast, alias Heinrich Köselitz, resembled a mask of the eighteenth century that he put on the face of his time.

6.   The Musical Clown

Some four years after Nietzsche wrote about Wagner's mask and actor-like behaviour Ruggiero Leoncavallo (1858-1919) finished his striking two act opera *I Pagliacci* (the Clowns). Tonio, the personified prologue ("io sono il Prologo"), announces in a costume in the style of the *commedia dell'Arte* that the author of the libretto and music, Leoncavallo, regarded truth as his inspiration. Ironically, his libretto became an object of controversy. Leoncavallo was accused of having plagiarized Catulle Mendes's play, *La Femme de Tabarin*.

The first act of the opera introduces the comedians as they arrive in a bustling Calabrian village. We meet the leader of the players Canio, Nedda his unfaithful wife, Silvio her lover, and Tonio he onlooker. The act concludes with Canio's famous heart-rendering aria ("ridi Pagliaccio") in which he deplores his fate as betrayed husband condemned to sorrow but compelled to make others laugh – as ever at his expense. This aria is one of the defining moments in the history of the clown on the musical stage

> Perform the play! While am racked with grief,
> Not knowing what I say or what I do!
> And yet … I must … ah, force myself to do it!
> Bah! You are not a man!
> You are Pagliaccio!
> Put on the costume, the powder and the paint:

The people pay and want to laugh.
And if Harlequin steals your Columbine,
Laugh Pagliaccio, and all will applaud you!
Change all your tears and anguish into clowning:
And into a grimace your sobbing and your pain ...
Laugh, Pagliaccio, at your shattered love!
Laugh at the sorrow that has rent your heart!
(*Grief-stricken he goes out through the curtain.*)[16]

Canio's aria reaches the truth about deception; it describes a man trapped, even imprisoned in costume and mask. The second act mirrors on stage what had happened before in the village. The *commedia dell'arte* characters perform their own lives, the betrayal and revenge, except that jealous Canio/Pagliaccio stabs his Columbine and her lover for real. In a tragicomic turn at the end Tonio/Taddeo, the former prologue personified proclaims after the murders were committed "The comedy is ended" – *La commedia è finita!* At the end, stage and life are but one thing.

The fate of the clown and with it his mask are musical events – this was Leoncavallo's approach. But in the history of the clown music itself had become an object of clownery. The clown, Grock and Charlie Rivel in particular, can turn every object into a quasi musical instrument. He may insist on playing but one chord; f-sharp minor seems to be preferred by clowns, perhaps due to the peculiar melancholy this chord radiates. The musical clown, more so than any other performer, is surrounded by silence. This silence serves as the space of resonance for the magic that unfolds through the clownesque performance no matter how basic the means of musical imitations.[17]

7.   The Virtue of Masks

Is the mask therefore an instrument for the redemption from reality or is mask in need to be redeemed itself? This is the question Leoncavallo associated with *I Pagliacci* and Nietzsche with Wagner as composer of the *Ring* and *Parsifal*. Nietzsche saw Wagner wearing the mask of Wotan, Klingsor and Parsifal at the same time, and regarded Wagner as a clown who liked to mimic his guests, act as his own impresario and avoid confrontation with reality. And Nietzsche himself? Can his works be read as parodies on the philosophical tradition, as works of an author who playfully exchanged the masks of sage and satyr at his convenience?

Nietzsche's preoccupation with masks reflects his concern about the possibility of speaking the truth. For masks could be regarded as facial lies, as it were, images of lies that cover man's face or, almost by the same token, revelations of what a person feels it should look like. Two of Nietzsche's last major works, *Antichrist* and *Ecce homo*, open with references to the face.

Nietzsche wanted to make his readers to look into each other's face (*Antichrist*) and look *through* their various masks in order to detect their real and true character. What do they find? "We are Hyperboreans" that is to say people who *believed* to have lived beyond the North Wind in a sunny land. But, in fact, this surprising result of people's (and Nietzsche's!) all too sudden mutual recognition can but confirm a life in self-deception; for the Hyperboreans have only *believed* to be in the eternal South untouched by the harshness of the elements. The question of where they *really* are remains as open as the meaning and ultimate purpose of Nietzsche's attempted "revaluation of all values." In *Ecce homo* Nietzsche sets out looking into his own face and in that of his *œuvre*. *Ecce homo* was his main autobiographical project designed to unmask his life. This ambition was driven by Nietzsche's fear that he could be "mistaken for" someone or something else ("Verwechselt mich vor Allem nicht!"[18]). For once, Nietzsche, the analyst of modernism's ambiguities, endeavoured to become, and remain, recognisable as a thinker who can command the use of masks if it enhanced the colourfulness of his argument but without losing his very own, as he professed, unambiguous identity. But even in *Ecce homo* Nietzsche insisted that it is "Spiel" (playfulness) that provides us with the one and only mode of dealing with the "great tasks."[19] To the very end he lived up to his own expectation of being a *philosophus ludens* who found the style of writing and presenting his thoughts an indispensable tool for executing his intellectual artistry. In *Ecce homo* he unmasked the nature and purpose of his various works thus implying that his books may well have served him in the past as masks. About himself, including the state of his health, he appears as frank as he can be even though he introduces himself in the form of a riddle suggesting that he had already died as his own father, but continues to live and grow old as his very own mother.

8.   Ecce Homo and Other Performances

Ecce homo introduces a specific way of self-analysis that eventually amounts to the process of unmasking turning into the most bizarre of masks. For at the end Nietzsche emerges from this process as the bearer of a double mask, namely that of Dionysus and the Crucified. To be precise, he finds himself being caught between them or by their antagonism ("Dionysus *gegen den Gekreuzigten*"[20]).

Immediately after finishing *Ecce homo* Nietzsche embarked, as we seen already, on revising his Zarathustra-inspired *Dionysus-Dithyrambs*[21] and preparing them for publication. As we have pointed out earlier these poems celebrate in more than one way the truth of lying as well as the multi-perspectivism of which Nietzsche had declared himself a master in *Ecce homo*. In addition to the previously made point that, the first dithyramb in particular, amounted to a shameless mocking of Plato's diatribe against the arts there is another aspect which needs to be considered in our context. The fool-poet presents himself as a suitor, if not punter, of the decaying truth. And one of the most striking words Nietzsche uses in connection with the fool-poet is "Larve," meaning both larva, grub and (Venetian) mask. The fool-poet in this poem speaks through the "Larve" in the most colourful of manners. The colourfulness of his speech is emphasised repeatedly. Moreover, we see the fool-poet climbing on deceiving bridges of words ("herumsteigend auflügnerischen Wortbrücken") and even on lying rainbows ("Lügen-Regenbogen"). The larva in a biological sense, however, implies a development into a different form of existence by metamorphosis. But it is difficult see how this fool-poet, who is longing to be dispelled by truth, could engage in any form of further development. He remains what he is already: fool and poet. His mask is a well of words and, at the same time, a dark mirror for all those who look at him.

At the end of *Ecce homo* Nietzsche suggested that by now he may have become a buffoon which he preferred to ending up as a "saint."[22] This suggestion is consequential for it illustrates his preoccupation with the mask and delight in the art of lying. As explained earlier, Nietzsche had not always written in praise of masks. In *The Birth of Tragedy* he underlined that the Greek stage characters until Euripides had been little else than "masks of Dionysus,"[23] later he claimed that even Euripides himself had turned into a "mask," through him, according to Nietzsche, spoke Socrates and with him the destruction of myth and *genuine* tragedy. It is surprising though that Nietzsche did not explore the use of mask by actors and choruses in ancient Greek plays more fully. Had he embarked on discussing this important feature of the Greek stage then he would have been likely to come to his positive understanding of the mask even earlier which may well have had consequences for his conception of truth in *Human All Too Human*.

If ever there was any proximity between analytical reason and sheer clownery with thoughts, highly sophisticated intellectualism and sheer foolishness then in the works of Nietzsche. But the only real clown-like figure that Nietzsche ever came in contact with was indeed Wagner. Yet, in the history of philosophy there is another such encounter, namely between Adorno and Charlie Chaplin after the Second World War in Chaplin's Hollywood mansion. At a party Adorno was introduced to a famous actor who, unbeknown to the young philosopher, had lost both hands in the war. Adorno wanted to congratulate him on his achievements in the film *The Best Years of our Life* but was profoundly shocked when he realized that he was shaking a cold metal hook instead of a hand. Chaplin then imitated Adorno's reaction. This non-verbal mimesis, which Chaplin commanded with rare perfection, is seen by some of Adorno's critics as one of the main features of the philosopher's own style in the sense that he, too, wanted to diffuse through writing in a particular way moments of tension that occur when something terrifying happens.[24]

It is, perhaps, consequential that through the figure of the clownish fool a whole new understanding of opera was introduced – not by Leoncavallo but Arnold Schönberg in 1912. His operatic melodrama is based on Albert Giraud's poem *Pierrot Lunaire* in which the clownish protagonist imagines himself to be executed by the blade of the moon. Schönberg portrays imagination as a form of self-torture which can only be redeemed by indulging in nostalgia and *kitsch*. This Pierrot, too, cannot discharge his mask.[25] But the musical underscoring of his feelings reflects a mind that plays to the tune of self-deformation. Pierrot's identity is drifting between associating himself with the fatally seductive moonlight and identifying with unfulfilled yearning for a final homecoming.

The masks of Pierrot, Canio and, not to forget, Till Eulenspiegel in Richard Strauss's musical narrative are icons of modernism. Perhaps Nietzsche worried about this very prospect that the actor and clown could become the godfathers of artistic innovation; hence his decidedly ambiguous praise of the mask. "Everything profound loves the mask" did not imply that masks themselves possess profundity. Masks, according to Nietzsche, were ultimately the result of misinterpretations – both of texts, statements of the "profound spirit" or any of his utterances and gestures. This may have tragic or comic effects. But this conception illustrates that the truth of any "profound" matter can only be a truth about its mask-like image.

But how do we feel about this state of play with masks? We have by now become the sorcerer's apprentices of progress in civilisation. In order to cope with this situation we seem to need the assistance of more clowns and magicians in order to distract and comfort us. If we watch them carefully we will see in their mimicking the growing of our very own masks; and they are expanding at the expense of the faces they once pretended to protect.

Notes

[1] Rainer Maria Rilke, "Die Aufzeichnungen des Malte Laurids Brigge," in *Werke*. Kommentierte Ausgabe Vol. 3, ed. Manfred Engel, Ulrich Fülleborn, Horst Nalewski, August Stahl (Frankfurt and Leipzig: Insel Verlag, 1996), 507.

[2] In Oscar Wilde, *The Complete Works*, ed. J. B. Foreman. With an Introduction by Vyvyan Holland (London and Glasgow: Collins, 1984), 1078.

[3] Seamus Heaney, *The Redress of Poetry. Oxford Lectures* (London: Faber & Faber, 1995), 86.

[4] Friedrich Nietzsche, *Die fröhliche Wissenschaft*, in *Sämtliche Werke. Kritische Studienausgabe* Vol. 3 (= KSA), ed. Giorgio Colli and Mazzino Montinari (Munich and Berlin: Deutscher Taschenbuch Verlag/de Gruyter, 1988), 433.

[5] In Friedrich Nietzsche, *Sämtliche Briefe. Kritische Studienausgabe*. Vol. 7, ed. Giorgio Colli and Mazzino Montinari (Munich and Berlin: Deutscher Taschenbuch Verlag/de Gruyter, 1986), 44 (written on 7 Mai 1885).

[6] Ibid, 48 (written on the same day 7 May 1885).

[7] Ibid, 52 (letter of 20 Mai 1885).

[8] In KSA 5 (40), 57. Transl. from R.J. Hollingdale (Friedrich Nietzsche, *Beyond Good and Evil. Prelude to a philosophy of the future*. With an Introduction by Michael Tanner (Penguin Books Harmondsworth, 1990), 69.

[9] In George Orwell, *Complete Works*. Vol. X (London: Peter Davies. Secker & Warburg, 1999), 504.

[10] See Rüdiger Görner, "Spuren ins Unwegsame. Notiz über das Absurde bei Nietzsche und Levinas" in Rüdiger Görner, *Mauer Schatten Gerüst. Kulturkritische Essays* (Tübingen: Klöpfer & Meyer, 1999), 148-154.

[11] One of the first studies on the court jester was written by Carl Floegel, *Geschichte der Hofnarren* (Liegnitz 1789).

[12] In Friedrich Hebbel, *Briefwechsel*. Historische kritische Ausgabe in fünf Bänden. Wesselburener Ausgabe Vol. 1, ed. Otfried Ehrismann et al. , (Munich: iudicium verlag, 1999), 272 (letter of 12 December 1838).

[13] Jochen Klepper, *Der Vater. Roman eines Königs* (Stuttgart: Deutsche Verlags Anstalt o.J.), esp. 204.

[14] Nur Narr! Nur Dichter!/ Nur Buntes redend,/ aus Narrenlarven bunt herausredend,/ herumsteigend auf lügnerischen Wortbrücken,/ auf Lügen-Regenbogen/ zwischen falschen Himmeln/ herumschweifend, herumschleichend – /*nur* Narr! *nur* Dichter! /[…] Das – der Wahrheit Freier? […] KSA 6, 378.

[15] Ibid, 39.

[16] In Pietro Mascagni, *Cavalleria Rusticana*. Ruggiero Leoncavallo, *I Pagliacci*. Philharmonia Orchestra Riccardo Muti. Electrical & Musical Industries 1954, 30.

[17] See Annette Fried andJoachim Keller, *Faszination Clown* (Düsseldorf: Patmos Verlag, 2003), 151-157.

[18] KSA 6, 257.

[19] Ibid, 297.
[20] Ibid, 374.
[21] Ibid, 377-410.
[22] Ibid, 365.
[23] KSA 1, 71.
[24] Jürgen Habermas, *Philosophisch-politische Profile*. Erweiterte Ausgabe (Frankfurt am Main: Suhrkamp Verlag, 1987), 167.
[25] See Wilhelm Sinkovicz, *Mehr als zwölf Töne. Arnold Schönberg* (Vienna: Paul Zsolnay Verlag, 1998), 141-150.

Bibliography

Floegel, Carl. *Geschichte der Hofnarren*. Liegnitz 1789.

Görner, Rüdiger. *Mauer Schatten Gerüst. Kulturkritische Essays*. Tübingen: Klöpfer & Meyer. 1999.

Habermas, Jürgen. *Philosophisch-politische Profile*. Erweiterte Ausgabe. Frankfurt am Main: Suhrkamp Verlag, 1987.

Hebbel, Friedrich. *Briefwechsel*. Hist.-krit. Ausgabe in fünf Bänden. Wesselburener Ausgabe. Edited by Otfried Ehrismann et al. Munich: iudicium verlag,1999.

Heaney, Seamus. *The Redress of Poetry. Oxford Lectures*. London: Faber & Faber, 1995.

Klepper, Jochen, *Der Vater. Roman eines Königs*. Stuttgart: Deutsche Verlags Anstalt, 1954.

Nietzsche, Friedrich. *Sämtliche Werke*. Kritische Studienausgabe. Edited by Giorgio Colli and Mazzino Montinari. Munich and Berlin. Deutscher Taschenbuch Verlag/de Gruyter, 1988.

—. *Sämtliche Briefe*. Kritische Studienausgabe. Edited by Giorgio Colli and Mazzino Montinari. Munich and Berlin: Deutscher Taschenbuch Verlag/de Gruyter, 1986

—. *Beyond Good and Evil. Prelude to a philosophy of the future*. With an introduction by Michael Tanner. Harmondsworth: Penguin, 1990.

Orwell, George. *Complete Works*. Edited by Peter Davies. London: Secker & Warburg, 1999.

Rilke, Rainer Maria. *Werke*. Kommentierte Ausgabe Vol. 3. Edited by Manfred Engel, Ulrich Fülleborn, Horst Nalewski, August Stahl. Frankfurt and Leipzig: Insel Verlag, 1996.

Sinkovicz, Wilhelm. *Mehr als zwölf Töne. Arnold Schönberg*. Vienna: Paul Zsolnay Verlag, 1998.

Wilde, Oscar. *The Complete Works*. Edited by J.B. Foreman. With an
        introduction by Vyvyan Holland. London and Glasgow: Collins,
        1984.

Clowning Around at the Limits of Representation: On Fools, Fetishes and Bruce Nauman's *Clown Torture*

Maxim Leonid Weintraub

For centuries artists have been drawn to the figure of the clown and its metaphorical potential regarding representation and self-representation, perhaps never more so than in the last quarter of the twentieth century – a period which saw such varied artists as Ugo Rondinone, Mauricio Cattelan, Roni Horn, Jack Pierson, Paul McCarthy and Cindy Sherman, to name but a few, incorporate the iconography of the clown into their art. But perhaps the most provocative use of a clown figure during this time occurs in the art of Bruce Nauman, an American artist born in Fort Wayne, Indiana, who in the 1980s made a series of video and installation pieces in which a clown appears, foremost among them his 1987 installation *Clown Torture*. Since the 1960s Nauman's art has consistently probed the fundamental nature of both words and images – a career-long preoccupation with the possibilities and limitations of representation and signification, I argue in the essay that follows, in which the figure of the clown will prove crucial, and *Clown Torture* central.

Variously described by critics as "disorienting," "unbearable," "excruciating," "unsettling," "abrasive," and "repellent," Nauman's video installation *Clown Torture* is indeed an experience that produces in spectators a "fussy anxiety [that] swamp[s] us with dread."[1] *Clown Torture* consists of an enclosed room with two pairs of stacked video monitors placed atop pedestals and two large video images projected onto opposite walls by overhead video projectors. Each screen and wall projection shows footage of a clown engaged in some absurd activity. [Figure 1]

On one monitor in particular we see a clown dressed in typical clown attire, complete with colourful bulbous nose, wig, and make-up looking directly into the camera and reciting the following joke: "Pete and Repeat are sitting on a fence, Pete falls off. Who is left? Repeat. Pete and Repeat are sitting on a fence, Pete falls off, who is left? Repeat." [Figure 2]

Figure 1. Bruce Nauman, Clown Torture 1987
(detail) © Bruce Nauman / Artists Rights Society
(ARS), New York

Figure 2. Bruce Nauman, Clown Torture 1987
(detail) © Bruce Nauman / Artists Rights Society
(ARS), New York

Dutifully restarting each time the punch line is delivered with its
imperative to begin again, the increasingly exasperated clown seems trapped
in the joke's perpetual linguistic loop. Indeed, the clown's predicament

constitutes the entirety of a videotape that is itself viewed in a continuous loop, factors that contribute further to an overall impression of endless circularity. Each remaining monitor and wall projection presents in similar fashion a different clown performing an equally repetitive activity, from balancing a fishbowl on the end of a long stick to repeatedly walking through a door and getting doused by a bucket of water that comes crashing down. In *Clown Torture*'s darkened room the installation's multiple video monitors and the "aggressive reverberations" of their loud and competing soundtracks produce a cacophonous, percussive visual and sonic environment, one that on curator Robert Storr's account makes *Clown Torture* "excruciating to watch or hear," and that critic Peter Schjedahl concludes causes the spectator to "glaze over, tense up and flee."[2]

Nauman's *Clown Torture* marks one of the first—and certainly the most striking – of several appearances of a clown-like figure in the artist's oeuvre. And while much has been said about this complicated work – by many accounts one of Nauman's most important – my tasks in this essay are relatively modest: to examine the artist's rather remarkable decision to use a clown as the protagonist of his video installation, and in so doing to offer a reading of *Clown Torture* and its raucous environment that will help us to better appreciate why it prompts the strong reactions from viewers that it does. Indeed, this essay takes seriously these bewildered critical responses to Nauman's work, as I believe that they are important and heretofore unexamined indices of *Clown Torture*'s productive force.[3]

To this end, I concentrate my analysis primarily on one particular aspect of Nauman's *Clown Torture*, namely the aforementioned "Pete and Repeat" clown – admittedly but one element of a complex whole, yet one that I believe is emblematic of the concerns Nauman explores in *Clown Torture* specifically and in his artistic practice generally. In this essay I argue that Nauman's use of a clown suggests that the issue at hand in *Clown Torture* is in fact the issue of representation itself, a reading that reframes the figure of the clown in a postmodern context and ultimately provides an interpretation of the work's jarring environment and its impact on us as viewers. By way of beginning then, it is important to briefly note that *Clown Torture*'s engagement with the problem of representation does not alone grant it a unique status in Nauman's oeuvre, for as we shall see, Nauman's art has consistently been engaged with representation and its limitations from the outset.

Indeed, some of Nauman's earliest art demonstrates this career-long concern with representation, as his photographic pun *Eating My Words* from 1967 and his neon sign word play *Eat/Death* from 1972 suggest.[4] Nauman made these works, each in its own way a succinct indictment of a verbal or visual sign's illusory stability, at a time when contemporary philosophy was also engaging with the implications of the gaps, breaks, and absences in representation's structure.[5] As is well known, the 1960s saw a renewed interest in the fundamental distinction between signifier and signified posited decades earlier by the Swiss linguist Ferdinand de Saussure. Ultimately, a number of theorists began calling attention to the fact that the very system upon which language's signifying function and coherence depends also contains within it the spectre of its own incoherence, as each signifier constitutionally 'is' nothing more than its difference from other signifiers. Indeed, it is precisely these same differential gaps that make words legible and meaning possible that also raise the radical possibility of a word's *il*legibility and meaning's *im*possibility. And it is this capricious and arbitrary aspect of signification and representation that Nauman has probed and exploited in his art from the outset.

With his visual puns and word play in mind – of which *Eating my Words* and *Eat/Death* are but two examples of many – we see that Nauman was exploring representation's seams and fissures at a moment when such considerations were also at the fore of contemporary theoretical concerns.[6] For *Eating my Words*, the photograph in which Nauman consumes letters made of bread that spell out "words," and *Eat/Death*, in which one neon word seemingly emanates from another, both conspicuously point to representation's differential structure and equivocal nature – the former by featuring how words and phrases can readily assume unforeseen significations, and the latter by rendering literal the way in which words and meanings are inflected by and acquire meaning through the absent presence of other words and meanings.

Of course, in our everyday lives we effectively and understandably disavow representation's imprecision – that is, we suppress in the name of unity and continuity such discontinuities as those put forward in Nauman's puns and language games. Understandable as well is the anxiety that this acknowledgment of representation's illusory coherence can provoke, a point which returns us to Nauman's clown for reasons that will be made clear shortly. As I see it, puns and anagrams are central motifs in Nauman's art precisely for their divisive operations on representation, their dismantling of our normalising systems of meaning production and their subsequent effect on us as viewers.[7] But how *Clown Torture* manifests Nauman's artistic concern with representation's precarious structure, and why it prompted the reactions that it did are questions not yet answered. With these questions in mind, then, let us now turn our attention back to the figure of the clown, and begin by considering his role in the overall performance that is the circus.

As provider of comic relief and diversion, the clown is a figure that distracts us between the circus' feature acts. Performing his antics during the interval required to disassemble one big number and make ready the next, the clown diverts our attention so that we might not notice the necessary breaks in the performance. And it is of course not the clowns and their antics but the bigger, more elaborate numbers with their spectacular feats and breathtaking grand finales that draw us to the circus, and that we anticipate seeing and remember long afterward. Performing in the interstitial moments of a larger extravaganza, the clown is but an entr'acte, an interludinal figure meant to entertain not *as* a feature act but *between* them. The clown is, in other words, an incidental figure effectively operating in the gaps of the representation that is the circus, whose function is to cover over those necessary breaks that literally make the circus possible in order to create the illusion of the show's seamlessness – an illusion to which we as viewers of the spectacle willingly acquiesce.

However, contrary to circus convention, Nauman's "Pete and Repeat" clown's performance is neither brief nor functioning as a discreet transitional bridge between acts. Rather, Nauman's clown performs an endless routine in the fixed glare of a spotlight not typically meant to linger on such a figure. His divertissement, quickly emptied of any diversionary power or entertainment value with each retelling of his not-so-funny joke, seems abruptly ill fitted for his sudden feature-act status. With its clown transposed from an incidental and provisional figure into protagonist, *Clown Torture* presents to us the sideshow without the main event. Indeed, in *Clown Torture* the sideshow *is* the main event.

Elsewhere the dutiful custodian of representation's illusory unity in the context of the circus, Nauman's clown instead marks representation as *dis*unified, precisely because the clown's essential function as the suppressor of that fact has been thrown into relief. And if we begin to consider the clown in the context of Nauman's larger artistic concerns, the importance of the figure – as fetish and more abstractly as metaphor – becomes clear. If Nauman's punning and word play expose the gaps in representation by foregrounding a sign's incapacity to fully represent, then *Clown Torture* does likewise by foregrounding a fetish figure meant to maintain the illusion of representation's seamlessness – an overexposure that unravels the delicate conditions upon which our disavowal depends and renders transparent the machinery of representation's own masquerade.[8] And this proposition that *Clown Torture*'s clown is indeed functioning as a metaphor for representation is impressed on us not only by the circumstances of his performance but also by its content: the "Pete and Repeat" joke.

Of course, much can be said about the constitutional repetition of the "Pete and Repeat" joke, including the way in which its Sisyphean form collapses narrative structure and suggests language's self-referential nature. Indeed, as frustrating tautology endlessly looping back on itself, the clown's repeating joke can productively be read – as so much of Nauman's work can – as a critique of our collective desire for a sense of meaningful telos and definitive resolution, as it emphatically complies with neither. But the very fact that Nauman's miscast clown repeats a self-reflexive joke *about* repetition suggests once again that his clown functions as a metaphor for representation. After all, if gaps and absences are one essential requirement for representation then iteration is the other, since signs—be they verbal or visual – are only identifiable as such through their ability to be repeated, reiterated.[9] And like a pun's discursive operation, the "Pete and Repeat" joke does not simply reveal the mechanics of representation in its form and content but also yields the consequence of those differential processes, as the "Pete and Repeat" clown fails at his task of achieving closure to his joke, and does so repeatedly.

That *Clown Torture*'s clown functions as a metaphor for representation seems ever more certain when we consider that Nauman employs a protagonist whose very nature makes it the perfect emblem for just such a task. For those same elements that identify the clown as such – namely the exaggerated artifice of its dress and makeup – operate quite candidly according to the conditions of a sign, wholly dependent as they are on their iterability and recognisability. Indeed, the very "essence" of the clown hinges on a clichéd idiom of signs embalmed in its cosmetics and woven into its costume that signal different stock character types (a happy or sad clown) and traits (clumsiness or naiveté). As ultimately nothing but a surface of signs, the clown is a figure inscribed in and prescribed by representation, one whose effect hinges on an acknowledgement from its audience of its own status as a sign. In short, a clown *is* only what its excessive makeup and costume signifies – there is nothing behind the mask.

With this understanding of the clown in mind the affinity between *Clown Torture* and Nauman's puns and word play becomes increasingly clear. Both in the end about representation's inadequacy, pun and clown expose the seams in representation's fragile masquerade – the former through each semantic slippage and the latter as an emblem of the very lack that it is meant to conceal. And while *Clown Torture* is arguably the most provocative articulation in Nauman's oeuvre of this fundamental concern, it is not the only instance in which the artist employed a clown-like figure performing absurd antics to suggest representation's limitations.

Indeed, clowns appeared in a series of works by Nauman from the late 1980s, most notably *Clown Torture: Dark and Stormy Night with Laughter* (1987), *Clown Torture: I'm Sorry and No, No, No, No* (1987) and *Double No* (1988) [Figures 5, 6, 7]. Closely related to Nauman's original 1987 *Clown Torture* in form, content and chronology, it is nevertheless in the interesting ways that the clowns in these works differ from *Clown Torture*'s protagonist that interests us here, as such differences will ultimately supply further corroboration of what I have been saying about Nauman's "Pete and Repeat" clown vis-à-vis the question of representation.

While clearly related to the "Pete and Repeat" clown in their make-up and mannerisms, the aesthetics of the characters in these three other works by

Nauman additionally conflate the basic iconography of the circus clown with that of a court jester, most notably in their donning of the jester's motley garment, mock sceptre and cap and jingle bells.[10] And while a comprehensive consideration of such an archetypal character as the jester is beyond the limited scope of this essay, a brief review of the figure's historical role as an emblem of folly and its societal function will, I believe, help to explain Nauman's simultaneous interest in both jesters and clowns, and in the end further our understanding of *Clown Torture*.[11]

Like the circus clown, the jester traditionally performs as entertainment and diversion. However, the jester traditionally offers more pointed and overt social criticism and commentary than does the clown, as the often quick-witted jester couches within his courtly foolishness a certain wisdom. As such his actions, unlike those of the clown, serve more of a mimetic function with regard to society writ large. Indeed, historically the figure of the jester acted as a foil to the power, authority and order symbolised by the king and his court. Apparent in his riddling, sometimes nonsensical utterances and emblematised in his multicoloured motley, the jester embodied ambiguity and irrationality and personified the lesson that chaos, unreason and death were ever-present and always poised to irrupt within order, reason and life. In fact, centuries old pictorial and literary traditions explicitly link the jester to death, and quite often subsumed the figure with the personification of death itself.[12]

Subversive by nature, the jester sowed the ideas of unreason and finitude in a place where such ideas were otherwise disavowed – the comforts of the royal court. An emblem of the return of the repressed the riddling jester, like the pun and the "Pete and Repeat" clown, exposes the contrived and arbitrary nature of symbolic conventions, boundaries and structures while simultaneously staging for us as his audience our own equally contingent existence within those conventions. Indexing the spectre of unreason that always haunts order, the jester seems an apt figure for what I have been arguing is Nauman's career-long critique of the ways in which we perceive our world, and assures us that we are indeed on the right track concerning our present reading of *Clown Torture*'s clown.

Nauman's interest in this other fool figure at about the same time that he made *Clown Torture* allows us to more fully appreciate the way that his "Pete and Repeat" clown operates as fetish and as a metaphor in the service of its own critique of representation, and also makes possible our return to and final accounting for *Clown Torture* and the "fussy anxiety" that its assaultive space incites. Consider for a moment that if the exploits of Nauman's clown ultimately point us to representation's lack, it also compels us to acknowledge *our* role as spectators vis-à-vis the clown as spectacle, and exposes a more profound connection between the clown and us, one already signalled by the jester's historical association with unreason and death.

If, as post-structural theory and Nauman's language games have made clear, representation attempts and fails to summon forth its referent, to ultimately cover up the gap between word and world, then *Clown Torture*'s clown thematises not just representation's constitutive failure to re-present but also *our* desire to disavow this fact by calling attention to precisely those fetishistic conventions that are meant to remain invisible and unspoken. And this last fact brings to the fore one of the most compelling aspects about the figure of the clown and Nauman's decision to employ it: the circus clown performs his diversionary antics *for our benefit. Clown Torture* conspicuously foregrounds a figure that, by its very existence, manifests *our* desire as spectators to suppress representation's lack.[13] Thus the question at hand is not simply that of the clown *per se*, but also what is invested in the clown as a necessary object; for the spectacular nature of the clown invariably marks and bears *our* desire.[14] After all, if the clown is a necessary spectacle so that the show can indeed go on without interruption, it is a figure in whose very existence we see our own complicity since the clown's theatrics – indeed the figure itself – ultimately indexes our desire as spectators for representation to be seamless.

All of this is to say that if *Clown Torture* ultimately bespeaks a sign's impossible task of faithfully re-presenting the thing to which it refers, and if we understand the fetish as that which absorbs our anxiety and therefore enables us to persist in the face of an unsettling and threatening absence, then the need for such enabling strategies – embodied here in the figure of the clown in the context of the circus – indicates that we have much invested in representation's unity, which is to say in the concealment of representation's *dis*unity. Representation's lack – whether gestured to in the form of the pun or the fetishistic artifice of the clown – prompts such anxious disavowals ultimately because representation's disunity threatens our own imaginary organization, constructed as we are as subjects in and through the same insufficient systems of image and word.[15]

And it is here that we might return to and finally account for the remarkable tenor of the critical response to *Clown Torture* cited at the outset of this essay, and consider the possibility that Nauman's installation not only symbolise s representation's limitations, but also effects an experience of those very boundaries.[16] With this newly proposed reading in mind, let us consider more closely the reactions to Nauman's installation, beginning with the way in which the artist himself describes an encounter with his clowns.

Asked in an interview about his decision to use clowns in his videos, Nauman replied that he likes them because "[...] they become very disconcerting. You, I, one, we can't make contact with them."[17] By way of Nauman's remark—aside from its striking pronominal excess being a testament to language's insufficiency – we might begin to glimpse why *Clown Torture* prompts the reaction that it does. For on Nauman's account the trouble with *Clown Torture* seems to lie in our failure as viewing subjects to cognitively and perceptually apprehend the clowns as objects before us, as his ungraspable clowns, like personifications of a pun, somehow elude our collective subjective custody.

Now failure is certainly a significant trope in *Clown Torture*, as the repeated frustrations of the "Pete and Repeat" clown can do doubt attest to. But Nauman's statement also gestures to a failure of a more profound and intimate order – one at the level of *our* perceptual process. And it is by way of this new sort of failure that *Clown Torture* moves from being simply one more meditation on the nature of representation to being an experience that literally takes us to the very limits of representation itself.

If Nauman's quotation does indeed index a breakdown in our gestalt-based conventional expectations vis-à-vis the aesthetic object at hand, as I believe it does, then his sentiment regarding *Clown Torture* is not unique. Indeed, the critic Jean-Charles Masséra echoes the tenor of Nauman's reaction insofar as he too intuits an unsettling confrontation with an elusive, inapprehensible object, describing *Clown Torture*'s space as one in which, "Looking and listening become impossible and unbearable [...]"[18] And he concludes by stating, "Unable to say anything to us, [the] installation attack[s] us [...] as soon as you get in you have to get out."[19] Echoing then Nauman's acknowledgment about the work's failure to communicate we sense that on Masséra's account this disruption occurs not simply between viewer and clown but between viewer and the installation in its spatial and acoustic entirety. As such, Masséra's and Nauman's accounts, like those reactions cited at this essay's outset – for example Peter Schjedahl's description that *Clown Torture* compels the viewer to "glaze over, tense up and flee" – seem to be testaments to more than authorial contempt or intellectual unintelligibility. Their words instead collectively index something quite different and more visceral, something that I will provisionally describe here as a phenomenological disturbance produced by our inability to apprehend the work.

Constructed so as to "attack" us from all sides with sounds and images *Clown Torture* assails our holistic organization of space, our orientation within it and our relation to the objects at hand. Without a particular locus in its formal logic, *Clown Torture* does not simply elude perceptual apprehension but *overwhelms us* in its torrent of visual and sonic stimuli. Faced with an aesthetic object that defies apprehension – in psychoanalytic terms a pre-emption of object cathexis – *Clown Torture*'s force resides in its disruption of the conventions that structure our experience of the world around us and shape our perceptions. It is an environment that disregards the comforts of conventional expectation, not unlike the way in which Nauman's language games problematise a word or phrase's conventional signification; indeed, if his puns use humour to momentarily break us out of our perceptual or cognitive habits, *Clown Torture* shocks us out of them. And it is through the effect of *Clown Torture*'s shocking space on us as viewers that the installation as a whole turns from an expression of representation's inadequacy to an enactment of it.

As I have emphasised throughout, *Clown Torture*'s clown is a figure that marks representation's lack and our efforts to suppress that fact. But the pain generated by *Clown Torture*'s overall environment – a discomfort exemplified by Masséra's compelling observations that the work is "unable to say anything to us" and that "as soon as you get in you have to get out" – suggests that Nauman's installation not only thematises representation's lack but also puts us in an uncanny and overwhelmingly proximate relation to it. In other words, if Nauman's clown signals what is repressed in representation, then *Clown Torture*'s space gestures to that which is repressed in our self-representations by staging the limits of those representational strategies in a manner befitting the notion of torture suggested in the work's title. Let me explain.

Whatever the particular words or expressions invoked to describe the nature of *Clown Torture*'s visual and sonic assault, what is self-evident in such reactions is the installation's infliction of suffering, an infliction that prompts many critics to openly wonder "whether the [work's] title means the clowns are being tortured or you are."[20] This inversion, remarked upon in this instance by the art critic Michael Kimmelman but commonly expressed by others, is important not only as another testament to *Clown Torture*'s unaccommodating, if not threatening and oppressive space, but in its recasting of subject-object dynamics, in its repositioning of us as the object-victims of another's torture. And while such an observation does add a new, Nauman-esque twist to the work's suddenly polysemous title, the tenor of Kimmelman's and the other critical reactions to Nauman's installation seems fraught with more than mere hyperbole, bespeaking instead a more fundamental relationship between our disquieting experience and the work's titular motif of torture that requires further examination.

The act of torture is characterised by an infliction of mental or physical pain that is too much to bear, an experience whose analogue – if the responses to Nauman's work are any guide – can be found in the operations of *Clown Torture*'s environment.[21] The overwhelming extremity and immediacy of torture results in an experience that is inexpressible; it is a torment indifferent to any attempts at its symbolisation, its representation. Indeed its intolerability and excessiveness annuls the very processes of signification by rendering word and image inadequate. Faced with torture's unrepresentability, its refusal to coalesce into a legible sign, we encounter a gap between our victimised bodies and our processes of representing it, a breach in our self-knowledge and self-mastery that excises our social selves from the very site of torture.[22] In this breakdown of the social framework of meaning and the interruption of our relationship to our (intimately) external world the tortured body, unmoored from the social, becomes an abject object, and in self-representation's place there is for the moment only a void. In short, by exceeding culture and convention, torture disrupts our social selves and places us in close proximity to the Real.

Torture then, as a momentary intrusion of the Real, as a denuding of the process of (self-)representation, returns us once again to Nauman's *Clown Torture*, as both clown and torture – that is, both *Clown* and *Torture* – ultimately signal representation's lack. If the clown's "Pete and Repeat" joke exposes and parodies those narrative conventions and structures that bestow meaningful form to our "reality," it is a critique of representation that we see embodied in the form of Nauman's jester and clown. But it is the bewildering extremity of *Clown Torture*'s environment that transforms Nauman's installation from a simple meditation on representation's limitations to a work in which we encounter ourselves *at the site* of representation's inadequacy. If *Clown Torture* exposes the clown as a fetish and, ultimately, as a symbol of representation's lack, then the installation space's pre-emption of meaning production and apprehension momentarily produces that lack. What Nauman's clown and earlier puns thematise, in other words, *Clown Torture*'s environment effects.

Indeed, what we see indexed in the unsettled, belated reactions of Masséra, Nauman and others is *Clown Torture*'s failure to submit to the conditions and conventions upon which our representation of reality and our selves depend. Thinking again of the compelling statements by Nauman and Masséra concerning the way in which *Clown Torture* eclipses our position as viewers before an apprehensible object, it seems that the force of *Clown Torture* lies in the way it reveals the limitations of representation by effecting an experience momentarily devoid of culture or convention.[23]

The consequence of *Clown Torture* is, like the act of torture itself, the experience of an excessive space within which the limits of our perceptual processes and self-identity are laid bare, an environment that Parveen Adams has elsewhere called an "anamorphic space."[24] Generating the condition of our selves innocent of convention and unmoored from the gestalt project of self-organisation and self-representation, what *Clown Torture* is about is producing this anamorphic moment by instancing those very gaps emblematised by Nauman's clown.[25]

Significantly, if perhaps by now unsurprisingly, as early as 1975 Nauman had already explicitly expressed his concern with representation's inadequacy when he wrote in a textual accompaniment to another installation piece that, "No thing and no mask can cover the lack, alas."[26] Twelve years later, *Clown Torture* unmasks representation's masquerade by putting a masquerade of representation onto centre stage. Moreover, in light of Nauman's 1975 melancholic resignation to representation's lack, *Clown*

Torture embodies a striking manifestation of one artist's desire – if not compulsion – to effect an experience that might, if only for a moment, eclipse our perceptual and conventional fetishes and allow another modality of experience from the site of that lack.[27]

At this essay's outset I noted that for generations artists have employed the figure of the clown in their art for its rich metaphorical potential with regard to representation and self-representation. And in closing, we can say that in *Clown Torture* we encounter two intersecting lacks of representation: that evidenced by Nauman's clown and engendered by *Clown Torture*'s "disorienting," "unbearable," "excruciating," "unsettling," "abrasive," and "repellent" environment. That in *Clown Torture* we confront the lack about which Nauman wrote in 1975, and which we encounter in so many other of Nauman's works, confirms what I have been arguing throughout: that the problematic of representation (and self-representation) is indeed at issue in *Clown Torture*, a complex installation within which we find ourselves immersed in a bewildering, disconcerting, and potentially liberating experience at the very limits of representation.

Notes

[1] Neal Benezra, "Surveying Nauman," in *Bruce Nauman*, ed. Joan Simon (Minneapolis: Walker Art Center, 1994), 138; Ingrid Schaffner, "Circling Oblivion/ Bruce Nauman Through Samuel Beckett," in *Bruce Nauman: 1985-1996. Drawings, Prints, and Related Works* (Ridgefield, Connecticut: Aldrich Museum of Contemporary Art, 1997), 28; Jean-Charles Masséra, "Dance With the Law," in *Bruce Nauman*, ed. Christine van Assche (London: Hayward Gallery, 1998), 26; Robert Storr, "Flashing the Light in the Shadow of Doubt," in *Bruce Nauman*, ed. Robert C. Morgan (Baltimore: The Johns Hopkins University Press, 2002), 159; Kathryn Hixson, "Nauman: Good and Bad," *New Art Examiner* (December 1994): 34; Joan Hugo, "Bruce Nauman," in *Bruce Nauman*, ed. Robert C. Morgan (Baltimore: The Johns Hopkins University Press, 2002), 222; Paul Mattick, "Bruce Nauman," in *Bruce Nauman*, ed. Robert C. Morgan (Baltimore: The Johns Hopkins University Press, 2002), 226; Ronald Jones, "Bruce Nauman," *Bruce Nauman*, ed. Robert C. Morgan (Baltimore: The Johns Hopkins University Press, 2002), 229.

[2] Brooks Adams, "The Nauman Phenomenon," *Art & Auction* 13 (1990): 118; Robert Storr, 159; Peter Schjedahl, "The Trouble with Nauman," *Art in America* (April 1994): 85.

[3] I first encountered Nauman's *Clown Torture* at the Museum of Modern Art in New York, on the occasion of the artist's 1995 retrospective exhibition. I should say here that my own reactions to the work in question were analogous to those expressed by those voices that I quote in the main text. Nevertheless, as my argument hinges on *Clown Torture*'s effect on the viewer, for rhetorical purposes I have chosen to give particular weight in this essay to the documented critical reactions of others, rather than my own, in support of my thesis.

[4] Regarding this essay's emphasis on representation in both verbal and visual form, I would note here that Nauman's art has consistently violated the arbitrary division between word and image at every opportunity, treating both as equal semiotic material.

[5] See for example Jacques Derrida essay, "Structure, Sign, and Play in the Discourse of Human Sciences," in *Writing and Difference*, trans. Alan Bass (Chicago: University of Chicago Press, 1978), 278-294.

[6] The link between Nauman's concerns with the issue of representation and those of contemporary philosophy are quite explicit at various moments in Nauman's oeuvre, one of the most notable examples being one of the first, a 1968 lead plaque titled "A Rose Has no Teeth," the title and text of which were appropriated by Nauman from Ludwig Wittgenstein's *Philosophical Investigations*.

[7] This is a point that I have argued in my unpublished Master's thesis, "The Innocence of Becoming: Bruce Nauman's Art of Anxiety."

[8] I am indebted to Professor Isabelle Loring Wallace for her help in my formulation of this idea, and it is to her that I also owe a larger debt of gratitude, as her scholarship and thoughtful, generous advice have been invaluable to my own work on Bruce Nauman. I would also like to take this opportunity to thank Professor Lisa Saltzman for her constructive criticisms and guidance.

[9] See Jacques Derrida, "Signature Event Context," in *Margins of Philosophy*, trans. Alan Bass (Chicago: University of Chicago Press, 1982), 307-330.

[10] Of course, it needs to be remembered that these works do also differ in significant ways from both *Clown Torture* and from each other.

[11] For a thorough history of the jester figure, see William Willeford, *The Fool and His Scepter; A Study in Clowns and Jesters and Their Audience* (Evanston: Northwestern University Press, 1969).

[12] Among innumerable visual representations of the jester/fool as death in the history of art, Hans Sebald Beham's *Tod in Narrengestalt und Mädchen* (1541) and Hans Holbein's *The Queen* from his *Dance of Death* series (1538) count among the earliest and most striking.

[13] It is worth noting here the resonance between the clown and its evocation of childhood memories and Sigmund Freud's positioning of the initial lack – namely the lack of castration – in childhood.

[14] Significantly, the structure of the clown's joke hypostatises desire's metonymic slippage that is, like the joke, propelled by an unfulfillable lack.

[15] It is worth noting that Nauman created *Döppelganger/UFO* (1988) around the same time that he made *Clown Torture*, as it is a work whose title evokes in the figure of the döppelganger a haunting and uncanny reminder of our divided and mortal status.

[16] Nauman has often alluded to his efforts to produce art that effects a rupture in the perceptual habits and expectations of viewers, including when he likened the effect of certain of his works to, "[...] going up the stairs in the dark, when you think there is one more step and you take the step, but you are already at the top and have the funny [...] or going down the stairs and expecting there to be another step, but you are already at the bottom. It seems that you always have that jolt and it really throws you off." See Willoughby Sharp, "Two Interviews," in *Bruce Nauman*, ed. Robert C. Morgan (Baltimore: The Johns Hopkins University Press, 2002), 259.

[17] Joan Simon, "Breaking the Silence," *Art in America* 76 (1988): 203.

[18] Masséra, 26.

[19] Ibid.

[20] Michael Kimmelman, "Space Under a Chair, Sound From a Coffin," in *Bruce Nauman*, ed. Robert C. Morgan (Baltimore: The Johns Hopkins University Press, 2002), 210.

[21] For a related discussion of torture's effect on the body, see Elaine Scarry, *The Body in Pain: The Making and Unmaking of the World* (New York: Oxford University Press, 1985), 27-59.

[22] Significantly, the discrepancy between oneself and one's image is a prominent motif in Nauman's oeuvre, being a central feature in many of his mirror and video corridors from the late 1960s and 1970s.

[23] What is also suggested by Nauman's and Masséra's remarks is the way in which *Clown Torture* exposes the desire at work in our own spectatorial gaze. This confrontation with our own desires for identification with the art object is, as I have already pointed out, already realised in the clown's very necessity, perhaps signaling that another of *Clown Torture*'s effects is its reminder that our look is riddled with desire.

[24] Parveen Adams, *The Emptiness of the Image: Psychoanalysis and Sexual Differences* (New York: Routledge, 1996), 141-142.

[25] In 1988 Nauman described his art in terms quite relevant to my argument concerning *Clown Torture*'s visceral effect and his aspirations to effect an immediacy in his art in excess of symbolisation, having stated that he tries to

make art that "[…] was just there all at once. Like getting hit in the face with a baseball bat. Or better, like getting hit in the back of the neck. You never see it coming; it just knocks you down." See Joan Simon, "Breaking the Silence: An Interview with Bruce Nauman," *Art in America* 76 (1988): 142. For a valuable reading of the gestalt tendencies of our perception of the world see Richard Boothby's *Freud as Philosopher: Metapsycholgy After Lacan* (New York: Routledge Press, 2001).

[26] The text is part of his 1975 installation *Consummate Mask of Rock*. See Joan Simon, 56.

[27] My use of the term "melancholy" here is not accidental, as this essay's concern with lack and repetition – privileged terms in Freud's conception of melancholia – points to my contention that Nauman's *Clown Torture* is but one part of his career-long preoccupation with expressing the anxiety-inducing truth of representation, and to somehow express in spite of that fact. It is a necessary imperative towards impossible expression that I liken to that articulated by Samuel Beckett on a number of occasions, most famously in 1965 (translated into English in that year from the French original of 1949), concerning the artist's task as one involving "The expression that there is nothing to express, nothing with which to express, nothing from which to express, no power to express, no desire to express, together with the obligation to express." Significantly, Beckett was one of Nauman's earliest and most important influences. Nauman's frustrated desire for meaningful expression through, and in spite of, representation's bankruptcy is palpable in many of his works, of which I will only mention here a 1973 lithograph *Pay Attention*, whose text exhorts the viewer to "Pay attention Mother Fuckers," and a collage, also from 1973, that forlornly implores "Please Pay Attention Please."

Bibliography

Adams, Brooks. "The Nauman Phenomenon." *Art & Auction* 13, no. 5
        (December, 1990): 118-125.

Adams, Parveen. *The Emptiness of the Image: Psychoanalysis and Sexual
        Differences*. New York: Routledge, 1996.

Benezra, Neal. "Surveying Nauman." In *Bruce Nauman*, edited by Joan
        Simon, 13-46. Minneapolis: Walker Art Center, 1994.

Derrida, Jacques. "Structure, Sign, and Play in the Discourse of Human
        Sciences." In *Writing and Difference*, translated by Alan Bass, 278-
        294. Chicago: University of Chicago Press, 1978.

Hixson, Kathryn. "Nauman: Good and Bad." *New Art Examiner* 22

(December, 1994): 32-35.

Hugo, Joan "Bruce Nauman." In *Bruce Nauman*, edited by Robert C. Morgan, 221-223. Baltimore: The Johns Hopkins University Press, 2002.

Jones, Ronald. "Bruce Nauman." In *Bruce Nauman*, edited by Robert C. Morgan, 227-232. Baltimore: The Johns Hopkins University Press, 2002.

Kimmelman, Michael. "Space Under a Chair, Sound From a Coffin." In *Bruce Nauman*, edited by Robert C. Morgan, 208-211. Baltimore: The Johns Hopkins University Press, 2002.

Masséra, Jean-Charles. "Dance With the Law." In *Bruce Nauman*, edited by Christine van Assche, 20-33. London: Hayward Gallery, 1998.

Mattick, Paul. "Bruce Nauman." In *Bruce Nauman*, edited by Robert C. Morgan, 224-226. Baltimore: The Johns Hopkins University Press, 2002.

Scarry, Elaine. *The Body in Pain: The Making and Unmaking of the World.* New York: Oxford University Press, 1985.

Schaffner, Ingrid. "Circling Oblivion/ Bruce Nauman Through Samuel Beckett." In *Bruce Nauman: 1985-1996. Drawings, Prints, and Related Works*, edited by Jill Snyder, 15-31. Ridgefield, Connecticut: Aldrich Museum of Contemporary Art, 1997.

Schjedahl, Peter. "The Trouble with Nauman." *Art in America* 82 (April, 1994): 82-91.

Sharp, Willoughby. "Two Interviews." In *Bruce Nauman*, edited by Robert C. Morgan, 233-261. Baltimore: The Johns Hopkins University Press, 2002.

Simon, Joan. "Breaking the Silence: An Interview with Bruce Nauman." *Art in America* 76, no. 9 (September 1988): 140-149, 203.

Storr, Robert. "Flashing the Light in the Shadow of Doubt." In *Bruce Nauman*, edited by Robert C. Morgan, 155-162. Baltimore: The Johns Hopkins University Press, 2002.

An American Circus: the Lynch Victim as Clown

Barbara Lewis

The summer of 2000 in New York, I saw a photograph in the Museum of the City of New York that was taken one hundred years before. What was manifest in the image staggered my mind. There in front of me hanging on display was a lynched man placed, slack-bodied, in a chair. His face was decorated, post-mortem, as though he were a clownish figure, a masked fetish. The sepia-toned photograph of the seated corpse seemed to beckon me closer so that I could take a longer look. Something about it was magnetic, drawing me to it and holding my attention with a strange, insistent power. I could not keep my distance. The scenario portrayed was expressive of a macabre link that I, a cultural historian, had long suspected but had never found a way to put into words. Now, it was graphically evident. Lynching, the ultimate ritual banishment of outsider bodies from the privileges and protections of American citizenship, was related to minstrelsy, a masked performance genre emergent in the nineteenth century with roots in the circus. In minstrelsy, white males, many of them immigrants, costumed and masked themselves as black men – on occasion as black women – and danced and sang, played musical instruments, and told jokes on a wide variety of stages, official and impromptu, and later also in film. In this photograph, the black male body was manipulated into a role that satisfied the expectations of an original spectatorship that colluded in its extinction. The role of choice for those viewers was minstrel characterisation, which codified in performance the relationship between slave and master, subservient and dominant, seated and standing, with the master possessing ultimate ownership in the slave, inclusive of its right to life.

The clown image in the photograph exploded with drama, the kind few people talked about, a murderous and mean-spirited kind of racial drama climaxing in a death that was viewed as comic entertainment and sanctioned by many eyes. A black man had been lynched, his life taken away in a public ceremony in which white men officiated and took pleasure. In the crowd observing the lynching, if this lynching was like so many other spectacle lynchings conducted at that time, there were also women and children in attendance, eager to participate in the festivities. After it was slaughtered, the body was costumed as a minstrel clown. The corpse was desecrated and positioned in a chair by men who handled the body as though it were their bauble, a puppet festooned and controlled like a gossamer kite in the wind. The body was malleable in their fingers, and they made it into what they wanted it to be, a grotesque representation, a symbolic trophy and source of amusement. This picture of the simulated clown linked lynching, a carnival of death, to the wildly popular history of blackface performance or minstrelsy, its other, if lighter, side.

Without Sanctuary Plate 1.
The bludgeoned body of an African American male. Circa 1900, location unknown. Courtesy of the Allen/Littlefield Collection.

Perhaps it is strange that I would describe the communal meting out of a death penalty, summarily enacted, as carnival. For Bakhtin, carnival was a joyous occasion in which the community came together on a time-dependent basis, whether in response to a crisis or cyclical transition point, to push past its quotidian boundaries and emancipate its anxieties through revelry and role-reversal. This concentrated period of excess gave vent to energies that, if allowed to accumulate, threatened to destabilize social equilibrium. Those who were poor could pretend to be rich, and the rich could impersonate and even serve the poor, if they chose. Contrarieties were brought together in carnival. After indulging in difference, it was easier to return to daily functions and the usual round of obligations with renewed spirit. Carnival was salutary and rooted in cathartic laughter. Lynching was conducted in a festive atmosphere, as was carnival. In the public mind, the fire would begin to smoulder when news of the dastardly crime that was sure to bring down on the head of the culprit the deserved retaliation would be reported. When the culprit was apprehended and the lynching was certain, schools would be closed, and special excursion trains added to accommodate all the travellers clamouring to witness the fun. Lynching claimed the full attention of those involved, as did carnival. According to Bakhtin, "everyone participates because its very idea embraces all the people."[1] The men as well as women and children who took a hand in the American tradition of ritual killing were convinced they were doing the vital work of enforcing the social walls of their world, shoring up their integrity against attack and infringement. Also in lynching, the border between spectator and victim was easily crossed, as was the case in carnival. The crowd pressed close together to partake in the death. It is as though they became one body, an aggregate body. The victim body, however, was transgressed and perforated, sometimes even pulled apart. Its integrity was denied. In lynching, the body of the victim was claimed as communal property, and the citizens came together to partition it as relics for display, sale, and distribution. The daily tensions of living in a racially divided society were expiated through lynching, which momentarily eliminated the symbolic intruder presence. Once the ritual of death that expelled the disturbance was complete the world could travel at its normal pace again.

The link between blackface performance and carnival is explicit in Dale Cockrell's commentary on Jim Rice, the first international minstrel celebrity, who jumped Jim Crow in a way that called attention to the lower body, the carnivalesque bodily zone par excellence. Rice emphasised "dancing and the body and laughter, and how the performance of joy and pleasure can remake a less than perfect world."[2] By bringing the tradition of riotous and outrageous carnival street performance indoors to the stage, where it erupted into an extraordinary rush of popularity, minstrel performers mediated the betwixt and between character of carnival, which celebrates the end of one world or time and the beginning of another. During the formative period of minstrelsy, performers created a visual image of a grotesque otherness that modelled their ideal world, with them in absolute control. Other carnival elements were present in minstrelsy. Both privilege the present. Responding to and being fully in the moment was a key skill in the arsenal of minstrel performers. They were comics. They spoke to the everyday, sized up their audiences, and gave them what they wanted. They were improvisers. Carnival, as well as minstrelsy, juggles difference. Both thrive on the energy of opposition. Finally, each is disruptive, topsy turvy, chaotic, expressing the quality of a world turned upside down.

In minstrelsy, which seems to be all about release into the otherness of blackness that is liberating and fun-filled, playing and dancing in the streets of another reality has a darker face. The masking of minstrelsy, which constructs a doubled body that is neither black nor white, has a political dimension. It defines who, among the citizenry, can wear the mask and under what circumstances. It determines who laughs and who serves as the butt of laughter. It also fixes in the public mind the acceptable and exaggerated image of otherness, how it is to be perceived as clownish and inferior, bumbling and inept, dismissible. Lynching takes that perception to the extreme. The person who is lynched is abnormal, criminal, defective, deserving of elimination. Minstrelsy and lynching stalk the other side of carnival, the one Bakhtin did not explore. He specifically links death and carnival, which acknowledges as well as forestalls with laughter the onslaught of time. Bakhtin also divides the carnival spirit into phases, the medieval one with which he is concerned, and a subsequent Romantic era, out of which there came a more abusive carnival sensibility. It was during the Romantic phase that minstrelsy as well as lynching emerged. Then, according to Bakhtin, the world was full of terror needing to be controlled. Bakhtin describes this changed order that evokes a darker carnival sensibility:

> All that is ordinary, commonplace, belonging to everyday life, and recognised by all suddenly becomes meaningless, dubious and hostile. Our own world becomes an alien world. Something frightening is revealed in that which was habitual and secure.[3]

Radical departure from expectation characterises what was occurring when lynching took hold in America in the closing decades of the nineteenth and early decades of the twentieth centuries. The old order, built on the certainties of slavery, was dying. Transition was hard. The desire was to have a hand in shaping the future in line with the profile of the past. The men who engineered the lynching of the man made clown and also conceived and carried out this unusual lynching finale are outside the frame of the picture, but the hand of one man is apparent in the photograph. This insider yet outsider status, this doubleness, underscores the carnival narrative presented in the image. There are three key players in the creation and preservation of this visual narrative: the clown victim, the photographer whose hand is unseen, and the enabler, whose hand is implicated. The clown victim serves as the performer, the person whose action or, in this case, inaction and appearance give pleasure to the spectators who have been multiplied through the activity of the photographer, himself a facilitator for those who will be visually taking in the constructed image across boundaries of space and time, from one generation to the next. The hand that holds in place this telling tableau represents the regulatory ego that attempts to arrange everything and everyone it encounters in accord with its views. The tripartite constitution of ego, object, and witness in this scenario advertises its hostile comic intent, which fixes the representative subservient body in an unchanging status. In discussing wit and the comic, Freud identifies the comic turn to hostility as a process requiring three people: the ego, the object, and the stranger or observer.[4]

What was depicted in the photograph that riveted my eyes and mind was not violent in the conventional way that lynching scenes are violent. The victim's body, the visual focus in this tableau, was not stripped to the skin. His back and his legs were not whip slashed and disfigured with gaping scars. He was not hanging from the branch of a tree, from a bridge, or telephone pole. His hands were not rendered helpless behind his back. His flesh was not charred to stumps, his clothes were not ripped and soaked in blood. He did not appear to be castrated. He was not dismembered. The violence inflicted on him was not only reductive – in the sense of eliminating his life – but also additive. His face was painted and he was made to appear as a clown. Cotton tufts – most likely allusions to the recent agricultural slave past – were affixed to his pate and to the sides of his face. His eyebrows are exaggerated and redefined with white paint; so is his nose and mouth. In death, he is made outlandish, freakish, the main attraction in an improvisational circus of American violence. This photograph is one of the more disturbing and arresting images in *Without Sanctuary*, the book and accompanying exhibit of lynching photography that has travelled to several major cities in the United States and attracted world-wide attention and debate since its opening in a New York gallery in January 2000. As a result of the popularity of the book and exhibit, the subject of lynching has received new attention from the public and in academia. Simultaneous with a showing of the *Without Sanctuary* exhibit in Atlanta in the fall of 2002, the first international conference on lynching was held at Emory University in October 2002. Lynching has only recently become a subject removed from the academic ashcan. Now, it can be studied with scholarly concentration and examined from a variety of perspectives, including its situation within the history of American performance and entertainment.

The connection between lynching and the clown and thus implicitly minstrelsy, also identified with the clown, is highlighted in this sepia-toned photograph. Minstrelsy was the most pervasive performance genre in America in the nineteenth century. In his provocative as well as seminal book on minstrelsy in the antebellum era, Eric Lott wrote that:

> [M]any minstrel performers began their careers in the circus, perhaps even developing American blackface out of clowning (whose present mask in any case is clearly indebted to blackface), and continually found under the big top a vital arena of minstrel performance.[5]

In the first half of the nineteenth century, minstrelsy defined how the black body could be presented in public and visually consumed. Minstrelsy not only set how blacks were seen, it also ritualised how white males saw themselves. They saw themselves in command, sovereign over blacks. This absolute power was regularly reinforced by white males, who claimed the look and motion of the black body as within their prerogative to create. Lynching also assumes the sovereignty of white over black, and this sense of entitlement over the black body is expressed in the clown photograph with the rod that keeps the corpse in place. The chair in the clown photograph suggests a passive or sedentary rather than active relationship to power and recalls that in the antebellum period as well as subsequently, minstrel clowns often performed on stage in a chair. "Gentlemen, be seated" was the phrase that initiated the early minstrel show.

Located prominently on the half title page of *Without Sanctuary*, this image of the lynch victim as clown is set apart from and juxtaposed to the other one hundred photographs that fill the pages of the book. The clown photograph differs from the typical lynching iconography by not humiliating the victim in the usual way. Here, the corpse is seated rather than strung up. It is supported, not suspended. The corpse is fully clothed. Attention has been paid to the face of the corpse. It is built up. It is adorned. The uniqueness of this photograph is acknowledged by James Allen, who, through happenstance, began collecting these photographs over twenty years ago and now, with his partner James Littlefield, has amassed over one hundred of them from the second half of the nineteenth and the first sixty years of the twentieth centuries:

> This is perhaps the most extreme photographic example extant capturing the costuming of a victim of extra-legal violence. What white racists were unable to accomplish through intimidation, repressive laws, and social codes – namely, to mould the African American male into the myth of the emasculated "good ole darkey" – they have here accomplished by violence and costuming.[6]

The "good ole darkey" is tamed, reduced psychologically, degraded. The minstrel characterisation – here reference in the costuming of the clown – took the barb out of blackness. That was also the ultimate intent of lynching.

We know very little about the victim. Not his name, not where he was lynched, not what transgression he committed to draw upon himself this kind of punishment. We do, however, know the approximate year of his death. He was killed around 1900, in the crossover between one century and the next, a time of transition. Four other photographs (nos. 15, 16, 27, and 77) in *Without Sanctuary* depict African Americans lynched in or circa 1900. In addition to the simulated clown, these seven African Americans (four victims are shown in no. 16) are anonymous as well. Their identities were not important enough to record. They were effaced. What mattered was not who they were but what was done to them. The ritual enactment of death was key. The locations in three of the four photographs are unknown, and their crimes are not specified. In contrast, another photograph (no. 7) bearing the date of January 20, 1900 shows the double lynching in Fort Scott, Kansas of two white men, George and Ed Silsbee, who were accused of murder. Their bodies were cut down the next morning, a courtesy not generally accorded to black bodies that were left swinging in the wind and could be further victimised by vandals taking fleshly mementos of the communal deed.

During the changeover between centuries, racial restrictions, which had loosened a bit in the era of Emancipation, were being drawn tighter and tighter to insure that those who had been enslaved remained on the bottom politically and economically. Even those African Americans who had managed to establish some financial and social standing were not immune to the onslaught of lynching. In fact, their ambitions sometimes increased their vulnerability to attack. They were not conforming to the clown stereotype of ineptitude. Because he wore a matched suit, minus the jacket, we can speculate that the victim in the clown photograph may have occupied some fairly respected position in the community. Perhaps he was a clergyman, a teacher, a businessman, an editor, or a prosperous farmer. His suit trousers, vest, and long-sleeved white shirt indicate that he took pains with his appearance and presented himself as a professional who earned a better than average income. In some towns, having more than two dimes to jingle together in a pocket was enough to get a black man killed.

Some of the men who executed him as a group activity spent their final moments with the trophy that was his body, fashioning it into an object for their delight. In so doing, they demonstrated their attitude toward the representative black male body. Whether dead or alive, it belonged to them and they could do with it what they chose. Having absolute control of their victim gratified them. They invested their time, energy, and emotions into transforming his corpse into an icon or effigy of their desire. They treated the victim's body as clay that they could shape and manipulate into their ideal image, the image that gave them the most pleasure and comfort. And so they created a clown, the key figure in a circus. Lynching has much in common with the circus. Both pursue a specific format to a conclusion. Both appease the appetites of huge crowds. Both communicate meaning. Both connote risk and danger. Both depend on a ratio of one in contrast to the many, which, according to Paul Bouissac, is standard entertainment format:

> The circus presents in a ritualistic manner, spectacular events that are remarkably patterned and highly meaningful for large audiences. The one-to-many relationship of the production of its "message" qualifies it as one of the mass media of our culture.[7]

When the nameless, well-dressed African American was lynched, the country was forging its post-bellum and modern identity through visual as opposed to narrative means. Photography was still a relatively new invention, and cinema was in its infancy. The visual also impacted lynching, and spectacle lynchings, a kind of *ad hoc* outdoor theatre that emphasised a chase and capture format, began to occur more frequently and attract hordes of people. In the age of rapidly changing technology in transportation and communication media, some lynchings became media events. A number were well-patronised:

> attended by thousands, captured in papers by reporters who witnessed the tortures, and photographed for those spectators who wanted a souvenir and yet failed to get a coveted finger, toe, or fragment of bone.[8]

Many of the lynching photographs from *Without Sanctuary* have put the eager and delighted faces of men, women and children behind the ability of lynching to visually magnetise and pull together into one location many thousands of spectators.

Like the circus, lynching was ritualistic behaviour that reinforced the viewer's sense of normality. He or she was not anomalous, but connected to the community that preyed together. In the comic world of contrast, inflicting pain on the other generated pleasure in the spectators, a sense that they could control their world, keeping all threats incapacitated. At the end of the nineteenth century, segregation, which separated the races and encouraged continuing oppositional relations, took over from slavery as the prevailing racial regime. While segregation, often designated as Jim Crow after the minstrel clown, was being institutionalised, lynching climbed to its highest incidence, occurring in the 1890s roughly every two days in some part of America, rural as well as urban. Ritual and ideology go hand in hand, and ideology is given vent in ritual. The ideology of increased access to power that briefly obtained during the Reconstruction Era began to lose favour toward the close of the nineteenth century. Racial attitudes akin to those that had held sway during slavery were reinvoked and celebrated in the onslaught of lynching that swept the country in the nineteenth and twentieth centuries. Segregation and slavery depended on the premise that the man or woman of African lineage was inferior to the European. As the loser in the comparison, the African could be ridiculed and humiliated publicly. This comic humiliation took two corporal forms, lynching and minstrelsy. Lynching truncated corporal expression and minstrelsy pinpointed it. Minstrelsy, which was born in the circus, and lynching are connected through the minstrel clown. In minstrelsy, the African American was psychologically contained within the frame of white expectation and demand. Lynching made the African American body inanimate and stationery, incapable of any progress. Both forms of public entertainment sought to limit and fix the African body in a particular place, where it could be seen and contained.

The lynch victim and the clown have more in common than generally assumed. Each stands apart from the norm, from the everyday and the cultural convention, differentiated through dress and/or some physical marking. Each occasions the release of accumulated emotion in a viewing public. Each is seen as childlike and irresponsible. In addition, both are objects of ridicule that serve a cathartic as well as an instructive purpose within a society. The plight of the lynch victim, like the clown, is seen as amusing, even though he or she symbolises what is sad. That frontier of meeting between contraries, between the comic and the tragic, is what makes the clown or lynch victim a danger to the community. The remedy is to either scoff at or exorcise the threat. The clown occupies an extreme location, being either too funny or too terrible, that threatens social equilibrium. As the one who is out of step with the status quo, the clown or lynch victim represents what is to be incorporated or excommunicated to insure communal survival along terms that comport with tradition. The clown opposes the given, at the same time that he or she is in conversation with it. Through this challenge and its resolution, the community reinforces the borders of its identity. The clown stands outside the frame of the usual and expected. So does the lynch victim. The disruptive potential of each is reduced by derision, a form of distancing.

It might seem strange to be discussing lynching in comic terms. But comedy is about renewing and continuing the status quo. That is the reason so many comedies end in marriage, because comedy replenishes the old. Those who engage in lynching consider that social endeavour, ratified by the communal whole, as a means of maintaining group integrity by annihilating those considered unworthy to participate in the American contract of citizenship. The lynch victim is seen as an agent of disorder that must be expelled for the polity to thrive. Not every lynch victim is a clown, but every lynch victim falls into the outsider group where the clown also resides. Lynching is seen as a salutary and a necessary act that releases the noxious influences threatening the state. Violence is not outside the range of comedy, which can be cruel. And comedy is about doubles. So is lynching. The false double, the pretender to privilege, is sent out into the wilderness of forever through lynching.

According to Bouissac, clowns function inside the realm of "a basic dichotomy in the status of the participants."[9] Such a structured, built-in discrepancy in power reassures those who belong to the dominant class, making them receptive to the machinations of the clown. Clowns, who personify failure, make non-clowns feel good. The clown represents inferiority, and those who consume and clamour for the clownish fare can perceive of themselves as superior. That was essentially the appeal of the minstrel clown, "the most persistent and influential image of blacks in American history."[10] Working class whites who had the price of admission to a minstrel performance could walk out after its conclusion feeling that the world was theirs to command. The imperfect minstrel clown mirrored back the excellent possibilities of the world they inhabited. Minstrelsy fixed those who were black inside specific parameters, and gave absolute leeway to those who were not. Minstrelsy codified the permissible interactions between black and white. It communicated the limits within which their lives and their public display must be conducted. That was also part of the object of the lynching ritual, to communicate to the African American community the extreme penalty for departing from predetermined limits.

There are several ways to read the white clown markings that were applied to the victim's eyebrows, nose and mouth. One interpretation is that the masking is symbolic reintegration. Once the corpse was punished and cleansed of unacceptable behaviour, the disciplined body could be readmitted into the fold through the familiar and popular figure of the minstrel clown. From another perspective, the white markings could represent a commentary on the European tradition of white-faced clowns, symbols of authority and artistic accomplishment. In Bouissac's description, "[t]he white-faced clown behaves elegantly and authoritatively. He knows how to play the most sophisticated musical instruments."[11] Around 1900, when the lynching that was a prelude to the clown photograph took place, African Americans had started performing regularly on the minstrel stage, and many were distinguishing themselves as musicians. The white markings, the handiwork of the lynchers, might also indicate the boundaries that the victim crossed. He might have tried to assert himself within what was considered the province of whites, and so his punishment was to enter eternity with his face bearing white designs, the mark of his transgression, turned into the mark of his degradation.

In order to decorate the body, it had to be touched. This is in contrast to the regime of segregation that obtained at the time, which decreed that there should be no touching between black and white bodies. Laws were legislated to keep the races apart in public and in private. There is the suggestion that the taboo or phobia against physical contact masked a desire to touch and to look at the black body, which was the object of the gaze in minstrelsy and in lynching. The desire to be involved with the corpus of blackness is revealed or at least hinted at in this photograph. Care was taken with the preparation of this body for its final photograph. Lynching, at least in terms of the stories that were bruited about in newspapers, in parlours, in saloons, and on street corners, retaliated for inappropriate intimacies between the races. Yet, there was also an inclination to get close, to run one's fingers over the skin of blackness.

This covert desire for closeness contrasted with and was masked by the overt desire for separation. The need to keep a controlling distance between the empowered and the disempowered is explicitly symbolised in this photograph by the pole that keeps the corpse from falling and is held in the fingers of a white male. This pole, which suggests the slapstick that clowns often carry, also links these two figures in a comic paradigm that expresses a comparison of unequals. The black male and the white male exemplify the contrasting couple basic to comedy. As Bouissace writes, "[a] clown act always has [...] a basic dichotomy in the status of the participants. Two strings of signs symbolise, respectively, the cultural norm and the absence of that norm, either as nature or as anticulture."[12] The figure of the lynch victim as clown is sitting outside what appears to be a barn with symbols of nature and growth all around him. There are dried leaves and other debris at his feet. His location is external, exposed, and he is situated in the midst of rootless, disposable objects. The white male, who is primarily seen in shadow (almost as though he is too powerful to be looked at directly), wears a brimmed hat, probably made of felt, which serves as an emblem of status and belonging as well as protection. He has covered up his nature, and thus has dominated it.

The only part of the white male body that is actually visible in the photograph is from hand to the wrist. This is his power zone. We can also see the slightest bit of white cuff, which suggests refinement. The hat and the long-sleeved shirt suggest that he is not wearing the overalls of a labourer, but rather more middle-class attire. There are over forty photographs in the book that include full frontal views of the white men who participated in lynchings, from the end of the nineteenth century through the first few decades of the twentieth. In *Without Sanctuary*, photograph number 15, which encompasses two pages, was also taken at a lynching in 1900. The victim is slung, face down, across a horse. Like the victim in the clown photograph, he cannot stand on his own and his name has not been recorded for posterity. In photograph number 15, the faces of fifteen white males, members of a lynching posse, are visible. Two of them are astride horses and two others are short, probably boys rather than mature men. All of them, the boys included, are wearing dark trousers, long-sleeved white shirts and brimmed hats. The conformity of their clothing suggests the regularising character of their role as members of a posse, self-deputised to oust the threat to their social cohesiveness and continuance. Their clothes, almost a uniform, are similar, if not identical, to the apparel of the white man in the clown photograph. The posse and the lone white man in the clown photograph are dictating the terms of interaction between white and black men. In each case, the white male takes control of the body of the black male. Figuratively, that is also the situation in minstrelsy, where the black body becomes the virtual puppet of the white male body.

In minstrelsy, the black body is physically assumed, taken over, dispossessed, and thus virtually destroyed. In lynching, the black body is vanquished, deprived of breath and future. In the eternal present of the photograph, the eradicated lynch victim cannot lift himself from the horse or from the chair that holds his body. He is passive in the hands of his captors, which is just what the crowd that extracted his death wants from him. His passivity, his inability to assert his own will or raise his hand, his lifelessness, was its ultimate goal. The concept of the comic double is useful in looking at the link between minstrelsy and lynching. Both are competitive in spirit. In the former, the competitiveness is expressed through imitation that is invidious. The minstrel performer mocks his opponent and substitutes his own body for that of his rival, erasing it. This is symbolic banishment. Lynching expresses its animus in ritual chase and capture, the terms of which are uneven. The individual is no match for the mob. For all its humour, minstrelsy operated on the premise of grotesque African American difference and inferiority. Lynching also cast the African American outside the human federation. That is what these photographs show, that lynching celebrated the suffering of the black body and was male-dominated entertainment just as minstrelsy was.

The minstrel clown was a circumscribed figure, whether that circumscription was psychological or physical, enacted on stage or in the public sphere. In minstrelsy, the African American was psychologically contained within the frame of white expectation and demand. Lynching made the African American body stationery, incapable of any movement or progress. Being incapable of independent movement is akin to death. In the 1890s, when lynching reached its numerical height, minstrelsy was in its decline. According to Robert Toll, who has written a standard work on the history of American minstrelsy, the most popular entertainment genre of the nineteenth century "lost its dominance [...] in the 1890s."[13] Also, in the 1890s, as a new century approached, America was coming to grips with the loss of slavery as an ordering principle as well as with the aftermath of a fratricidal war. The anxiety built up by major and cataclysmic societal change was masked in the carnivalesque of lynching. Originally, the minstrel mask was created and applied to the face of white men, by their own hand, and they revelled in the release and possibility it provided. Where were they to get that release now that minstrelsy was on the wane? In the lynching scenario depicted in the clown photograph, white men have superimposed a mask of whiteness on the face of an anonymous black male, which they have converted into a canvas for their fantasies. The release in this case is not afforded to the one wearing the mask, but to those who have applied the mask to an immobile, powerless body. Using modern visual technology, they have broadcast their total ownership and manipulation of this black male body, and many other bodies like it, declaring for themselves and for posterity their ability and entitlement to dictate every aspect of the body of blackness, its life and its death. In minstrelsy, the mask was black but the face that wore it was white. Here in this photograph, the markings on the mask are white but the face that is made to wear it is black. The inverse relationship between minstrelsy and lynching is revealed in this image of a sacrificed clown.

Notes

[1] Mikhail Bakhtin, *Rabelais and His World* (Bloomington: Indiana University Press, 1984), 7.
[2] Dale Cockrell, *Demons of Disorder: Early Blackface Minstrels and their World* (Cambridge: Cambridge University Press, 1997), 84.
[3] Bakhtin, 39,
[4] Sigmund Freud, *The Basic Writings of Sigmund Freud* (New York: The Modern Library, 1995), 703.
[5] Eric Lott, *Love & Theft: Blackface Minstrelsy and the American Working Class* (New York: Oxford University Press, 1993), 24-5.
[6] James Allen et al. *Without Sanctuary: Lynching Photography in America* (Santa Fe, New Mexico: Twin Palms Publishers, 2000), 165.
[7] Paul Bouissac, *Circus and Culture: A Semiotic Approach* (Bloomington: Indiana University Press, 1976), ix.
[8] Grace Elizabeth Hale, *Making Whiteness: The Culture of Segregation in the south, 1890-1940* (New York: Vintage Books, 1999), 202.
[9] Bouissac, 164.
[10] Gary D. Engle, *This Grotesque Essence: Plays from the American Minstrel Stage* (Baton Rouge: Louisiana State University, 1978), xiv.
[11] Bouissac, 165.
[12] Ibid, 164.
[13] Robert Toll, *Blacking Up: The Minstrel Show in Nineteenth-Century America* (London: Oxford University Press, 1974), 274.

Bibliography

Allen, James et al. *Without Sanctuary: Lynching Photography in America.* Santa Fe, New Mexico: Twin Palms Publishers, 2000.
Bakhtin, Mikhail. *Rabelais and His World*, translated by Helene Iswolsky. Bloomington: Indiana University Press, 1984.

Bouissac, Paul. *Circus and Culture: A Semiotic Approach.* Bloomington: Indiana University Press, 1976.

Cockrell, Dale. *Demons of Disorder: Early Blackface Minstrels and their World.* Cambridge: Cambridge University Press, 1997.

Engle, Gary D. *This Grotesque Essence: Plays from the American Minstrel Stage.* Baton Rouge: Louisiana State University, 1978.

Freud, Sigmund. *The Basic Writings of Sigmund Freud,* translated and edited by Dr. A. A. Brill. New York: The Modern Library, 1995.

Hale, Grace Elizabeth. *Making Whiteness: The Culture of Segregation in the South, 1890-1940.* New York: Vintage Books, 1999.

Lott, Eric. *Love & Theft: Blackface Minstrelsy and the American Working Class.* New York: Oxford University Press, 1993.

Toll, Robert. *Blacking Up: The Minstrel Show in Nineteenth-Century America.* London: Oxford University Press, 1974.

The Court Jester in Nigerian Drama

Kayode Gboyega Kofoworola

Pre-amble:
What , then is the true knowledge which is
only to be found by ascent from the cave to
the light of the sun?

1.   Introduction

Even now after many ages, decades and years since the emergence of the ruling system by dynasties, the mystery of the origin, functions and impact of the court jester, still smacks us in the face. We are amazed by the insightful knowledge of the man who is conventionally regarded as the fool in the societies of mankind, but is yet the epitome of wisdom and knowledge.

Strolling down the paths of history in the royal courts of several nationalities, race and colour, this man called the fool seems to be the wisest of them all. He is the court jester. He is regarded as the meanest of the courtiers and men in corridors of power and authority. Yet he could be reckoned as the strongest when sensitive issues of the state and human affairs are involved. Philosophers first sighted him in his humble genesis as the priest when knowledge was still imprisoned within the caves of the ancient religious mysteries, rituals and festivals. Then he was observed to have re-emerged from the tunnel of darkness into the bustling light of the court royalty. He is at the centre of the political and administrative events of the rulership of many palaces. From the oral traditions of historical developments in the courts and palaces, he is always in peace and partnership with the kings. With the emergence of the literary traditions, he became transformed as some one to be reckoned with. An example is the Shakespearian Hamlet, the prince of Denmark. His role in the Elizabethan theatre of the Shakespearian era provides a high insight into the duality of his role and person, whether in courts or on the theatre stages. Demonstrating the courage and confidence of Thespius, his progenitor of the Greek theatre, he is the only one who dared looked at the kings in the face, as he releases his message of truth. State affairs are ususally marked by extreme sensitivity and delicateness. This is why the actions of the court jester can be regarded as courageous, for he dares to walk where even angels would tread with fear and trepidation.

In the hierarchy of mankind he belongs to the common stock. He is often referred to as the fool, jester, comedian, and clown. Yet his stock in trade has acquired for him a place in the palace and among men of timber and calibre. This chapter will analyse the exploits of this man over several ages. It will attempt to unravel the mystery of his origin within the enclave of the hegemony of the Emir's court rulership in Hausa society in northern Nigeria. It will also touch briefly on his counterpart in the Yoruba chieftaincy kingdom as well as how he is revealed in some selected play texts. What is significant about him is the fact that his audiences are not limited to the courts and palaces. That the broad scope of his audience incorporates both the powerful and the pauper, is a major achievement of the court jester

2.   The Origins

The court jester is a very important feature in the Hausa dramatic repertoire, like in many societies where the influence of royalty holds sway. Often it is emphasised that the court jester plays a vital socio-political role in such societies. It is from this background that the origin of the court jester or the Wawan Sarki, as the court jester is known among the Hausa of Northern Nigeria, can be traced. Zikky O. Kofoworola and Yusuf Lateef have attempted to do just that in their book *The Hausa Performing Arts and Music*. They assert:

> The origin of this character of traditional performing art has been traced to an ancient religious practice – possibly an ancient version of the bori ritual festival. It is believed that the Wawan Sarki first appeared as part of the entourage involved in ritual performance which A. J. N. Tremearne documents in his report.[1]

A quote from Tremearne's report provides an insight into the nature of this socio-political involvement:

> The dance of the king and priests around the sacred tree is interesting. One informant said only the priestly king wore the hide, but Haj Ali maintained that all did so in order to obtain albarka. It was first dried in the sand and after the chief and the three senior priest had worn it, the fourth called the dan wawa (fool although he was not really silly) put it on and danced foolishly before the people at some distance from the tree so as to distract their attention from the other four secret rites at the foot of the tree.[2]

Consequently we find that the court jester within the Hausa community can be explained in a religious context. The significance of this is that the origin of the court jester may not be separated in any significant way from the symbolism of the king's performance of his socio- religious duties, roles and responsibility.

Just as kingship within the Hausa community is hereditary, so is the profession of the court jester. He has his place in the Emir's court. His entertainment of the court is thus an hereditary duty in the same way as kingship is hereditary. Because of this origin and tradition the court jester's role is still being played today, though to a lesser degree, within the socio-political context of the court activities and organisation.

Drama and the dramatic are at the centre of court entertainment. Consequently, within the Hausa dramatic repertoire, the court jesters were previously grouped into two broad categories: the Wawan Sarki and the Dan Kama or Yan Kama (plural). Today the Dan Kama is less recognised as a court performer and more as a performer for the commoners. At a particular point in history it is believed that the dan kama also performed primarily for the royalty. But over time a transformation took place that made it possible for commoners not only to partake of the dan kama's witticism and innuendoes but also gradually appropriate it, thus effectively ending their palace existence. Unlike the Dan Kama, however, who performs in both the palace and the public, the Wawan Sarki's performance is basically for the Sarki (king). Thus he is not only a person of the court but also the personal comedian of the king. Simply put, he works to ensure that the king rules.

In some other parts of northern Nigeria, precisely within the Sokoto emirates, the Wawan Sarki is also sometimes called Sarkin Karma. This seeming change in title has generated a lot of controversy. This is probably because the word "Karma" bears a close resemblance to the word "Kama" (see above). However, it is important that historical origins of this name be taken into account as well as the linguistic difference between different groups of the Hausa peoples.

3.   The Functions

Traditionally the court jesters operate within a setting prescribed by age-long traditions. The Wawan Sarki is not just the personal court jester of the king (Sarki); he is also recognized as the traditional arbitrator of peace. He acts out the role of a middleman between the Sarki and his subjects. In a nutshell he can be described as the people's representative in the Emir's court and a servant to the king. He serves to let the courtiers and the ruling authority know the feelings of the people about the administration. This role is to maintain the balance between the two, so that the rulership is not overbearing and the followership is not complacent. He plays the role of the modern press but is immune to the travails of the modern press. For instance he could say things for which he may not possess hard documentary evidence and still be free from libel even if they are eventually found to be untrue.

The court jester's immunity against libel for any expression of opinion on pressing social, political and economic issues constitutes a big asset in his traditional role. The following comment elucidates this issue in a more succinct manner.

> Contrary to the experience of the journalist, he cannot be sued for libel. In addition he is not constrained by any decree in his exposition of any vital information which though embarrassing is considered as essential part of his duty to achieve the necessary checks and balance between the Sarki, the ruling class and the ordinary citizenry. Wawan Sarki is immune from any accusation or persecution for making any statements or comments. He warns sarki when he feels there is something wrong with his administration. Any courtier or official who is fond of misbehaving or committing acts which are capable of bringing the administration into disrepute is exposed and in fact rebuked by Wawan Sarki.[3]

Often this greater duty of the court jester masks his other duties. For instance, he also includes the Sarki's entire household within his constituency of activity. For example, when the household suffers ill luck such as bereavement, the court jester acts out his role as a healing balm. He helps the Sarki and his household to deal with their emotions through his dramatic repertoire.

In an interview with the Wawan Sarki of the Emir of Zazzau, Zikky Kofoworola, an authority on Hausa performing arts, confirms the elating image of the king's court jester. Laced with comedy, his speech is laughter-provoking and imbued with the power to cause serious issues to be easily overlooked. The following translation of Wawan Sarki's words is only an approximation and lacks the nuance and flavour otherwise present in the original version (see endnote). Wawan Sarkin Zazzau says:

> Who owns the town?
> I am Wawn Sarki, the kings fool
> Sarki is the owner of the town
> Ask me, I am his court jester
> As for me, I am his servant
> And throughout the landscape of northern Nigeria
> I am the greatest king's fool
> No one king's fool has ever been taken to Haj by Sarki
> Except me and my wife together[4]

4. The Performance

The court jester or Wawan Sarki can be described as the fool that makes the difference – difference in the sense that he occupies an intractable place in society's scheme for ensuring a balance of power between the ruler and the ruled. This social status reserved for the Wawan Sarki is inherited. However, much more important than the roles bequeathed to him by tradition is the performance of his office itself within the court, for it is this that enables him to fulfil his social responsibility. It is essential to note that the foundation of his performance is the dramatic techniques he employs. These involve slapstick, parody and satiric burlesque. His objective is to communicate serious messages in the form of jokes without creating any form of embarrassment. A universal correlation of this idea is found in the aspect of comedy that developed within Greek tragedy. As Hartnoll states:

> [T]he Greek drama was not confined to tragedy. Even at its most reverent, the human spirit needs relaxation, and comedy crept in with the revels which took place in the villages when the harvest had been safely gathered in. They were enlivened by the antics of the satyrs – half men, half goats – who were the attendants of Dionysus. It was from their fooling, and from the rough horseplay of other village festivals, that the first true comedies of the theatre developed.

The court jester in the Hausa tradition does not play musical instruments but relies on complementing his speech with body movements, designed to provoke and produce laughter. This sets him clearly apart performatively from the Yan Kama who employ comical forms that integrate elements of music, dance, song and satire. However, as previously asserted, although the Yan Kama originated from the palace, today they hold their forte mainly in the streets. Hence we are not surprised that their subject should be the banal and the mundane, since the main theme in their performance has to do with man's interaction with and attitude towards food.

It is essential to note that it is his theatrical spectacles that enable the court jester to fulfil his function through performance and thus protect the immunity which his function is guaranteed by tradition.

A. Differences in Performances

While the Wawan Sarki or Sarkin Karma are meant for the court, the Yan Kama performs for the commoners. This difference in patronage has perhaps also resulted in the difference in their acting styles as well as their thematic preoccupations. Today Yan Kamas are regarded as street comedians. However, they deserve mention since they are still in the business of foolery. They engage in social criticism, but deal less with serious issues of governance and administration. Significantly they cannot engage in criticism of the Sarki because they do not possess the immunity to do so. They are very strong in the art of imitation and their parodic statements are directed at themselves.

B. The Costume and Make-up

In the following quotation E. D. Morel relates the costume of the Wawan Sarki to his description of the dramatic spectacle in a performance of the Wawan Sarki:

> Rattle, rattle come the drums, mingled with long drawn-out notes of the tin or silver trumpets. Suddenly, a loud shout arises, a shout of merriment as a monstrous figure clad in skins of beasts and apparently, hung round with bladders, in his hand a long stick dashes out on the throng , cleaning the intervening space between it and the Emir' residence in a succession of frantic bounds. This is the court fool. And his appearance is quite in setting with the piece. For this whole scene is a scene out of the Arabian Nights and really one would hardly be astonished at the appearance of jins, or even eblis himself.[5]

However while this statement indicates to us the state of the appearance of the fool in his performative role, it does not explain nor give us details about the different attires and why they are worn. Zikky Kofoworola undertakes to supply this missing link thus:

> Wawan Sarki dresses in all sorts of pieces that make him appear liker a ridiculous character because of the odd collection of his costume. Wearing a threadbare cloth he hangs all sorts of animal skins round his waist. He wears all sorts of amulets on his waist and neck. The hair on his head is shaved off leaving only a small round piece that looks like small horn. The face is powdered with blue. Always in his hand is a long rugged stick with a curved head. The costume and his extraordinary make-up make him appear like a fool – a court jester indeed.[6]

This seems to bear a correlation with the comical satyr of the Greek theatre, which thrived on antics and in which the actors wore masks with shaggy hair and beards, pointed ears and snub noses. Their costume was made up of loincloth of fur, horse-like tail in rear and phallus in front.

Similarly the yan kama's costume according to Zikky Kofoworola is made up of big traditional baggy trousers called "buge" and a singlet or none. They carry a special wooden sword known as Turaye with which they engage in mock fights in the course of their performances. All sorts of imitative or fake objects are also at their disposition. For example, Dan Kama may make a rosary out of bean cakes or ground nuts – kuli-kuli – and imitate saying a prayer with it, when he is not hanging it on his neck. Since they are very fond of food they sometimes carry food about and even keep it in their pockets.

C. The Use of Language

There are obvious differences in the use of language among the two groups of court jesters. It is important to begin by restating that language use is determined not only by audience but also by purpose. One is concerned with royalty; the other is concerned with the commoner. One seeks to effect changes at the level of administration or rulership; the other seeks to do the same at the level of the followership. Together the fools become thus the linking symbol of togetherness in society. Consequently it follows that the language used and the illustrations utilised must be easily accessible to the audience and have the capacity to cause the audience to change direction with regards to a social policy or action if such a change is seen as imperative or required. Both, however, seek to use language in such a way that it motivates and generates laughter in itself. This is usually achieved either by pre-determined modulation in the tonal movements of words or in a language break.

More often the Wawan Sarki speaks fewer words than the yan kama. For the former, the effect is in the quality of words and subtlety of its delivery. For the latter it seems as though the effect is in the quantity of words and the rapidity of its delivery.

So far this essay has looked at the court jester from a rather strictly performative angle. In this respect it accurately serves as an overview of the court jester's role and place within the corpus of Hausa dramatic repertoire, tapering down to Hausa oral literature in particular. To this we hope to provide some correlatives from the corpus of Yoruba literature.

Consequently we shall examine the transformation of the concepts discussed thus far in literary play texts. Some of the texts employed for this analysis have been published. Others are unpublished but have been performed on stage.

5.   The Court Jester in Yorubaland and Some Selected Nigerian Play texts

We must realise the humanity of the court jester; his complete naturalness and unpretentiousness in the propagation of his vocation contrasts totally with the rulership, who often make pretensions to perfection. Indeed the Emir is perceived by the culture in this way. The court jester, however, knows better: society is not perfect, indeed no one is. This understanding is perhaps the greatest strength of the court jester and is strategic to his function.

Amongst the Yorubas of the south western part of Nigeria there are correlatives of the court jesters of northern Nigeria. Since these are diverse in nature, one particular example used here is that of court jesters in the palace of the Akarigbo of Remo. The delineation of the functions of the court jester in Remo seem to be a little more complicated than that of the emirates in the north. The court jester here does not only provide laughter through the use of highly technically proverbs, he is in fact the master of ceremony for virtually all courts activities. He introduces guests and visitors to the king. It is evident that he thus becomes the gateway to the king. This is different to the northern part of Nigeria, where the court jester mirrors the commoners' opinion of the king. The court jester in this Yoruba palace actually enables the commoners access to the king to express their own views. Often his dexterity is visible in his ability to combine speech with music. Like in most parts of Yorubaland the court jester here also doubles as the blower of the trumpets and horns that usher the Oba into his seat in the palace or herald his entrance at other state functions. Interestingly the court jester here is not without check, he does not possess absolute powers and could lose his immunity. This is dependent on his relationship to the Apena a right hand chief to the Oba. The Apena is also an Ifa priest, in fact he is the head of the Ifa priests in the Kingdom. Perhaps this is so because the court jester here is believed to possess social rather than divine roles.

A very interesting departure from the court jester of the Hausas is that in Yorubaland, especially among the Remos, there are several court jesters in the kingdom and the position is not in any way hereditary. In addition, in Remo, most of the court jesters are the wives of late or previous Obas. They are preferred because it is believed that they are already conversant with court traditions and would therefore not venture beyond their prescribed limits. They can be easily identified within the palace courts by their unusual appearance as well as the dedicated hairstyles. Often they interrupt the Oba's speech with praise, song and dance. Also worthy of note is that while court activities in the north are largely male-centered, women in Yorubaland of south western Nigeria are given room to participate fully in court activities, politics and intrigues.

In Wole Soyinka's *Death and the King's Horseman* Elesin Oba forms a correlative to the Wawan Sarki from the Hausa oral tradition and its literature. Set within the Yoruba royal court tradition he holds the balance in terms of the power and authority of the Oba's rulership. To put humorously, he eats with the Oba from the same bowl. However, he does not only enjoy the privileges and benefits of the court while alive. He is also given the hereditary privilege to die with the Oba. For, literary speaking, he must escort the Oba from this world into the next. His limitless access to the Oba also provides him with his poetic license. In addition the Elesin Oba is essentially a very instrumental link to the future of the race, for he is expected to bridge the gulf of transition through his being sacrificed to the god of iron – Ogun.

Like the god heroes in Greek tragedy and Ozidi in the play by John Pepper Clark[7] Ogun embodies that great energy which permits both awesome creativity and destruction. And like them also he unites the human and supernatural realms in his person, for it was Ogun in Soyinka's poetic mythology, who led the other gods down to earth to be re-united with man. Such characters as Eman in *The Strong Breed*[8] and Olunde in *Death and the King's Horseman* can be seen as Ogun figures whose tragic function it is to bridge the gulf of transition between the different areas of experience: the worlds of the living, the dead and the unborn.

It seems pertinent to assert here that, as in the Hausa Emir's court, the court jester's role within the Yoruba court, as reflected by the court jester in Akarigbo of Remo's palace as well as in the character of Elesin Oba and his son Olunde, was primarily and principally propriety and hence princely. That Elesin Oba refuses to die with the Oba can be regarded as a reflection of one of the main functions of the court jester within the Oba's court, which is to criticise society, but also to ensure this criticism is free of condemnation when related to the Oba.

A very interesting play that gives an insight into the court jester's acts in the king's court is *Queen Amina of Zazzau* by Wale Ogunyemi.[9] The play, though not the only one produced about the legendary historical Queen Amina, is probably the only one to be published and widely chronicled. Telling of the life and times of an Hausa warrior queen, it is an historical play that seeks not only to establish the place of Amina within the literary and historical lore of the federation of Nigeria, but also seeks to reinvent her as a progenitor of the latter's women liberation movement. It is therefore full of research. This inadvertently has meant that the historical has sometimes compromised the dramatic and, in the process, the expected rigid boundary lines in character delineation seem to have been lost. This process also affects the naming and the acting of the stock character – the convert jester in the play.

Ogunyemi justifies his creative enterprise here in quoting from Hilda Hope from the introduction to her play *A Witch in my Heart*[10] to:

> [A] creative writer is allowed greater freedom of expression and imagination. He is expected to personalize general experience, is permitted to develop his style and eccentricities, and encouraged to avoid technical formulation and conventions in making his own comments.

His idea may change without the criticism of inconsistency and his characters can express contradictions without evoking acrimonious review by scholars of other schools. He needs not explicitly distinguish between ideas and emotions and may deliberately use the ambiguity of words to extend the readers perception. Since he does not have to prove facts or test hypotheses, he may allow vision to replace reality. Its historical need not be chronological nor social, nor (his) cosmology computable. He may take for granted that the mind sets its own pace as it wanders through an existential labyrinth. He is permitted to be the blind sage of the Sogon without attempting to justify his existence. He is entitled to ecstasy.[11]

It is important to state that it is not for dramatic effect alone that Ogunyemi chooses to split the court jester into varying characters in terms of his roles and manifestations. This is evident because of the practical difficulty it would pose in a stage production for a single character to play the multiplicity of roles that the court jester has in this play. The several characters into whom Ogunyemi deconstructs the Wawan Sarki include priest (who Ogunyemi describes as a fortune teller), courtiers, Emissary chiefs, Sarki Yaki and herald. Three of these have been selected to illustrate our contention.

A. The court jester as a priest
    In *Queen Amina of Zazzau* he plays a very significant role as he also ironically functions as the people's historian. This position seems to be fortified by the subjects' perception of the priest as one whose office encapsulates both the present and the future. This perception is enhanced by his socially accepted role as the intermediary between God and man, a role that lends him a divine manner. He thus functions as a custodian of the people's trust and hence becomes an authentic force to forecast their future without fear of being intimidated by the king or queen as others, especially the chiefs within the court, may be. In this play, the priest initiates Amina into the Bori cult. The priest and queen thus belong to the highest cult in the land. Indeed it seems that the priest has an unacknowledged and tactical control of the queen. He becomes, by virtue of her initiation by him, her spiritual mentor. In this respect she is his protégé and is thus subject to him. Hence a power balance is maintained between them. No wonder in the text we find that wherever the priest is, the queen is also likely to be present. Like our original court jester, the priest has unlimited and unfettered access to the palace and must be listened to, even if what he has to say is unpleasant.

B. The court jester as a courtier

Here we not only see, but we feel the court jester as he plays his traditional role, as a singer of praises; as part of the king's household, concerned about not only the welfare of the queen, but that of everyone under her influence in the palace.

C. The court jester as a herald

In the Hausa language the herald is called "Sankira." He often announces the arrival and entrance of the queen into any arena or the palace. His announcement is not ordinary as he utilises the opportunity to eulogise the virtues and greatness of the queen. His role remains significant in that he serves as an amplifier to emphasise whatever the queen says. He often paraphrases the queen and extends the meaning of her original intention. Take this for example:

> Amina: I retire
> Herald: The greatest of the great retires.[12]

Another text entitled *Shaihu Umar*, which was originally written in Hausa by Alhaji (Sir) Abubakar Tafawa Balewa (First Prime Minister of independent Nigeria) and later adapted into a play by Umaru Ladan and Dexter Lyndersay[13], is perhaps one of the very first few published plays written in Hausa after independence. The Wawan Sarki or the court jester is allowed to remain one single character and thus consequently to retain his traditional roles and functions.

Perhaps one interesting departure from the way the court jester is portrayed in other texts is the creation of a female counterpart: the Jakadiya to the Wawan Sarki. The Jakadiya operates principally in the midst of the women folk as the king's emissary and his ear in their midst. Even though the appearances of these characters in the text seem to be brief, their statements – conditioned by their mentality – ensure that they are effective in the discharge of their roles.

In *Shaihu Umar* the Wawan Sarki remains a strong character whose language remains steeped in proverbs and the proverbial. With a mixture of praise and short jabs at his object the court jester exerts a presence that, though brief, ultimately emphasises his importance in the palace set-up:

> Wawan Sarki: This is the mother of them all. Today, dakaru, the month for sitting has ended, the rabbit has bought a dog. Who are those who want to become farmers of yam?[14]

In *Shaihu Umar* the court jester's questions, answers and interjections are so loaded with irony that while they provoke laughter , they also invite serious thought. Take this for example:

> Sarki: Or is there anyone who wants to support Macau?
> W/Sarki: Only his wife or Malam Buhari because he is his friend. He even said he wounded his hand for him. [15]

Perhaps a little comment on this will suffice. This encounter shows a situation where Macau, one of the Chief's and the Sarki's right hand men, creates intrigue among courtiers and, accused of betrayal of trust, is about to be banished from the land. The court jester's answer to the king's question would look at first glance inappropriate. But a closer look indicates that the answer is more of an advice or affirmation of the need for the king to proceed on the course on which he is set.

This chapter set out to look at the role and place of the court jester in Nigerian drama in foregrounding the discussion on the Wawan Sarki or the court jester as manifested in the Emir's court in northern Nigeria. In drawing comparisons between the activity of the court jester in northern and south-western Nigeria one thing that needs to be restated is the male-centric nature of court activity in the north as compared to the sexually liberal stance in the south where female participation in court activity is highly encouraged. Differences in costumes, language, music renditions, movements and perceptions of the origin of the court jester abound from the Yoruba to the Hausa segments of our discussion and this is also reflected in the literature that emanates from these regions. In conclusion there is humanity about the court jester that makes him relevant to all cultures and consequently deserving of study.

Notes

[1] Ziky O. Kofoworola and Yusef Lateef, *Hausa Performing Arts and Music* (Lagos: A Nigeria Magazine Publication, 1987), 84.
[2] A. J. N. Tremearne, *The Ban of the Bori, Demon and Demon Dancing in West Africa and North Africa* (London: Frank Cass, 1968), 21.
[3] Kofoworola and Lateef, 87
[4] "Wa masu gari?/ Na'am nine wawan sarki/ Sarki shike da gari/ Ni kuwa nine wawan sarki./ Ni kuwa nine bawan sa/ Duk kasan nan na Arewa Kuwa/ Nine babban wawan sarki/ Ba wanda sarki ya kai shi Haji/ Sai ni da matata ya kai mu." Kofoworola, 88-89. Please note that translations into English are

the author's and they only attempt to approximate what the original meanings might be.

[5] Morel, 11

[6] Kofoworola and Lateef, 86

[7] John Pepper Clark, *Ozidi the Saga*

[8] Wole Soyinka, *The Strong Breed. Collected Plays 1* (London: OUP, 1975).

[9] Wale Ogunyemi, *Queen Amina of Zazzau* (Ibidan: University Press Plc, 1999).

[10] Hilda Hope, *A Witch in my Heart* (Oxford University Press, London 1970)

[11] Ogunyemi, vii.

[12] Ibid, 46.

[13] Umaru Ladan and Dexter Lyndersay, *Shaihu Umar* (Zaria: The Northern Nigerian Publishing Company, 1978).

[14] "Wawan Sarki: Gatan'uwan nan. A Yau Dakaru Kuma watan zama ya kare, zomo ya sai kare! A wasu za su zama manoma doya!" Ibid, 8.

[15] "Sarki: ko akwai wanda zai goyi bayan Makau?
W/sarki: sai dai matarsa ko malam Buhari, domin kuwa abokinsa ne har yana cewa, wai ya ji ciwo a hannu." Ibid, 11.

Bibliography

Ahmed, Umaru B. "Queen Amina of Zazzau." Unpublished play text performed by the Ahmad Bello University, Zaria Centre for Nigerian cultural studies troupe; directed by Zikky. O. Kofoworola at several venues in Nigeria and at the theatre of nations in Sofia, Bulgaria.

Clark, John Pepper. *Ozidi The Saga.* Ibadan: Ibadan University Press/ Oxford University Press, 1997.

Crow, Brian. *Studying Drama.* Lagos: Longman Nigeria Ltd, 1983.

Dabo, Abba. *Queen Mina.* Zaria: Northern Nigeria Publishing Company, 1986.

Gidley, C. G. B. "Yakanmanci: The Craft Of The Hausa Comedians." In *Yemi Ogunbiyi's Drama and Theatre In Nigeria.* A Critical Source Nigeria Magazine, 1981.

Imam, Abubakar. *Magana Jari Ce.* Zaria: Northern Nigeria Publishing Company, 1980.

Isola, Akinwumi. *Olu' Omo.* Ibadan: Onibionje Press And Books Industries (Nig.) Ltd, 1983.

Jones, Eldred Durosimi (Ed). "Drama in Africa." In *African Literature Today*, 8. London: Heinemann, 1981.

Kofoworola, Ziky. O. & Yusef Lateef. *Hausa Performing Arts and Music*. Lagos: A Nigeria Magazine Publication, 1987.

Kofoworola, Ezekiel Oyegbile. "Hausa Performing Arts And The Emir's Court." PhD Thesis. Zaria: ABU, 1982.

Ladan, Umaru and Dexter Lyndersay. *Shaihu Umar*. Zaria: The Northern Nigerian Publishers Company, 1978.

Nigeria Magazine 142, 1982. Lagos: Dept of Culture, Federal Ministry Of Social Development, Youth And Culture.

Ogunyemi, Wale. *Queen Amina of Zazzau*. Ibadan: University Press Plc, 1999.

Ricard, Alain. *Theatre and Nationalism: Wole Soyinka And Leroi Jones*. Translated by Femi Osofisan. Ile-Ife: University Of Ife Press, 1983.

Soyinka, Wole. *Myth, Literature and the African World*. Cambridge University Press, London. 1978

Soyinka, Wole. *The Strong Breed Collected Plays* 1. London: OUP, 1976

—. *Death and the King's Horseman*. London: OUP, 1975

Tremearne, A.J.N. *The Ban of the Bori, Demon and Demon Dancing in West Africa and North Africa*. London: Frank Cass, 1968.

Work In Progress, No 6. Zaria: Ahmadu Bello University Press Ltd., 1988.

"Fratello Arlecchino": Clowns, Kings, and Bombs in Bali

Ron Jenkins

1.   Introduction: Harlequin & Penasar

After improvising a comic scene with a Balinese masked clown at an international theatre festival in Copenhagen, Dario Fo embraced the Asian artist and shouted, "Fratello mio, Arlecchino!" ("My brother, Harlequin!")[1] The Nobel Laureate instinctively sensed that the Balinese clown was a kindred spirit to the character Fo had been playing all his life, the archetypal Harlequin, who in Fo's vision of clowning is a descendant of the medieval giullare. Fo noted that the Balinese clown's half-mask, mercurial gestures, split-second timing, and deft audience rapport all reminded him of the giullare, the improvising street jester of the middle ages on whom Fo has modelled much of his work. Since Fo's judgment was based on a simple observation of performance technique, he was not aware of the historic, literary, and political roots of Balinese clowning which suggest that the parallels between the two traditions might run even deeper than he imagined.

In his monologue "The Birth of the Giullare," Fo envisions an origin myth for the medieval clown that links the giullare to the tragedy of social injustice, and to the populist religious traditions that painted Christ as a revolutionary hero. After his wife was raped by the soldiers of an aristocrat who stole the land he had worked on for years, a destitute peasant tries to commit suicide, but is interrupted by Christ, who encourages him to spread the news of the injustices he has suffered as a warning to others. In Fo's story Jesus gives the tongue-tied farmer the ability to tell stories with satiric bite by kissing him on the lips. After Christ's kiss miraculously endows him with verbal gifts of comic virtuosity, the prototypical giullare in Fo's fable tells his audience that he feels his tongue "whirling like a corkscrew [...] like a knife that cuts and slashes [...] shaping words and phrases as clear as the gospels." The giullare describes his divine transformation into a clown as follows:

> a wisp of flame touched my lips [...] my tongue began to trill and twist like a water snake. New words wiggled and rolled around inside my brain. Every thought turned itself over [...] every idea came out upside down.[2]

In his new incarnation as a satirist who attacks injustices perpetrated by the powerful, the giullare proclaims: "I'll show you how to transform words into razor sharp blades that instantly slit the throats of infamous imposters [...] and other words that become drums to wake up sleeping minds."[3] Fo's fictional manifesto of the giullare is echoed in the seventeenth century Balinese manuscript known as "Dharma Pawayangan" ("The

Responsibilities of the Shadow Puppet Artist"), that is studied by Balinese clowns in all performance genres as a guideline to their art. Written in the first person voice of Twalen, a Balinese clown archetype still beloved throughout the island for his appearances as a servant character in shadow puppet plays, a section of the text reads:

> I am Twalen who holds the jesting conversations [...] I have the power to tread on the heads of kings and lords [...] Gods remain silent, kings remain silent, all my enemies remain silent [...] I Twalen have no fear.[4]

The fearless clown Twalen is the prototype for the clown figures who appear regularly in all genres of traditional Balinese performances, including the masked Topeng tradition that Dario Fo encountered in Copenhagen. All of these clowns are servants to the gods and kings whose stories form the main plots of the dramas, which are often eclipsed by the popularity and bravura of the clowns who weave local gossip and political commentary into their improvised jokes. Serving as intermediaries between the past and the present, the sacred and the profane, the nobility and the commoner, the Balinese clowns make the old religious and historical stories relevant to current events by joking about contemporary issues in the context of classic tales like the Ramayana, the Mahabhrata, or the chronicles of the island's kings.

Like the giullare in Fo's monologue, Twalen and the other Balinese clowns are linked to the near mystical powers of language. The performances in which Balinese clowns appear are usually linked to religious rituals and ceremonies in which sacred texts are quoted in the Sanskrit-based language known as Kawi. One of the roles of the clowns is to translate these texts into the vernacular so that they can be understood by the audience. In Kawi the word for the smallest unit of language, the syllable, is "aksara." Literally, "aksara" means "that which cannot be destroyed." Because of their responsibility for passing on the wisdom of the sacred texts and the meanings of the syllables they contain, Twalen and the other Balinese clowns in the shadow puppet plays are sometimes referred to collectively as "Aksara", or literally "those who cannot be destroyed." The clowns who appear in two couples (a pair of servants to the protagonists of the story and another pair that serves the antagonists) are often associated with the healing powers of the sacred texts they translate and joke about, so much so that a performer quoted in the Dharma Pawayangan attributes his personal safety to the fact that he is possessed by the voices of the clown characters in his play: "The four imperishables (aksara) enter my body [...] I escape the curse of age, disaster, and calamity."[5]

The healing powers of the four clowns are linked to their connection to the four guardian spirits that the Balinese believe are born with each human being, known as "kanda empat" (the four siblings). At birth the first physical manifestations of the guardian siblings are the amniotic fluid, the umbilical cord, the blood and the afterbirth. Later in life the kanda empat are manifested in numerous other invisible and visible forms, one of them being the four imperishable clowns. The Kanda Empat are important presences in the lives and ritual ceremonies of the Balinese people.

Another clue to the significance of the clown in Balinese performance can be found in the term "penasar" which is used to collectively refer to the two pair of comic servants that appear in almost all traditional plays. (In the shadow plays this quartet is usually named Twalen, Merdah, Sangut, and Dalem, but they have different names in other genres like masked Topeng). Literally the word penasar means "foundation" and the four clowns are regarded as the foundation on which the performance is built. The most talented and well-educated actors play the roles of clowns and they are the ones given the responsibility to choose the stories being performed before the play begins (this decision is usually made during a pre-performance discussion that takes place at a meal provided by the host and sponsor of the play). The penasar are also the ones who assign the roles to the other actors as well as determine the length and structure of the scenario through their improvised dialogue during the performance. In addition to making the jokes, the clowns quote pearls of wisdom from ancient texts that are intended to provide insight into current problems experienced by the audience.

The Balinese clowns embody Fo's vision of the medieval giullare in their reliance on the power of language to inform and protect their audiences from harm and injustice, and in their mystical connection to the invisible world of the spirits. Although Fo is an atheist, the Dionysian pagan vision of Christianity that he envisions in "Mistero Buffo," "The Peasants' Bible" and other fantastic tales have some similarities to the pantheistic animist tradition of the Balinese Hindu-Buddhist faith. In Fo's imagined landscape of Medieval populist religion Christ and the Virgin Mary appear as intimately familiar friends and protectors to peasants, fishermen, and thieves, part of an eccentric pantheon that includes an Earth Mother and a comic devil. Balinese cosmology presupposes a similar intimacy between gods, humans, and demons. And in both world-views the clowns play a crucial role, not simply as laugh-makers, but as semi-mystical protectors, dispensers of spiritual and political wisdom, and guardians against injustice. Central to the techniques that endow these two clown traditions with their impact on the audience are the use of paradox, historical memory, and a belief in the power of art as a weapon.

2   Paradox & "Ruabineda"

In Fo's depiction of "The Birth of the Giullare," the gift of comic virtuosity is equated with an aptitude for verbal inversion. "Every thought turned itself over," says the giullare after his tongue has been kissed by Christ, "every idea came out upside down." Paradox is essential to all of Fo's writing and performance. In an interview in Delphi, Greece Fo explained:

> I'm interested in discovering the basic contradictions in a situation through the use of paradox, absurdity, and inversion. This enables me to transform one reality into another reality, not as a rick, but so people will understand that reality is not flat, but that it is full of contradictions and reversals, and that often absurdity is a reality which is closer to the truth than those things which seem to be sacred and absolute, but are almost always false.[6]

Balinese clowns refer often to a basic Balinese principle of paradox and contradiction that is known as "Ruabineda." A Balinese clown feels that it is his responsibility to reveal the unity of opposites that is central to the Balinese Hindu/Buddhist/Animist tradition. In this world view, good and evil are necessary and inter-related, as are death and life, heaven and hell, happiness and sadness. In a monologue performed at a temple ceremony shortly after the 2004 elections, a respected clown named I Ketut Kodi commented on political campaigning by playing with the connection between silence and speech, sense and nonsense. He lamented the passing of bygone eras in which political speeches were unnecessary:

> In those times when people made election campaigns, they did not have to use their mouths. As long as campaigners are using their mouths it is considered a lower form of campaigning. The problem now is how can we get people to understand us without speaking. That is what happened in the kerta yuga era. Nobody during that time had to use their mouths to speak, but people heard their voices very clearly, because they performed good deeds and did not need others to promote them. Now there is too much talking. Even long before the campaign officially began there was a lot of speaking without saying anything and empty chatter. We need to learn how to speak loudly without using our mouths. Without using words, we can still make people listen. That is what it will be like when everyone achieves the harmony of "tri kaya pari suda" (the harmonious unity of speech, thought, and action).

Nowadays "tri kaya pari suda" is just an empty motto, spoken about, but not observed. It is something that just decorates the mouth [...] in fact there is nothing there.[7]

Mocking empty language as useless mouth decoration, the clown uses the paradox of meaningless speech to illustrate the power of Ruabineda and the necessity of meaningful silence. He is living up to the credo of fearlessness expressed in the "Dharma Pawayangan" by the archetypal clown Twalen who claims the right to mock the powerful. He concluded his performance by suggesting that if everyone followed the principles of "tri kaya pari suda" and actually backed up their words with actions that were true to their ideas, hell would go out of business. "The department of hell would have to close down because the demons would have nothing to do."[8]

3.   Historical Memory and "Kali Yuga"
     The prototypical giullare in Fo's fable tells his audience that he will present them with "words that become drums to wake up sleeping minds."[9] Using comedy to stimulate thought is a basic principle in Fo's work, particularly when the thoughts being stimulated are about forgotten lessons of history which leave people vulnerable to repeating the mistakes of the past. "Forgetfulness is the world's most dangerous disease,"[10] remarked Fo to an audience of Sardinians attending a museum exhibition about his work in 2000. He invented a fable to make his point, alluding to the mythic times of ancient Greece, when King Minos of Crete is said to have attempted to bring the island of Sardinia under his rule. "Minos asked his court inventor, Daedalus, to fabricate a giant who would stand guard over Sardinia in the king's name," Fo conjectured:

> But when the people of Sardinia invited the giant to their feasts and dances, he was so moved by the beauty of their culture that he set them free. Monos then commanded Daedalus to concoct a potion that would make people forget their past, and put it in the drinking water of Sardinia, so that it would be easy to conquer them once they had forgotten where they came from.[11]

The cure for the disease of forgetfulness, of course, is memory. And Fo believes that memory is an essential component of the art of the clown, historical memory, personal memory and even fictional memory which embellishes the past with truths of the imagination. "Memory [...] everything begins from there," mused Fo in a press conference in Cagliari shortly after his speech in the Sardinian museum:

Not only for remembering things, but for learning the
significance, the place, and the time that are inside and
behind every word. I'm an actor [...] for me memory has to
enter through the mouth [...] to listen means to move your
lips, your feet, articulate your face, stretch your throat, learn
to speak [...] to become the instrument of your own
memory, as if you were looking for a piece of music on a
guitar. Then your imagination takes you a step further. It
enables you to remember more.[12]

Fo sees imagination as an extension of memory. "There is not only a
mechanical truth," says Fo, "there is also a mythical truth that is sometimes
more important than the truth of facts and numbers."[13] The Balinese clowns
also rely on historical, personal, and invented memories to, in the words of
the seventeenth century "Dharma Pawayangan" "escape the curse of age,
disaster, and calamity."[14] Whenever historical chronicles are re-enacted in
the Balinese chronicle plays known as "Topeng," it is the clowns who make
the metaphoric connections between the past and the present. In the period
after the Bali terrorist bombings of 2002 that shattered the island's tourist-
driven economy, clowns took on the responsibility of performing plays that
told stories of people surviving disaster and recovering their fortunes. "Kali
Yuga" is a Balinese phrase that refers to the "era of Kali," a time in Balinese
Mythology when the Hindu deity Shiva took the form of the demon Kali, and
ushered in a time of devastation. In 2002 and 2003 many clowns invoked
"Kali Yuga" as a metaphor for the hard times endured by the Balinese in the
aftermath of the bombings.

In August, 2003, shortly after the trial that condemned the Muslim
extremist Amrozi bin Nurthasyim to death for his role in the bombing, a
troupe of clowns put on a historical drama in the village of Kerobokan, a few
miles away from the site of the tragedy. The plot was based on a fifteenth
century story about a disastrous situation under the rule of King Medang
Kemulan. No one in the market could sell any of their products and the
King's subjects became desperately poor. The solution proposed by the priest
in the story, after he was possessed by a visit from a goddess, was to tell the
people that they had become too greedy, focusing more on making money
than honouring their gods. When the people gave up their selfish ways and
made offerings to their forgotten gods, prosperity returned to the kingdom.

The audience of villagers watching the play had suffered a similar
economic tragedy, so the story's metaphor hit them close to home. Many of
them were descendants of King Medang Kemulan, and some of them
responded to the performance by going into trances that were manifested by
weeping and convulsions that continued until a priest blessed them with holy
water and mantras. These blessings took place at the same time that a masked

figure in the play called Sidha Karya (whose name means "the end of the ceremony") was performing similar rituals of blessing for the characters in the story. Before long Sidha Karya was chanting mantra and sprinkling holy water over the audience as well as the actors. The boundaries between the emotional world of the play and the emotional world of the village had dissolved in tears. The conflated realms of historical fiction and contemporary reality shared the sadness caused by economic disaster and both realms resolved the problem through ritual.

This play and countless others performed during that period advocated an extraordinary response to the terrorist bombings. Instead of demonising and attacking the bombers and other Muslims as the Americans had done after the September 11 bombings, the Balinese clowns were suggesting that their fellow islanders follow an example from past history in which the Balinese responded to disaster by looking inward to their own flaws and examining the possibility that they themselves might be partially responsible for the era of destruction because they had created an environment of spiritual imbalance in which religious devotion was eclipsed by conspicuous consumption.

As usual the clowns had made the connections between the past and present clear with their extra-narrative improvisations. One clown in the fifteenth century story wearing a buck-toothed mask came out stuttering and lunged into the audience. He immediately apologised for his aggression by reassuring the public: "Don't worry. I'm not Amrozi". Another clown jumped at the sound of a slamming door. "Whenever somebody farts," he said, "I think it's a bomb." [15]

After the performance, Ketut Jagra, who played the central role of clown narrator in the drama reflected on the intensity of the audience response. "The trance is proof and witness that the ceremony was successful," noted Jagra. "Maybe the bomb was a warning to the Balinese to wake up and pay more attention to worship and "yadnya" (ritual obligations to the gods)." [16] Jagra's attitude echoes Fo's vision of the medieval giullare as a performer who uses "words that become drums to wake up sleeping minds" [17] at the same time that it recalls the function of the clowns invoked in seventeenth century Balinese manuscript "Dharma Pawayangan" to escape the curse of age, disaster, and calamity." His sense of responsibility to the well-being of his audience is heightened by his position in his home village of Sanur where he is a "kepala dusun," a local leader. One of his jobs is to keep track of Muslims who emigrate from Java and to minimise tensions between newcomers and Balinese Hindus. His role as protector and guardian is both political and artistic.

---

4.   Culture Weapons & "Kebudayan Senjata"

In Fo's legend, the "birth of the giullare" in the middle ages was accompanied by a common man's realisation that comic language could be used as a form of power. "I'll show you how to transform words into razor sharp blades that instantly slit the throats of infamous imposters," says the peasant-turned-giullare to his audience of peasants.[18]

Throughout Fo's career, he has viewed comic performance as a weapon that can be used by the powerless against the powerful. Verbal, extra-verbal, and body language are all components of cultural power that give Fo's comic heroes their ability to overthrow the forces of tyranny and injustice. Fo's description of the Italian film comedian Toto reveals his vision in terms that read like the manifesto of the giullare:

> When speaking Toto touches his interlocutor, but does not content himself with laying a hand on his arm or shoulder. He grabs him everywhere – in the face, by the hips, by the hand, by the elbow, by the foot. The violence of the comic tradition is replying to the violence of power. Toto is the timid person in revolt who, at the moment of giving in, in order to win the struggle or at least to re-establish equality in the face of power, begins to act – that is to say, to make gestures. He uses all his body – at first to resist and then to pass over to violence and madness. The play of madness and of the illogical is fundamental to Toto's theatre. Toto works on the basis of paradox – at the limits of paranoia: he insults, he strikes, pretends to cry, shouts, and – this is fundamental – spits. He spits, bites, scratches, uses his elbows, sometimes gives great kicks in the stomach, sneezes. This famous prolonged sneeze accepted as a cry, a pang, a sexual spasm, and presented as madness and frankness at one and the same time. Why so? Because the character who is Toto, a man who is crushed, humbled, excluded from society, attempts by means of paradoxical violence, absurd violence, to re-establish an equilibrium in the face of power, which is immobile and static. Toto moves, writhes, runs about, shouts, screams, weeps, sneezes, spits, and makes obscene gestures in order to succeed precisely in destroying whatever is sacred and essential in power, to destroy it at the heart of that pyramid which assures its stability.[19]

The image of the powerless clown turning his comic arsenal against figures of authority appears regularly in the Balinese theatre. During the celebration of the Balinese religious holiday of Nyepi, a troupe of clowns known as "Salju" were invited to perform at a party for the employees of the government's Department of Religion in Denpasar. The clown show was preceded by a serious lecture given by a professor of religious studies. Shortly after the serious lecture, one of the clowns, dressed as a woman, took the podium and performed a parody of the lecture. The transvestite clown, known by his stage name of Sugama, also mocked the government officials in the audience when their cell phones sounded, and commented on the parliamentary elections that were about to take place. He evoked much laughter from the crowd with a pun that equated "Ca-leg" with "Ca-lug." The simple transformation of the vowel changed the word, caleg, commonly used to refer to legislative candidates ("calon legislatur") into an invented insult, "calug," which the clown explained was short for mosquito candidates ("calon lugu"). The change was appropriate, he said, because after they are elected, the legislative candidates become mosquito candidates, "sucking the blood of the people."[20] The audience not only laughed at the punch line, they applauded, indicating an even more enthusiastic response to the clowns satirical swipe at government corruption.

The topsy turvy comic battle between the transvestite and the government officials was all the more remarkable because it took place under the auspices of a government ministry, the department of religion. In the course of the madcap revolution in the government offices, the transvestite and his clown colleagues also made several serious points about the historic meaning and origins of the Nyepi holiday, including a story that legitimised the use of culture as a weapon. According to Sugama, the origins of the caka calendar which coincide with the origins of the Nyepi holiday go back to 79 A.D. when war broke out between the militarily powerful Uesci ethnic group and the militarily weak Caka ethnic group. "There was an ethnic war," explained Sugama to the audience of government bureaucrats.

> The ethnic group Uesci emerged as the winner and ruled over all the other ethnic groups [...] and during the reign of the Uesci, the ethnic group of the Caka changed their battle strategy. They changed from physical battling to cultural battling [...] and the struggle resulted in transforming their enemies into friends.[21]

Sugama explained the power of culture as a weapon at the same time that he was using it to satirise the government officials who had invited him to explain the meaning of a holiday whose historic roots are linked with the birth of Balinese cultural warfare. In Indonesian the term "Kebudayan Senjata" means cultural weapon, and the phrase is heard often in performances throughout the island. It was particularly common during the period after the terrorists bombings of 2002, when the Balinese knew they had been attacked by Muslim extremists, but had no desire to respond to the attack with direct violence. As the only Hindu island in the largest Muslim country in the world, Bali had a long experience negotiating for their cultural survival with a national government dominated by Muslims. Instead of responding to the bombing with a physical attack, the Balinese resorted to their weapons of culture, surviving the devastation through theatrical and ritual re-enactments that played a large role in the spiritual and eventual economic revival of the island's fortunes. The story of the 79 A.D. clash between the Uesci and Caka ethnic groups recounted by the transvestite clown Sugama, had obvious resonance with the contemporary tensions between the Balinese Hindus and the Javanese Muslim majority that dominates Indonesia's government. And like the militarily weak Caka clan, the Balinese have learned how to successfully substitute cultural weapons for other forms of violence. The skilful wielding of those cultural weapons was demonstrated by Sugama at the Ministry of Religious Affairs and at temple performances staged regularly by hundreds of other clowns throughout the island of Bali.

5.   Conclusion: "Puputan"

When the Balinese commemorate the 1906 massacre of their people by the Dutch colonial soldiers (an event that has been named "Puputan," Balinese, a term that means "the end"), the performances that accompany the speeches are marked by a curiously festive feeling. The roles of the Dutch soldiers are played by clowns wearing buffoonish masks with long protruding noses that suggest the ridiculously acquisitive motives of their conquest. Modern Balinese audiences laugh at the Dutch soldiers, secure in their knowledge that in spite of losing the short-term battle in 1906, they eventually won the long-term cultural wars and won their independence from the Dutch more than half a century ago.

The yearly procession of buffoons mocking the colonial powers that once dominated Bali is emblematic of the comic spirit that links Balinese clowns to the medieval giullare cited by Dario Fo, and the succession of comic artists through history, including Fo himself, who have used laughter to battle against injustice and oppression. Both traditions use comedy as a cultural weapon, shaping historical memory into paradoxical humour that awakens thought, and linking laughter with the social responsibility to protect the weak against abuses of power. Reading Fo's comic manifestoes honouring the medieval giullare together with the seventeenth century Balinese manuscript "Dharma Pawayangan" reveals the deep, sometimes spiritual similarities between the European giullare and the Asian clowns whose representative was greeted by Fo as "fratello Arlecchino."

Balinese Temple performer I Nyoman Catra prepares for his masked Topeng performance in a ceremony that includes ritual incantations of sacred texts. Photo by Franziska Blatter © 2005

Notes

[1] The author observed this meeting at the Danish Sessions of the International School of Theatre Anthropology in October 2000 at the Louisiana Museum in Copenhagen.

[2] Dario Fo, *Teatro* (Torino: Einaudi, 2000), 316. Translated by the author.

[3] Ibid.

[4] C. Hooykaas, *Kama and Kala* (Amsterdam, North-Holland Publishing Company, 1973), 133.

[5] Ibid, 23.

[6] Ron Jenkins, *Artful Laughter: Dario Fo & Franca Rame* (New York, Aperture, 2001), 8.

[7] The author observed this performance by Ketut Kodi in Singapadu, Bali on April 7, 2004. Translated by the author with Nyoman Sedhana.

[8] Ibid.

[9] Fo, *Teatro*, 316.

[10] Jenkins, 23. Quotation translated by this author.

[11] Ibid, 38.

[12] Ibid.

[13] Ibid.

[14] Hooykaas, 23.

[15] Ron Jenkins, "In Bali, All the Post-9/11 World's a Stage," *New York Times*, 12 October, 2003, Arts & Leisure Section, 5.

[16] Ibid.

[17] Interview with the author in Sanur, Bali on 12 August, 2003.

[18] Fo, *Teatro*, 316.

[19] Jenkins, 152.

[20] The author observed this performance by the "Salju" theatre troupe in Denpasar, Bali on March 30, 2004. Translated by the author with Nyoman Sedhana.

[21] Ibid.

Bibliography

Fo, Dario. *The Tricks of the Trade.* London: Methuen, 1991.

Geertz, Clifford. *Negara: The Theatre State in Neneteenth Century Bali.*
    Princeton: Princeton University Press, 1980.

Hooykaas, C. *Kama and Kala.* Amsterdam: North-Holland Publishing
    Company, 1973.

Jenkins, Ron, *Artful Laughter: Dario Fo & Franca Rame.* New York:
    Aperture, 2001.

—.   *Subversive Laughter: The Liberating Power of Comedy.* New
    York: Free Press, 1994.

Scaramouche: The Mask and the Millenium.

Stephen Knapper

In this chapter I want to explore the picaresque elements of the *commedia* mask of Scaramouche in three parts: to examine its provenance in early modern Neapolitan carnival; give a necessarily selective and episodic whirlwind overview of the character as a theatrical mask in the early modern period; and then to concentrate on the most recent interpretation of it rendered by Justin Butcher in his play *Scaramouche Jones* (2002). The essay will explore themes dear to this volume, namely the role of the clown and its relation to both carnival itself and carnival theory in an exploration of the machinations of grotesque realism.

At the outset I would like to discuss the carnivalesque origins of the mask. The first depiction of the figure appears in Jacques Callot's celebrated series *I Balli di Sfessania* (1621).

Jacques Callot, "Scaramucia," *I Balli di Sfessania*.
Photograph by Gilbert Mangin. Courtesy of Nancy Museum of Fine Arts

Without doubt this was the iconographical model for George Sidney's 1952 eponymous Hollywood version of the stage figure. In this, Stewart Granger's first appearance as Scaramouche is preceded by a frame portraying a poster for the travelling players which depicts Callot's Scaramucia.[1] As well as that, the first costume Granger wears as Scaramouche in the film also appears to be modelled on the engraving. Similarly Carlo Boso's Scaramuccia in the mask's late twentieth century return to the theatre in Tag Teatro's *Scaramuccia* (1986) bears a striking resemblance to the original.

Although the influence of the Callot engravings on later recreations of the *commedia* has been widely acknowledged it is far from universally accepted that the depiction could refer to a real actor. *I Balli di Sfessania* have been dismissed as grotesque, contorted flights of fancy with no bearing whatsoever upon the performance reality of the *commedia dell' arte*.[2] They depict, according to Donald Posner's influential 1977 article in *The Art Bulletin*, solely the *Sfessania*, a *mattacino* or *moresco*-type sword dance of Maltese origin probably performed by fairground performers sharing the same names as the professional actors of the *commedia* or invented by Callot himself.[3] Posner dismisses previous hypotheses that the figures form part of a *commedia dell' arte* company as either "wrong or, at least, seriously misleading" and posits his own notion that they are fairground performers on the basis that in Garzoni's *La Piazza Universale* (1586) there appears an acrobat named Scaramuccia Venetiani [sic]. He notes that:

> If one version of the Scaramuccia type evolved and achieved fame in the impromptu theatre, another must have continued to practise the original, more modest, profession, appearing on the fairgrounds, tumbling or rope-walking, and dancing moresche, as he does in the Callot print.[4]

More recent research however has returned to the earlier hypothesis that the Callot engravings do refer to companies of actors who performed at the Teatro Baldracca, otherwise known as the Stanzone delle Commedie or Teatro della Dogana, in Florence in the first two decades of the seventeenth century, while Callot was working as a kind of pictorial chronicler for the Medici court.[5] Working from the findings of Anna Maria Evangelista, Sara Mamone has noted the similarity between many of the names of the masked figures and actors from these companies (Gli Uniti, Gli Accesi, I Fedeli and I Confidenti)[6] among them the Neapolitan, Giovan Battista Fiorillo, *in arte* Scaramuzza. He, in the light of evidence recently discovered, seems more likely to have been the model for the engraving subtitled Scaramucia/Fricasso than a descendant of Garzoni's acrobat. It should be noted that while Scaramucia appears in the engraving with Fricasso, seemingly about to bump into each other in what appears to be a comic duel scene, another engraving in the series has Taglia Cantoni, who seems the double of Scaramucia, facing a Fracasso, again in a duel scene. This seems to be the reverse of the former in that the same figures are now facing each other instead of appearing back to back.

Is it then merely a coincidence that in Act 2, scene 11 of the first play published by Giovan Battista's father, Silvio Fiorillo, *Li Tre Capitani*

Vanagloriosi (1621), the Spanish Capitan Mattamoros' Neapolitan parasite Scaramuzza appears to attack Capitan Cortes Rincones' servant Fracasso with the words: "Take this blade and parry this blow"?[7]

The Neapolitan didascalies of *I Balli di Sfessania* have been explained with reference to popular songs published in the renascent dialect literature of Cortese, Basile and Sgruttendio[8], contemporaries of Silvio Fiorillo, who, together with his fellow actor/author, Bartolomeo Zito, championed Neapolitan over Tuscan in his plays and poems.[9] There is no firm documentation as to whether or not Callot ever went to Naples. If he did not, perhaps the Fiorilli were instrumental in diffusing their meridional culture to him through their performances in Florence. It has also recently been speculated that Callot's representation of a bearded Pullicinielo in the series is a depiction of Silvio playing the theatrical part which he, at least according to the *commedia* actor/author Pier Maria Cecchini, invented. [10] Callot's images could thus acquire a more precise documentary quality and the mystery they may contain as evidence of a performance reality may need to be re-examined.[11]

The connection made by Posner to carnival has been reinforced by the Neapolitan anthropologist, musicologist and theatre director Roberto De Simone who has used his own studies of the phenomenon in the region of Southern Italy to inform his productions of early seventeenth century Neapolitan theatre. According to a Campanian oral tradition cited by De Simone, his own and other interpretations of Jacques Callot's *Balli di Sfessania* and tantalising pointers from secondary sources, the origins of the mask, and therefore primary meanings, are to be found in carnival.[12] De Simone sees the origins of the mask of Scaramouche in a practice indulged in by young men at carnival time in Southern Italy who would parade beneath the balconies of young women holding a pole suspended from which was a pot to which a rope was attached. When the rope was pulled a giant phallus would spring out of the pot and frighten the women back into their houses. A folk tale is told of how Sgarra-Muscia, a phallus, finds a uterus on a mountain where she has been abandoned by two testicles who had accompanied her there and left after she had told them they were good for nothing. She offers him a home for life if he will help her but without those "due coglioni" (two testicles). This primal association between the mask and the phallus is highlighted in De Simone's interpretation of its etymology[13]; a fusion of the dialect words "sgarrare" (to err in a duel) and "muscia" (a cat, and sixteenth century symbol for a uterus), the compound effect being that of a character failing in the act of love. Further connotations of impotence are indicated by the fact that "musciò" also means soft, and "muzza" means cut off. Here, we have something of a paradox with a carnival practice symbolising virility juxtaposed with a name signifying impotence.

Further complications arise from the word "sgarrare" implying connotations of duelling – albeit in this sense metaphorically – which can also be ascribed to the etymology of the Italian noun "scaramuccia," sharing the same meaning as the English word "skirmish" and the French word "escarmouche," all stemming from the Frankish root "skirmjan" (to defend) which is also the origin of the verbs "schermare" and "escrimer" meaning to fence.[14] Indeed the Scaramucia of Callot's engraving, is wielding a rapier and a cloak in a very competent en garde position about to collide incompetently into the back of Fricasso. There is a paradox inherent in this double image whose binary nature is typical of the Mannerist principle of discordia concors – the juxtaposition of opposites in the same form. Here we can see the figure in the context of the sixteenth and seventeenth century artistic movement. One art critic has seen this binary quality as being typical of the whole Mannerist movement's dependency on:

> a tension between classicism and anti-classicism, naturalism and formalism, rationalism and irrationalism, sensualism and spiritualism, traditionalism and innovation, conventionalism and revolt against conformism for its essence lies in this tension, the union of apparently irreconcilable opposites.[15]

Callot has been described as one of the last exponents of Northern Mannerism[16] and not only may his images be a potentially rich source for information about outdoor staging but they may also supply us with keys to the origins of the masks in carnivalesque festivities and folk festival. In spite of this a theatre historian who has made a valuable contribution to the artistic context of the early *commedia dell'arte* has found himself so impressed by the power of the images that he is moved to conclude his discussion of them by saying:

> The etchings are intertwined with the identity of the *commedia dell'arte*. The prints stand out not only for their excellent technique but also because they represent a different vision of the theatre. The gestures are at once ambiguous and celebrative, energetic but poised, grotesque yet amusing. This is part of the *commedia dell'arte* that escapes narrative; refusing to be captured by the literary, it eludes meaning.[17]

What then of the meaning of Callot's Scaramucia, or for that matter De Simone's Sgarra-Muscia, or even of what I have chosen to give the generic name "the mask of Scaramouche" in my study of the mask? Can they therefore be interpreted at all or is that meaning fundamentally ambiguous and ultimately ironic? Perhaps, but we may need to go beyond the antiphrastic sense of irony as it has been defined by Umberto Eco:

> irony asserts the contrary of that which is considered to be the case, and is effective only if the case is not explicitly stated. Irony means saying "-p" when, on the contrary "p" is the case. But if one asserts "-p", and immediately afterwards informs one's interlocutor that "in fact, as you know 'p' is the case,, the ironic effect is destroyed.[18]

The postmodernist writer and critic, Linda Hutcheon sees irony as being relational, inclusive and differential.[19] Relational in that it operates between meanings and people, between the said and the unsaid, therefore – in the case of the double image of Scaramucia – between the seen and the unseen: the master fencer about to collide incompetently with his adversary, where the artist is ironist, the viewer interpreter and Scaramucia the target. Inclusive, in that the meanings signified by the name Sgarra-Muscia, or Scaramucia, are simultaneously double, moving between the said and the unsaid, creating a third meaning of something between the two – thus a comic effect is obtained as Sgarra-Muscia may be at the same time virile and impotent, Scaramucia, competent and clumsy. The name or the sign is therefore polysemantic and Hutcheon's third category of the differential highlights the fact that one signifier, for example Scaramouche, may have two or more different though not necessarily opposed signifieds. Thus the name Scaramouche may connote both skill with a sword and impotence, the further historical irony here being that in a sketch for one of the masques at the Stuart court made by Inigo Jones derived from Callot there appears "a fantastical lover Scaramuzo" [20] and the beatings suffered by the Scaramuzza of *La Lucilla Costante* at the hands of Volpone and Policinello are hardly indications of a mighty swordsman.

If irony is the key to the interpretation of the many and contradictory meanings of the mask then it may also be possible to link Scaramouche to the etymological origins of the trope itself in the dissembling Greek stage figure of the *eiron*. The Scaramuzza of the Fiorillo plays is certainly referred to as a parasite, a character with antecedents in *commedia erudita*, Roman and Greek Old, Middle and New comedy. Indeed Enid Welsford has identified this figure of the parasite with the Greek laughter-maker, [21] whom she sees as the origin of the medieval buffoon, and new light may be thrown on the Scaramucia of Callot's *Balli di Sfessania* by the probability that the Sfessania dance, referred to in Del Tufo's 1584 poem describing the Neapolitan carnival as having magical powers of healing,[22] was a derivation of a Maltese *moresco* sword dance.[23] Welsford has noted the importance of the buffoon in similar folk forms in early modern Europe:

> The French term "les Bouffons" – the Italian term "Il Mattacino" – makes clear the character of the sword-dance, which is related probably to the morris dance and the German *Fastnacht Spiel*, and certainly to the English mummer's play. The dance is a dance of fools who perform a kind of combat in which swords are leapt over, clashed together and woven into various patterns, culminating in a figure in which the swords are entwined over the heads of one or more of the performers, this figure bearing in a Spanish example of the dance the significant name of "la degollada," "the beheading," and suggesting, as Dr. Chambers has convincingly pointed out, that the sword-dance is not in origin a martial affair, but an agricultural and sacrificial rite. This theory is supported by the fact that in some of the dances one of the grotesques interferes with the action, is killed, and brought back to life again. [24]

The themes of death and resurrection are very close to the Bakhtinian crowning/decrowning structure so essential to his notion of carnival. As he puts it: "All forms of ritual laughter were linked with death and rebirth, with the reproductive act, with symbols of the reproductive force." [25]

In the scripted plays by the early modern *comici dell'arte*, Flaminio Scala and Silvio Fiorillo, the characters of Scaramuccia and Scaramuzza supply us with plentiful examples of grotesque realism in their debasing of official discourse to the realms of food, sex and the body. Similarly in its ironic movement from significations of potency to impotency (Sgarra-Muscia); martial competence to clumsiness (Scaramucia); man to woman (the transvestite strategies of Scaramuccia in Scala's *Il Finto Marito* and Scaramuzza in Fiorillo's *La Lucilla Costante*); servant to master (Tiberio Fiorilli's Scaramouche) the paradox inherent in the shifting early modern understandings of the mask evokes the dualistic and ambivalent structures of carnival laughter.[26]

The first evidence of the character of Scaramuzza that we can link to a known actor appears in a scripted play by the Neapolitan actor/author Silvio Fiorillo entitled *Li Tre Capitani Vanagloriosi* (published in 1621). Fiorillo, the theatrical creator of the Policinela character, was predominantly a specialist in the role of the Spanish Capitano Matamoros who played with the first wave of Italian *commedia* actors to tour in Italy and France and here his servant is the Neapolitan dialect speaking parasite Scaramuzza, probably played by his son Giovan Battista as a second *zanni*. He is introduced in the first scene as a tavern dwelling ne'er-do-well, whose plot function, while minimal, is to engage in the typically carnivalesque structure of levelling the bombastic hegemonic discourse of his Spanish master – the Spanish being in control of seventeenth century Naples: -

> MATAMOROS: Thus like the supreme and most resplendent Phoebus shineth between the white moon and silvery stars; holding the victorious standard of great splendour and beauty and the palm of triumph, so do I among the famous warriors and brave captains, strong courageous and brave, bring the glorious flag.
> SCARAMUZZA: Just like the innkeeper of the Cerriglio in this noble city of Naples claims to know how to cook tripe from beef and veal, and roast quails, pheasants, chickens, pigeons, so I claim to be, am and will be (despite my enemies) the greatest swallower, eater, drinker and tavern dweller of all the eaters, drinkers, drunkards and buffoons that can ever be found between the four winds of the Levant, the Ponente, the Scirocco and the Tramontana and so on, et cetera: and that's why everyone that knows me should stay alert and take great care for fear that I don't cut their throats, eat them alive and swallow them whole so starving am I.[27]

The captain's boasting is thus mirrored by Scaramuzza, whose invocation of a long list of Neapolitan dishes and whose pretensions to become the biggest drinker, glutton and buffoon in the western world effectively parodies the hegemonic megalomania of the captain, and by inference the Spanish. The reduction of the Captain's astronomical metaphors to Scaramuzza's stomach is typical of the lowering process inherent in Bakhtin's concept of grotesque realism. In the play, Scaramuzza engages in a duel with the servant Fracasso to whom he finally loses his love interest, the *servetta* Laudomia. Scaramuzza closes the play with a eulogy of the nuptial banquet or *komos-gamos* in the classic tradition of the *alazon-eiron*.

This obsession with food is of course symptomatic of the traditional concerns of the clown and it is echoed in Angelo Costantini's description of the first role undertaken by Giovan Battista's brother, Tiberio, who took over the role from him sometime after 1620, in *Le Festin de Pierre,* the source for Molière's *Dom Juan.* Tiberio was to enjoy stellar success in the courts of Europe from the late 1630s but in particular in France from the 1640s as Scaramouche. However, his comic biography *La Vie de Scaramouche* by his fellow actor Costantini in the latter stages of his long French sojourn is laced with picaresque elements of beggary, jesting, theft, romance, trickery of patrons, cuckoldery of others and then finally himself. One story in particular illustrates the subversive power of the mask in a fine example of its fusion with the actor, recalling the medieval tradition of the court jester, or natural fool, identified by Bakhtin as the permanent embodiment of carnival laughter. The anecdote goes so far as to mock both the King himself but also the divine right of kings and by implication religion itself. At a dinner at the palace Louis XIV poured a glass of wine for the actor, to whom Mazarin pointed out the honour of the gesture. Scaramouche's reply made everyone in earshot laugh. When the king asked for an explanation Scaramouche:

> said to His Majesty that when his Eminence had told him that he could boast that the greatest king in the world had poured him a drink, he had replied that he wouldn't fail to tell his baker about it. The King understanding by this speech that the honour he had conferred on Scaramouche didn't give him any bread responded immediately with an unequalled generosity, "You'll tell him that I am raising your pension by 100 pistoles." Scaramouche thanked His Majesty and retired very happy. [28]

The implication behind the jest is that the king, who claimed direct authority from God is being equated with a priest, or Jesus himself. The parody of the Christian mass is clear and squarely within the tradition of medieval festive popular culture outlined by Bakhtin. Costantini further strengthens the connection by his report of Fiorilli's death, reciting prayers and expiring with the words "Sicut in coelo et in terra" – in heaven as it is on earth – on his lips. The comic and grotesque levelling of all that is sacred (and in seventeenth-century France its embodiment was the person of the King) is given tangible form here. Dismissed as calumny by some on its publication a year after the great actor's death in 1694 there are many elements in the novella which are structurally more typical of the Spanish picaresque fiction popular throughout seventeenth century Italy, France and England (where a translation was made in the late 1690s) than likely events from the actor's life. Nevertheless, the broad lines of what we know from archive sources and more reputable contemporary accounts are more or less respected. Indeed the biography may well fill some of the gaps that archival study has failed to find. The myth of the picaro Scaramouche, to be adapted much later into a popular Italian TV series by the RAI starring the singer Domenico Modugno in the 1960s was thus consolidated. As an actor Tiberio Fiorilli shared two theatres with Molière and influenced his acting and playwriting particularly in the characterisation of Sganarelle and the solipsistic old men of his great comedies – Orgon, Harpagon and Argan. He successfully ran a theatre in Florence and companies of *commedia* actors in Italy, Paris and England – coming to London at the behest of Charles II at least twice in the 1670s. As a result of these visits the character of Scaramouch was naturalised into English farce, pantomime and puppetry. Fiorilli's characterisation of Scaramouche was famous for its eschewal of the mask, perhaps a fusion of the French *farceurs'* tradition of playing *enfarinée*, sporting the typical Spanish dress of a black costume with a white ruff. The actor's characterisation may have been a fusion of his father's Capitan Mattamoros character and the servant Scaramuzza pioneered by his brother. There is however a lot of evidence to suggest he continued playing the second servant role until the 1670s when his characterisation in the scenarios of what was known as the *ancien théâtre italien* seems to have become more fluid playing bourgeois characters such as the paterfamilias or lawyers. In this he seems to mirror the performance career of Molière, upon whom he undoubtedly had an influence. As his alter ego, Scaramouche Fiorilli was an ambassador of the Neapolitan carnival in Paris, filtrated and refined in Italian and French courts but at the same time preserved in the popular memory by such picaresque works as Costantini's comic biography. Fiorilli enjoyed something of the status of a court jester at the court of Louis XIV which seemed to give him a carnivalised immunity from reproach, that his more famous prodigy Molière was to marvel at, particularly in the long censorship battle he had over *Tartuffe*. It has been speculated that it was the nightmare climate of the five years' censorship of this satirical masterpiece that pervades the comic ingenuity of the Neapolitan world of *Scapin*. Here, in Molière's comic *chef d'oeuvre,* as in the earlier *Sganarelle* there is abundant evidence of Fiorilli's influence in the use of a physical, farcical style of acting that was described at the time as a *jeu naturel* and the use of facial grimacing which was allowed by the *enfarinée* white mask of the *farceur.*

This white mask and the reputation as a consummately physical comic actor, were significant historical influences in the gestation of Justin Butcher's *Scaramouche Jones or The Seven White Masks.* It is a reincarnation of Fiorilli's Scaramouche rather than the masked avenger of the cinema's adaptations of Rafael Sabatini's historical fiction that was the inspiration behind the play's central character. A picaresque anti-hero similar to that depicted in Costantini's biography, the provenance from carnival and the fusion of actor with mask are all discernible elements transposed from the seventeenth century to the twentieth. An embryonic version was first performed by the author in December 1999, the play was subsequently adapted for Radio 4 with Warren Mitchell in the title role and then rewritten in collaboration with the director Rupert Goold and the screen actor, Pete Postlethwaite with backing from the Bristol Old Vic to première at the Dublin Theatre Festival in Autumn 2001. A successful tour of the UK ensued and the play has now been to Australia, New Zealand and Canada. The picaresque characteristics of the mask have been retained in a 100 minute long monologue recounting the life of a clown born in Port of Spain, Trinidad on the cusp of the twentieth century, the son of a gypsy whore and an Englishman. A journey through the first half of the twentieth century ensues, taking in slave trading in Addis Ababa, child abuse on the way to Venice, perambulations in Poland and in the emotional climax of the play mass murder in a death camp in Split where Scaramouche is a gravedigger who discovers his eventual vocation as a clown by entertaining the children prior to their slaughter by Nazi guards with a parodic comic mime. On liberation incarceration with Nazis ensued only for the anti-hero to be freed by an English judge when the humanitarian nature of his clowning is recounted by survivors. He eventually arrives in the England he has sought since childhood in 1951 and meets his fellow Englishmen, a Trinidadian beggar who introduces him to other homeless people under Waterloo Bridge. Recounting the story of his life Scaramouche realises how "ultimately and irredeemably [...] ridiculous" it has been and resolves to become the clown which he will play for the next 50 years of his life.

The play is thus a meditation on the resilience of the comic spirit and the transformative power of laughter. The picaresque style of the monologue leads the spectator through some of the excesses of the twentieth century, British imperialism, class struggle and of course the Holocaust. The emergent clown is buffeted from one circumstance to another without betraying any emotional response typical of the other worldliness of the product of carnival. Indeed, carnival is present throughout with Scaramouche beginning life on the cusp of the twentieth century in a New Year celebration in Trinidad wherein elements of Canboulay have been transposed, if somewhat exoticised:

> A New Year's Eve carnival was whooping through the streets of Port o' Spain, firebrands held aloft by frenzied voodoo dancers festooned in feathers, black men with faces painted white...cavorting masquerade processions [...] [a] riot of wild festivities. A Clown's Nativity.[29]

There is a dionysiac frenzy to Scaramouche's life, structured through the diegetic device of seven white masks for each episode. The colour of the mask parodies the importance he ascribes to an imperialist notion of Englishness but at the same time signifies the purity of the innocence of the clown. Interestingly enough it was in discussions with the actor Pete Postlethwaite that this dimension to the storytelling was added after an idea of using seven eggs upon which clowns traditionally painted their make-up, representing their soul.

It is with the souls of the children whose final suffering Scaramouche temporarily relieved where I would like to leave your thoughts:-

My role in the "Final Solution" was to dig mass graves, even in bitterest winter when the shovel bent in the frozen earth, and then to stand by and watch as trailer-loads of dead bodies were up-ended into them. Sometimes, presumably for the sake of variation, huge droves of living victims were herded to the edges of the pits and then machine-gunned into the ground. However the corpses arrived, whether by gas, bullet or malnutrition, my task was then to shovel white lime all over their contorted limbs and twisted faces - like the painting of so many clowns. So many clowns, millions of clowns – Jewish clowns, gypsy clowns, homosexual clowns, children clowns – all with white lime to cover their faces. It used to sting and burn horribly if you got it on your hands while you were shovelling it out of the sacks, and so my sixth white mask was composed entirely out of lime, the pain of which has never left me.

An extraordinary thing happened: I discovered a certain facility for making children laugh […] yes […] when those ranks upon ranks of frightened, worn-down people were lined up for the machine-gun squads, naked and shorn, one by one the children began to catch sight of me with my funny white face, leaning on my shovel, waiting to resume my work […] and I would wink at them, pull faces, laugh hugely without a sound, cavorting and making fun of the guards behind their backs, acting out a silent pantomime of the execution that was about to take place, pretending to be a victim gunned down, falling down into the pit and having my face painted white, then rising, fluttering on an angel's wings, up into heaven. I got caught fooling around in this way plenty of times and my punishments were far from pleasant, but it seemed to me to be a price worth paying, to see those haunted little faces fixed on mine as they waited for the end […] and sometimes, just sometimes, one of them would almost break into a smile before the bullets ripped in to them from behind and they toppled down, down, down and beyond the reach of pain or fear for evermore. And so the common euphemism for extermination in our camp became not going to the showers, or going for a haircut, but "going to see the clown."[30]

Here Butcher is obviously playing with the redemptive power of laughter in an operation that might be seen as a direct inversion of the usual strategies of Bakhtin's concept of grotesque realism which works through a levelling strategy of taking the high to the low as evidenced in the early modern Neapolitan Scaramuzza's mocking of the hyperbole of his Spanish Captain master. The clown's mime of the passage of the victim to heaven is offering the children the chance of salvation and therefore freedom from their earthly suppression at the hands of their Nazi executioners. We are presented here in the litheness of Postlethwaite's performance of the mime with a kinetic response to the physical atrocities of twentieth century genocide. The movement here is from low to high and thus represents a newer, more spiritual form of carnival that might be termed grotesque idealism. It has been much in evidence in this new millennium in the playwright's most recent work which has turned to the energy of Aristophanic satire to respond to the Iraq war in a trilogy of plays entitled *The Madness of George W; A Weapon's Inspector Calls* and *Guantanamo Baywatch*. All three plays use grotesque imagery and debunking strategies to satirise the cant behind the Bush/Blair axis and highlight the hypocrisy, torture and injustice fundamental to the coalition's position in the Middle East. It is ironic that *Madness,* a transposition of Kubrick's *Dr Strangelove* to modern times, was written over Christmas 2002 and New Year 2003 just after I had interviewed Butcher about Scaramouche. As if a new Clown's Nativity was required as a necessary comic and idealistic response to the grotesque realities of war that almost four hundred years earlier Jacques Callot had depicted in his memorable series depicting the horrors of the Thirty Years War, *Les Misères de la Guerre*. The spirit of Scaramouche has thus informed the most comically spirited of the theatrical responses to war that the British theatre has seen so far into this new millennium. The debunking charge of the early modern instances of grotesque realism in Scaramuzza's dialogue with the Spanish Captain is echoed in the kinetic mime of the gravedigger mocking his Nazi masters mime in *Scaramouche Jones*. This in turn has been adapted by Butcher to deconstruct the politics of the Iraq war in the persona of the servant character, Yasmina the cleaner, a Palestinian member of Al-Qaida working against coalition forces in the American base of *Madness* and again reappearing in *Guantanamo Baywatch*. Through the comedy of servants and masters the carnival cycle of death and rebirth in the mask's artistic associations continues to reaffirm the life-affirming energies that its subversive qualities embodies. The picaresque journey that began in Neapolitan carnival has now left its traces upon the roadmap of the Middle East.

Notes

[1] Another poster in the film appears to be based on Callot's engraving of the *Capitano* or *Innamorato*. Sidney also used Callot's contemporary Abraham Bosse as a source for the execution scene of Milady in his 1948 version of *The Three Musketeers*. See Eric Monder, *George Sidney. A Bio-Bibliography,* (Westport, Connecticut and London: Greenwood, 1994), 161.

[2] Ferdinando Taviani dismisses Callot as a source for the performance technique of the *comici dell'arte* by contrasting the depictions of actors in the *Balli di Sfessania* with other engravings in the *Receuil Fossard* and Tristano Martinelli's *Compositions de Rhetorique* (1601). He applies Eugenio Barba's theories of the pre-expressive stage of the actor in performance and of his "energetic language" to conclude that the latter two sources are probably more reliable:

"Basta confrontare le incisione raccolte da Fossard con quelle dei *Balli di Sfessania* di Callot, per rendersi conto della distanza che separa il comportamento energico dell'attore dalla esagerazione contorsionistica. Callot sembra tradurre in immagini una fantasticheria sul teatro. Potrebbe essere assunto come documento di ciò che restava, di quel teatro, nella memoria eccitato di un spettatore. Ma certamente non è un documento di ciò del comportamento degli attori in scena." F. Taviani, "Un Vivo Contrasto. Seminario su attrici e attori della commedia dell'arte," in *Teatro e Storia*, 1 October (1986), 25-75, 53. See also F. Taviani, "Immagini Rivoltate" *Biblioteca Teatrale 37-38, Immagini del teatro*, (Rome: Bulzoni 1996), 59. His views regarding Callot's unreliability as a source are echoed by Marco De Marinis in "Appunti per un studio diacronico della commedia dell'arte" in *The Science of Buffoonery. Theory and History of The Commedia dell'Arte,* ed. D. Pietropaolo (Ottawa: Dovehouse Editions, 1989), 241.

[3] D. Posner, "Jacques Callot and the Dances called Sfessania" in *The Art Bulletin* 59 (1977), 203-216, 208.

[4] Ibid, 207, note 36.

[5] Documentation of the actors in these companies is provided by Annamaria Evangelista in "Le compagnie dei Comici dell'Arte nel teatrino di Baldracca: notizie dagli epistolari (1576-1653)," in *Quaderni del Teatro*, 24, (1984), 50-73.

[6] Sara Mamone, "Le miroir des spectacles:Jacques Callot à Florence (1612-1622)" in *Jacques Callot 1592-1635*, ed. Paulette Choné. Catalogue of an exhibition held at the Musée Historique Lorrain, Nancy, 13 June-14 September, 1992. (Paris: Éditions de la Réunion des Musées Nationaux,1992),183-87, 185.

[7] "Pigliate sta cortellata, e reparate sta stramazzone." To put the quotation into context, the servants are rivals for the same woman and the captains at loggerheads over marriage arrangements. Their exchange of insults breaks out into swordplay:

Scar: You cuckold gallows bird, do you think that I am scared of you?
Frac: Nor am I frightened of you, go on master.
Matt: This is the way in which one behaves with other gentlemen and so you come with men in ambush
Cort: Now I understand, you have hidden your army haven't you? Come now, we must each face one another's sword blows alone
Matt: Parry this reverse blow
Scar: Take this blade and parry this blow
Fra. You are already dead, go and be buried at your door
"Scar. A cornuto piezzo di catapiezzo, e che te piense cha io agio paura di tene.
Frac. No io di te mi spauento, innazzi padrone
Matt. Desta manera se tratta entre Caballeros ansi vienen con emboscados.
Cort. Rr. Ya entiendo, ascondido tiene l'exjercito? venga cadauano solo a solo tomase esta estocada.
Matt. Reparase este reues.
Scar. Pigliate sta cortellata, e reparate sto stramazzone.
Frac. Gia sei morto vattene à sepelir da tua porta"
Silvio Fiorillo, *Li Tre Capitani Vanagloriosi. Capricciosa Rappresentazione di Strani amorati auenimenti* (Naples: Domenico Maccarono, 1621), 78.

[8] Posner, *op.cit.* and a more detailed examination by Roberto De Simone in "Maschere e danze rituali carnevalesche, nella Napoli del seicento, in referimento ai 'Balli di Sfessania' di Jacques Callot" in Lucia Balbi, *Demoni e Santi. Teatro e teatralità barocca a Napoli* (Naples: Electa, 1984), 145-193.

[9] Silvio Fiorillo, *L'Amor Giusto* (Naples: Felice Stigliola, 1604).

[10] Domenica Landolfi, "Silvio Fiorillo: Un 'napoletano' in Lombardia," in Claudia Buratelli, Domenica Landolfi and Anna Zinanni, *Comici dell'Arte. Corrispondenze. G. B. Andreini. N. Barbieri. P. M. Cecchini. S. Fiorillo. T. Martinelli. F. Scala*, ed. S. Ferrone (Florence: Le Lettere 1993), 309. For a discussion of Silvio Fiorillo's Policinella see Monica Brindicci, "Il Pulcinella di Silvio Fiorillo fra vita teatrale del teatro e modelli letterari," in *Quante Storie per Pulcinella*, ed. Franco Carmelo Greco (Naples: E. S. I., 1988), 55-85.

[11] In her doctoral thesis Margaret Katritsky concludes that in the light of other iconographical evidence she has studied "it seems perfectly possible that they [the Balli di Sfessania] are based, however freely, on actual performance practice, either in the form of a commedia dell'arte troupe

capable of offering matachin dances in its own repertoire, or a temporary collaboration between troupes of actors and dancers. It would be going too far to suggest that all the characters discussed in this section are professional performers, let alone that *commedia dell'arte* companies typically employed matachins or buffoni, could routinely offer acrobatic spectacles such as the sword dance or human tower in their repertoires,or even that professional acting actually developed from such troupes of acrobatic dancers. However, in my interpretation, the widespread nature of the depiction of characters in buffone and matachin costume in conjunction with professional actors which I have been able to identify, particularly in the early iconography, by Flemish, German and Italian artists, is an indication that this is not simply an artistic convention, but reflects genuine performance practice." M.A. Katritzky, *A study in the Commedia Dell'Arte 1560-1620 with specific reference to the visual records*, D.Phil thesis, St.Catherine's College, University of Oxford (1994-5) 2 vols, vol. 1, 215-16.

[12] The stories cited are from the "pastore" oral tradition from Avellino in Campania and were told to me by De Simone in an interview on 10 March, 1993. See also his article on Callot of 1984 cited above and R. De Simone and A. Rossi, *Carnevale si chiamava Vincenzo, rituali di Carnevale in Campania*, (Rome: De Luca 1977). References to Scaramuccia as, respectively, a carnival mask, a Neapolitan *vecchio tipo* and a figure from the local tradition of the *sacra rappresentazione* are in G. B. Del Tufo, *Ritratto o modello delle grandezze, delitie e meraviglie della nobilissima citta di Napoli*, ed. C. Tagliareni, (Naples 1959); Brindicci 1988 *op.cit;* Domenico Scafoglio and Luigi M. Lombardi Satriani, *Pulcinella. Il Mito e la Storia* (Milan: Leonardo, 1992),.299. The mask has also been interpreted as having origins in religious ritual:

"From the ecclesiastical role of the Fan-bearer, in ritual; *esmoucher*, or *iscara-moucher*. Not being very active, the person who carried the fan tended to lounge; hence came the "moocher." This job required the wafting of the heavy incense in this or that direction; it is also hinted that he had to "keep the flies off" and in fact, a peacock feather fan became frequent in use, despite its oriental origin, in many churches." W. G. Raffé, *Dictionary Of The Dance,* assisted by M. E. Purdon (New York: Barnes & Co, London: Yoseloff, 1964), 447.

[13] There are echoes here of the origins of western comic theatre in the ancient Greek fertility rituals of the phallic songs. See F. W. Cornford, *The Origins of Attic Comedy*, (Cambridge: Cambridge University Press 1934), 41-3 and Anthony Caputi, *Buffo. The Genius of Vulgar Comedy,* (Detroit: Wayne State University Press 1978), 23-24 on the process by which ritual revels evolved into drama.

[14] See under *scaramuccia* in *Dizionario Etimologico Italiano*, ed. Carlo Battisti and Giovanni Alesso, Florence: Università di Firenze 1957 and *skirmish* in *The Oxford Dictionary of Etymology* (Oxford: Oxford University Press, 1966).

[15] Arnold Hauser cit. in Paul C. Castagno, *The Early Commedia dell'Arte. 1550 - 1621. The Mannerist Context.* American University Studies Series XXVI Theatre Arts Vol.13 (New York: Lang, 1994), 10.

[16] Ibid, 212.

[17] Ibid.

[18] Umberto Eco, "The frames of comic 'freedom,'" in *Carnival!* ed. Thomas A. Sebeok, (Berlin: Mouton, 1984), 5.

[19] Linda Hutcheon, *Irony's Edge: The theory and politics of irony* (London and New York: Routledge 1994), 58-64.

[20] K. Richards, "Inigo Jones and the Commedia dell'Arte", in *The Commedia dell'Arte from the Renaissance to Dario Fo*, ed. C.Cairns, (Lewiston, Queenston and Lampeter: Edwin Mellen, 1989), 212.

[21] See Enid Welsford, *The Fool. His Social and Literary History* (London: Faber and Faber, 1935), 4

[22] THE SFESSANIA DANCE
So you see that Maltese dance
That we call Sfessania in Naples
My women, free of charge
You will be cured of fever and migraines
"BALLO DI SFESSANIA
Cosi veder quel ballo a la maltese
ma a Napoli da noi det Sfessania,
donne mie, senza spese
vi guarirebbe alfin febre o mingrania"
Del Tufo *op. cit.*

[23] Daniel Ternois, "Balli de Sfessania" in *Jacques Callot 1992, op.cit.*, 216.

[24] Welsford, *op. cit.* , 70-71.

[25] Mikhail Bakhtin cit. in M.A.Rose, *Parody:ancient, modern and post modern* (Cambridge: CUP, 1993), 162.

[26] "Let us say a few initial words about the complex nature of carnival laughter. It is, first of all, a festive laughter. Therefore it is not an individual reaction to some isolated "comic" event. Carnival laughter is the laughter of all the people. Second it is universal in scope; it is directed at all and everyone, including the carnival's participants. the entire world is seen in its droll aspect, in its gay relativity. Third, this laughter is ambivalent: it is gay, triumphant, and at the same time mocking and deriding. It asserts and denies, it buries and revives. Such is the laughter of carnival." Mikhail Bakhtin,

Rabelais and His World, trans. by Hélène Iswolsky: (Cambridge, Massachusetts and London: The Massachusetts Institute of Technology Press 1968), 11.

[27] "MATAMOROS: Ansi, come el suberano y muy resplandeciante febo lunbre, entre la blanca luna y platedas estrellas; de may gran resplandor, y emorsura la vitorioso vandera y treofante palma tiene, ansi yo, entre los famosos guerroros y bravos Capitanes, de fuerca anima y balor, la gloriosa vandera traggo.

SCARAMUZZA: A cossi come lo Tavernaro precepale delle Cerriglio, de chesta nobilissima cettate de Napole; se pretenne de sapere buono cocinare; a cossi le trippe de Vaccha, come ancora chella de Vitella, e arrostire quaglie, fasane, polastre pernice, e pecciune a cosi io me pretengo, songo e saraggio (a despietto delle nemici miei) lo chiu gran cannarutu, magnatore, veuetore e tauerniero de quante vastase magnature, e beuettore, nbriacune, e buffune se punno mai trouare da Leuante ha ponente et da sceroco, a tramontana, e ba descorreno, e zettera: e perzo facce stare ncelleorillo, e a sticcheto, e con paura tutte chille che me canosceno, po che anno sospetione che no le scannarozzola, e me la magna viue e me gliotta sane tanto sto chino della gran famme e sto nolato appetitto."

Silvio Fiorillo, *Li Tre Capitani Vanagloriosi. Capriccciosa Rappresentazione di strani amorati auenimenti* (Naples: Domenico Maccarono 1621), 17.

[28] "dit à Sa Majesté que son Eminence luy avant dit qu'il se pouvoit vanter que le plus grand monarque du monde luy avoit versé à boire, il avoit repondu qu'il ne manqueroit pas de le dire à son Boulanger.

Le Roy comprenant par ce discours, que l'honneur qu'il avoit fait à Scaramouche ne luy donoit du pain, repartit aussi-tôt avec une generosité sans pareil: Tu luy diras aussi que j'augmente ta pension de cent pistoles. Scaramouche remercia Sa Majesté et se retira fort content."

Angelo Costantini, *La Vie de Scaramouche* (Paris: Barbin 1695), 92.

[29] Justin Butcher, *Scaramouche Jones or The Seven White Masks* (London: Methuen 2002), 6.

[30] Ibid 28-29.

Bibliography

Bakhtin, Mikhail. *Rabelais and His World*, trans. by Hélène Iswolsky. Cambridge, Massachusetts and London: The Massachusetts Institute of Technology Press, 1968.

Brindicci, Monica. "Il Pulcinella di Silvio Fiorillo fra vita teatrale del teatro e modelli letterari." In *Quante Storie per Pulcinella* edited by Franco Carmelo Greco, 55-85. Naples: E.S.I., 1988.

Butcher, Justin. *Scaramouche Jones or The Seven White Masks*. London: Methuen, 2002.

Caputi, Anthony. *Buffo. The Genius of Vulgar Comedy*. Detroit: Wayne State University Press, 1978.

Castagno, Paul C. *The Early Commedia dell'Arte. 1550 - 1621. The Mannerist Context*. American University Studies Series XXVI. Theatre Arts Vol.13. New York: Lang, 1994.

Cornford, F.W. *The Origins of Attic Comedy*, Cambridge: Cambridge University Press, 1934.

Costantini, Angelo. *La Vie de Scaramouche*. Paris: Barbin, 1695.

De Marinis, Marco. "Appunti per un studio diacronico della commedia dell'arte." In *The Science of Buffoonery. Theory and History of The Commedia dell'Arte*, edited by D. Pietropaolo, 239-256. Ottawa: Dovehouse Editions, 1989.

De Simone, R. and Rossi, A. *Carnevale si chiamava Vincenzo, rituali di Carnevale in Campania*. Rome: De Luca, 1977.

De Simone, Roberto. "Maschere e danze rituali carnevalesche, nella Napoli del seicento, in referimento ai 'Balli di Sfessania' di Jacques Callot." In Lucia Balbi, *Demoni e Santi. Teatro e teatralità barocca a Napoli*, 145-193. Naples: Electa, 1984.

Del Tufo, G. B. *Ritratto o modello delle grandezze, delitie e meraviglie della nobilissima citta di Napoli*. Naples: Agar, 1959.

Dizionario Etimologico Italiano, edited by Carlo Battisti and Giovanni Alesso. Florence: Università di Firenze, 1957. s.v. "scaramuccia."

Eco, Umberto. "The frames of comic 'freedom.'" In *Carnival!* edited by Thomas A. Sebeok, 1-9. Berlin: Mouton, 1984.

Evangelista, Annamaria. "Le compagnie dei Comici dell'Arte nel teatrino di Baldracca: notizie dagli epistolari (1576-1653)." *Quaderni del Teatro* 24 (1984): 50-73.

Fiorillo, Silvio. *L'Amor Giusto*. Naples: Felice Stigliola, 1604.

—. *Li Tre Capitani Vanagloriosi. Capricciosa Rappresentazione di Strani amorati auenimenti*. Naples: Domenico Maccarono, 1621.

Hutcheon, Linda. *Irony's Edge: The theory and politics of irony*. London and New York: Routledge, 1994.

Katritzky, M.A. *A study in the Commedia Dell'Arte 1560-1620 with specific reference to the visual records*. D.Phil thesis, St.Catherine's College, University of Oxford, 1994-5.

Landolfi, Domenica. "Silvio Fiorillo: Un 'napoletano' in Lombardia." In

Claudia Buratelli, Domenica Landolfi and Anna Zinanni, *Comici dell'Arte. Corrispondenze. G.B. Andreini. N.Barbieri. P.M. Cecchini. S.Fiorillo. T. Martinelli. F.Scala*, edited by S.Ferrone, 309-312. Florence: Le Lettere, 1993.

Mamone, Sara. "Le miroir des spectacles:Jacques Callot à Florence (1612-1622)." In *Jacques_Callot 1592-1635*, edited by Paulette Choné, 183-187. Catalogue of an exhibition held at the Musée Historique Lorrain, Nancy, 13 June - 14 September, 1992. Paris: Éditions de la Réunion des Musées Nationaux, 1992.

Monder, Eric. *George Sidney. A Bio-Bibliography*. Westport, Connecticut and London: Greenwood, 1994.

Posner, D. "Jacques Callot and the Dances called Sfessania." In *The Art Bulletin* 59 (1977): 203-216.

Raffé, W.G. *Dictionary Of The Dance*. Assisted by M. E. Purdon. New York: Barnes & Co, London: Yoseloff, 1964.

Richards, K. "Inigo Jones and the Commedia dell'Arte." In *The Commedia dell'Arte from the Renaissance to Dario Fo*, edited by C. Cairns, 209-225. Lewiston, Queenston and Lampeter: Edwin Mellen, 1989.

Rose, M.A. *Parody: ancient, modern and post modern*. Cambridge: Cambridge University Press, 1993.

Scafoglio, Domenico and Lombardi Satriani, Luigi M. *Pulcinella. Il Mito e la Storia*. Milan: Leonardo, 1992

Taviani, F. "Immagini Rivoltate." *Biblioteca Teatrale 37-38, Immagini del teatro*. Rome: Bulzoni, 1996: 39-59.

—. "Un Vivo Contrasto. Seminario su attrici e attori della commedia dell'arte." In *Teatro e Storia*, a.1, 1, October (1986): 25-75.

Ternois, Daniel. "Balli de Sfessania." In *Jacques Callot* 1992, *op.cit*. *The Oxford Dictionary of Etymology*, Oxford: Oxford University Press, 1966.

Welsford, Enid. *The Fool. His Social and Literary History*. London: Faber and Faber, 1935.

The Cinema of Masks: *Commedia dell'Arte* and Jean Renoir's *The Golden Coach*

Des O'Rawe

[The Golden Coach] was a film in which I tried to enclose one performance inside another. I tried, if you like, to erase the borders between the representation of reality and the reality itself. I tried to establish a kind of confusion between acting on a theatrical stage and acting in life. I don't know whether I really achieved my goal, but in any case it was truly interesting to try it.
Jean Renoir[1]

According to Eric Rohmer, *The Golden Coach* (1953) represents "the 'open sesame'" of all Jean Renoir's work."[2] Certainly, its theatrical qualities are in keeping with a very Renoirean attachment to the mysterious intimacy between theatre and life – the nature of role-playing and the paradox of performance: "Even when there is no theatre or stage involved, Renoir can give a feeling which is less film than theatre."[3] The theatrical, and the art of acting in particular, is as integral to the action and *mise en scène* of Renoir's early films – such as *Nana* (1926) and *La Chienne* (1931) – as it is to the *guignol* world of his last film, *Le Petit Théâtre de Jean Renoir* (1970). In *Boudu sauvé des eaux* (1932), the kindly Lestingois, in saving his "perfect tramp," inadvertently invites Dionysus to dinner. At the beginning of *Une Partie de campagne* (1936), the borrowed milk-cart that carries Dufour and his family into the countryside seems also to be conveying a troupe of unwitting players onto a new stage. In *La Grande Illusion* (1937), the prisoners' theatrical revue is suddenly interrupted by news from the front, by a reality from which there is no hope of escape. In this sense, *The Golden Coach* (like its contemporary companion pieces, *French Can-Can* (1955) and *Éléna et les hommes* (1956)) is no mere product of a "late Renoir" whose cinema had become disconnected from its own past. *The Golden Coach* – with its *mélange* of movement, colour and musicality – reaffirms the profound coherence of Renoir's cinematic vision and its debt to the bittersweet genius of *commedia dell'arte*.

Commedia dell'arte flourished in sixteenth century Italy and became a popular theatrical form throughout Europe before many of its comic routines (*lazzi*) and archetypical characters became assimilated into the more literary and moralistic dramas of the eighteenth century and after. *Commedia dell'arte*, as its name suggests, was above all an actor's theatre in which everything depended on witty improvisation, expressive gesturality, and the skilful use of mask and costume.[4] The set was entirely decorative and it functioned as a familiar prop rather than as an elaborate source of diegetic information. Normally distinguished from its more sophisticated counterpart, *commedia erudite* (which was scripted, devoid of masks and performed indoors), *commedia dell'arte* deployed a very visual and non-naturalistic style of performance that demanded remarkable agility from its actors. Any routines that were rehearsed (like the presence of stock characters: Columbine, Harlequin, Pierrot, Punchinello, and Pantalone, etc.) formed part of a template for comic improvisation and inventiveness. While *commedia dell'arte* was non-literary, it was not *a-literary*: virtually all performances (as with *The Golden Coach*) conformed to a three-act structure. Paradoxically, these and other dramaturgical conventions actually produced the myriad of improvisations – and that mood of general playfulness – with which *commedia dell' arte* has long been synonymous. The rules were the game and they guaranteed the *comic* authenticity of each action, gesture and comment: the sudden turn of a mask, the startling collision of two colours, the timing of a witty riposte.

Inevitably, there is much debate about the traditions and historical evolution of *commedia dell'arte*:

> Since the seventeenth century many myths have accumulated in many countries about *commedia dell'arte*: that it was a single entity, that it was artistically self-contained and well-defined, that it was spontaneously improvised, drew much on "popular" materials and was essentially of the "popular" meridian, that it trafficked mainly in "low" comedy, and was rooted in the physical and acrobatic antics of the masked players. The historical reality, however, was rather different. [5]

Renoir, for his part, was always less concerned with the reproduction of an historical reality than with a much more modernist enterprise: the cinematic rendering of a pure fiction that yields a moment of reality. For Renoir, *commedia dell'arte*, like the *guignol* and the Can-Can, was more than simply a rough theatre for the common people. While its exaggerations and comic directness were "carnivalesque" and had their origins in a pre-Enlightenment world of fixed social orders and strong communal ties, they also anticipated modernity. *Commedia dell'arte* was, after all, an essentially experimental art form in which prefabricated scenarios and archetypical characterisations liberated each performance from a requirement to be "realistic" in the naturalistic sense. This was "a purely artificial environment" that was not obliged to dramatise plots rich in psychological motivations, an environment free from the pursuit of a perfect clarity that amounts to a perfect banality, to paraphrase Orson Welles.[6]

What then was a *commedia* performance about? Ultimately, it was about itself, it was about its own fictions, its own theatricality. In this sense, it is hardly surprising that so many Modernist painters, composers and writers were drawn to the distinctive performative and visual characteristics of *commedia dell'arte*. The symbolic vitality and aesthetic openness of *commedia* has inspired everyone from Meyerhold to Pirandello, Picasso to Hockney. In her essay on the appropriation of *commedia* images and archetypes in the proto-modernist poetry of Appollinaire, for example, Susan Harrow states:

> Modernism achieves its dazzling, unassailable synthesis when Pierrot shares the stage with the modern-day pantomime artiste and Harlequin makes his entrance into the world of the street acrobat. It is in the work of the pioneers of Modernism – Appollinaire and Picasso – that we glimpse the liberating, transforming and ultimately regenerating powers of a movement which sets free the *zanni* from the *commedia*'s conventions, only to repossess them for the modern temper and re-present them in a radically new frame.[7]

It is hardly surprising then that within the history of the cinema – at one time, the modernist art *par excellence* – *commedia dell'arte* has proved an important – if generally implicit – point of reference for various film directors and actors.

Marcel Carné's *Les Enfants du Paradis* (1945) and George Sidney's *Scaramouche* (1952) are among the more obvious examples of films that derive their subject matter and some of their formal qualities directly from the *commedia dell'arte* tradition. However, while *Les Enfants du Paradis* is rightly regarded as a landmark film in the history of cinema, its formal elegance and theatrical content owes more to the nineteenth century cult of Pierrot than to the wider (and wilder) world of *commedia dell'arte*. Similarly, *Scaramouche* – a remake of Rex Ingram's 1923 version of Rafael Sabatini's eponymous novel – is remembered less for its representation of the actors and antics of an eighteenth century *commedia dell'arte* troupe than for the mesmerising choreography of its sword fencing sequences. Like numerous films of the fifties (*The Golden Coach* included), Sidney's *Scaramouche* exploits the new aesthetic possibilities of Technicolor and widescreen. However, its classical narrative structure and lavish cinematography is also consistent with a tendency within popular American and European cinema of this period to produce films that dealt with the themes of acting and artifice.

In his materialist study of Renoir's films, Christopher Faulkner offers a plausible explanation for this phenomenon:

The representation of the domain of art and artifice in the films of the fifties should not be thought of as a development peculiar to Renoir's work alone in these years. Its context is a world cinema that saw little innovation apart from experiments with flashy technology (3-D, widescreen) throughout a politically conservative decade retreating from the socially engaged film. It is remarkable just how many films of importance through the mid-fifties take art and artists as their subjects: *Le Plaisir* (Ophuls, 1951); *Lola Montès* (Ophuls, 1955); *An American in Paris* (Minnelli, 1951); *Lust for Life* (Minnelli, 1956); *Moulin Rouge* (Huston, 1952); *Limelight* (Chaplin, 1952).[8]

Although *Scaramouche* is not as important a film as any of those listed above (with the exception of Huston's cumbersome *Moulin Rouge*), it is a more intelligent film than Sidney's better-known MGM musicals (e.g. *Show Boat* (1951) and *Kiss Me Kate* (1953)). However, its conscientious adherence to the generic conventions of the day is certainly one of the reasons why it fails to engage with *commedia dell'arte* in a radical and formally inventive way.

In the case of both Carné's and Sidney's "commedia" films, the dissidence of *commedia dell'arte* is contained within a filmic environment that upholds the centrality of the script, emphasises the presence of individuated protagonists, and conforms to the technical procedures and production values of their respective studio systems. To a certain extent, this is also true of the comedies of Charles Chaplin, Harry Langdon, Buster Keaton and Harold Lloyd. Yet, the "clownesque" elements and slap-stick routines in these films does offer something closer – in spirit, if not substance – to more traditional *commedia* routines and techniques. In the silent, fragile faces of their heroes and villains, these post-vaudeville films easily reacquaint us with the masks of Pierrot, Columbine and Harlequin. Indeed, it is also a short (albeit, sideways) step from the burlesque antics of the Marx Brothers or the Three Stooges to the characters and situations of *commedia dell'arte* (although, it is probably "unlikely that the *commedia dell'arte* featured zanier *zanni* than Moe, Curley, Larry, and Shemp."[9]) Such films, particularly those of Chaplin, were an important influence on Renoir. According to Truffaut, for example, Renoir's *Tire-au-Flanc* (1929) "is a masterpiece of 'living cinema' in the tradition of Chaplin's *Shoulder Arms* [1919] and *A Night in the Snow* [1915]," while the closing scene in *Les Bas Fonds* (1936) explicitly pays homage to Chaplin's *Modern Times* (1936).[10] If the climactic chase sequences in *The Golden Coach* immediately recall similar sequences in earlier Renoir films, they also recall any number of chases and "body gags" from the golden age of the American slapstick comedy.[11]

The films and writings of Sergei Eisenstein also contain numerous allusions and references to *commedia dell'arte* and although Eisenstein was never an influential figure for Renoir and *vice versa*, both directors shared an enduring passion for the circus, puppetry and "Charlie." Throughout his career, Eisenstein sought to establish the artistic integrity of cinema through the development of montage techniques that – amongst other things – transformed the nature and function of film acting. Like Renoir, Eisenstein did not strive to exclude "theatricality" from cinema, rather he wanted to develop a cinema in which theatrical phenomena – particularly, "the comedy of masks" – become "transformed into a feature of the maximum purity of cinema."[12] Hence, the relationship between the concept of 'typage' and the *commedia dell'arte*: "The 'types' in *Battleship Potemkin* [1925] [...] represent the direct connection between the theatre and cinema and between the Theatre of Masks (*commedia dell'arte*) and "typage.'"[13] For Eisenstein, "typage" was a necessary element in the development of montage as a creative practice that would simultaneously revolutionise the cinema and eulogise the revolution. The types that one encounters in *Strike* (1924), *Potemkin*, and *October* (1927), for example, issue from a "film sense" that is fundamentally opposed to a cinema of spurious realism where the actions of heroic individuals merely serve to reaffirm any misguided notions we might harbour about love conquering all or life being determined by consciousness.

Although there are differences between the stock (masked) characters of *commedia dell'arte* and Eisenstein's (physiognomical) types ("The Spy," "The Priest," "The Worker," etc.), the rationale for their creation is remarkably similar: "What form of theatre is the most theatricalised? The comedy of masks. If you compare the principles of the comedy of masks with the principles of typage, you will see that they are two aspects of the same thing."[14] Eisenstein's ambitious (if ultimately unsuccessful) attempts to realise "typage" in his films of the 1920s discloses both the extent of his debt to theatre and, more specifically, his engagement with the theories of Vsevold Meyerhold. In *Strike*, for example, the presence of acrobatic techniques derived from the reflexological theories of Meyerhold and the avant-garde plays of the Moscow Proletkult are probably more conspicuous than the film's experiments with "typage." Indeed, it is probable that Eisenstein's interest in *commedia dell'arte* was a direct consequence of his earlier association with Meyerhold, whose revival of the *commedia dell'arte* was a direct challenge to the forms and conventions of Chekovian naturalism that dominated Russian theatre in the first decade of the twentieth century.[15]

Yet, there is more to Eisenstein's relationship with *commedia dell'arte* than "typage" experiments and the lingering legacy of Meyerhold. Eisenstein's fascination with circus clowns, his interest in the Japanese Kabuki and Bunraku theatrical traditions, and his more general resistance to the illusion ("ideology") of continuity and the supremacy of the script ("The presence or absence of a written script is by no means all that important"[16]) corresponds closely to the dramaturgical precepts of *commedia dell'arte*. This fact testifies to the complexity of Eisenstein's art while also emphasising the nature of Renoir's achievement in *The Golden Coach*. What is exceptional about this film is the seemingly ingenious way in which it both depicts *commedia* performances and characters whilst simultaneously integrating the essentials of *commedia* theatricality into the filmic *mise en scène*. While other filmmakers have incorporated elements of *commedia dell'arte* into their work and theories, only Renoir succeeded in transforming the material and formal characteristics of *commedia dell'arte* into a purely cinematic medium.[17] In this context, it is particularly important to stress the relationship between *The Golden Coach* and Renoir's earlier masterpiece, *La Règle du Jeu* (1939). Not only does *La Règle du Jeu* contain a cast of *commedia* types (principally, Jurieu/Pierrott, Christina/Columbine, Marcel/Harlequin), it also shares with *The Golden Coach* a very theatrical quality that intensifies its revelation of a truth about the appearance of truth: "I had [*La Règle du Jeu*] acted in somewhat of a *commedia dell'arte* fashion, a bit of pantomime style."[18]

Although Renoir never directly associated himself with the *avant-garde* movement in French cinema, throughout his career (and during the thirties in particular) he had freely experimented with new techniques; nurtured productive technical and creative collaborations; and secured for himself a reputation as one of the most artistically intelligent directors the cinema had ever produced. Not that this prestige counted for much when *La Règle du Jeu* was first screened to French audiences in the winter of 1939: the film outraged critics and spectators alike. *La Règle du Jeu* was shot on the eve of WWII; political commentary was pessimistic and prominent right-wing figures were already recommending further appeasement and "constructive collaboration" with Germany. Despite his involvement with the recently defunct Popular Front, Renoir did not respond to this situation by offering his anxious audiences a patriotic "call to arms" or a naturalistic correlative to the dire realities of the present situation. Instead, he turned to the classical French writers (Beaumarchais, Molière, and Musset), to the lightheartedness of *Les Caprices de Marianne*, and the sketchiness of *commedia dell'arte*.[19] In its conjunction of theatrical artifice and cinematic realism, *La Règle du Jeu* gradually reveals to its audience a society of the dead, a domain of mannequins and automatons, mechanical birds and dancing corpses. While *La Règle du Jeu* was a more elaborate (and controversial) work than *The Golden Coach*, the formal relationship between the two films is still worth emphasizing.

The Golden Coach was shot in Rome, at the Cinecittá Studios, in February 1952. It was the first Technicolor film to be made in Italy, and only Renoir's second colour film.[20] The narrative of the film – a free adaptation of

Prosper Mérimée's story, *Le Carrosse du Saint-Sacrement* (1829) – is as charming and insubstantial as the narratives of *French Can-Can* and *Éléna et les homes*.[21] A *commedia dell'arte* troupe arrives in a Spanish colonial town in eighteenth century Peru. Once they have built their theatre and established themselves, their leading actress (Camilla) is beset by a trio of suitors: Felipe (a soldier who eventually offers her an authentic life away from the theatre), Ramon (a bullfighter who offers her passion and fame), and Ferdinand (the Viceroy of the colony, who gives her the golden coach that has been voted to him as a symbol of his office and status). In the end, Camilla rejects them all and chooses the real love of her life: theatre, and its promise of "those two little hours on the stage." In the finale, Camilla donates the coach; the film's symbol of power and desire, to the people (through the Church) and order is restored. In true *commedia* fashion, this scenario is of course merely an appendage to the spectacle, to the movement of bodies, spaces and colour that is the real content of the film.

This scenario is openly allegorical and its fairy-tale subject matter seems to offer us a parable about art and the duty of the artist to acquiesce to the severe vocation of their craft, in this case, the artist as actor. In choosing theatre, Camilla chooses "nothing" (artifice) rather than "something" (i.e. marriage, fame, wealth, etc.): the truth that is in appearances rather than the appearance of truth. The coach becomes the soul of Camilla, the priceless emblem of her heroic generosity, which is itself the generosity of art. In the film, however, this "inner truth" about the function of art and the responsibility of the artist is not articulated – primarily, at any rate – through the diegetic rendering of Camilla's sentiments or speeches anymore than it is affirmed by the film's storyline. *The Golden Coach* is, first and foremost, a triumph of *mise en scène* over subject matter. Paradoxically, the film's transparent theatricality enables it to rediscover something of the true meaning and value of cinema. In demonstrating the extent of Renoir's achievement in this respect, it is important to attend to three particular aspects of the film's *mise en scène*: its tendency towards visual and aural excess; the "informality" of its editing and camera-work; and its endorsement of a decidedly anti-naturalistic (Brechtian?) style of acting, a style that continually draws attention to its own theatricality and, *a fortiori*, its own artificiality.

The Golden Coach opens to the sound of Vivaldi's *Four Seasons*. This blank "pre-credit sequence" is deliberately reminiscent of the dimming of theatre lights in the moments prior to a performance. Renoir famously referred to Vivaldi as his "principal collaborator" in the making of *The Golden Coach*: "I wrote the script while listening to records of his music, and his wit and sense of drama led me on to developments in the best tradition of the Italian theatre."[22] Extended excerpts from the *Four Seasons* are included to register the end of each of the film's three "acts" and throughout the credit titles at the close of the film. Ordinarily, the extensive use of music (particularly, something as vibrant and "voluminous" as the *Four Seasons*) would endanger the visual integrity of a film. Here, the effect is the reverse: we wait in anticipation not just for the film's opening shot but also for an image that might make Vivaldi's music visible.[23] This "first" image is itself an image of painted theatre curtains, over which the opening credits appear. The curtain rises to reveal another stage curtain, which opens on to a stage and the music fades. An important point is worth making about Renoir's adoption of Vivaldi and its relationship to the film's *mise en scène*. In a film free from the constraints of narrative clarity and "classical" coherence, the "excessiveness" of the music is entirely appropriate: the *Four Seasons* is not so much a soundtrack as an inadvertent narrator. It does not overwhelm the *mise en scène*, rather it assists in the evocation of a melodramatic mood that is entirely appropriate in a film that takes theatre seriously and that celebrates the courageous, precarious and mysterious art of acting. The vivacious naivety of the *Four Seasons* generates a "commedic" spirit of spontaneity and lightness of being that serenades the film's preoccupation with, and representation of, artifice. This is also a film in which the movement of colour is choreographed as much by the music of the moment as by abstract compositional principles.

Throughout *The Golden Coach*, the colour schemes acquire a remarkable physicality as they relentlessly scandalise the illusion of reality: the lavender costumes of the courtiers; the swirling spectrum of reds, blacks, greens and yellows of the stage performances; the bleached browns and yellows of the outside world; the blackness of Camilla's dress; the "golden-ness" of the golden coach. Shot compositions repeatedly contrast secondary and primary colour formations, and the cuts often involve a change from one colour palette to another, with one residual colour surging forward, insisting on its existence in the next shot or sequence: "In every shot there is some note off key – the decoration on a chair, the jewel on a cravat – that gives the whole harmony an added strength and vibrancy."[24] This joyously chaotic profusion of colour, like the film's momentary "reproductions" of famous *commedia* paintings (particularly, those of Watteau, Goya, Monet and Auguste Renoir) replicates the kaliescopic vigour of *commedia dell'arte*. The harlequinesque costumes of the players – particularly the child-acrobats – catch our eye and distract our attention, consistently drawing us towards the spectacle rather than the story:

> [S]ometimes a bright background flattens the perspective, or a matching of foreground and background colours confuses it, or a shrilly coloured detail insinuates itself into our attention [...] thus colour pixilates the sense of order and characters' subjectivities, and mediates between them in a capricious way.[25]

In true Renoirean fashion, the costumes of the *commedia* children "contain" all the colours while those of the adults are generally characterised by a concentration or confusion of particular colours and tones. Throughout *The Golden Coach*, the expressive and dynamic presence of colour – like the music of Vivaldi – serves to further disassociate the film from the confines of narrative realism. As in the *commedia dell'arte*, spectacle overwhelms representation. Instead of offering us the fantasy of identification, *The Golden Coach* creates a purely fictional space from which its "inner truth" can be revealed.

Anna Magnani as Columbine in *The Golden Coach*
Courtesy of BetaCinema

The informality of the camera-work and editing techniques further dissolve the film's "story" and generate all manner of visual distractions and narrative disorientations. Contradicting the normative approach to adapting theatre for film – an approach which traditionally uses montage and depth of field to diminish the presence of theatrical structure, space and time – *The Golden Coach* over-theatricalises rather than under-theatricalises its *mise en scène*. Everything is a signifier of performance. There are no reverse-shots and precious few matching shots (and even these can seem more coincidental than deliberate). The bullfight sequence, for example, abandons proscenium linearity altogether, making the spectators (and Camilla in particular) the real spectacle. The close-ups of Camilla are unashamedly melodramatic and often arrive "unannounced." This drama of distractions and inversions is contained within a set that presents itself as a complex of levels and rooms that refuse any release from a world of animation and artifice. The casual tracking and panning of the camera preserves the impression of scenes ("stages") that can only be viewed from one side only, set to screen the frame rather than to frame the screen. Sometimes, the tracking shots lead us through all manner of activities and objects only to leave us glimpsing a colour or a figure *en route* to another framing situation. During the backstage *mêlée* that occurs after each of Camilla's performances or in mesmerising chases and capers that take place in rooms of the Viceroy's palace, and in the actors' hostel, the camera seems to struggle to keep up with the manic to-ing and fro-ing of the protagonists. Needless to say, no character in the film is as elusive or difficult to "capture" as Camilla herself, played by Anna Magnani.

Although Magnani's (neo-) realist associations (what Renoir referred to as her "usual style") might have militated against the non-naturalistic gaiety of the film, Renoir had no doubts about her suitability for the part of Camilla: "If I had been dealing with a bourgeois type of actress, the film would have risked lapsing into affectation: the danger with Magnani was that it would go too far in the direction of what is called realism. Her dazzling interpretation forced me to treat the film as a light comedy."[26] Magnani's performance (itself a performance within a performance) is as profuse and free from the conventions of psychological realism as any other aspect of the film's *mise en scène*. Indeed, one of the film's chief qualities is related to the remarkable way in which the acting succeeds *because* it so readily betrays the pretence of method or the illusion of naturalness. The film is unapologetic in its rendering of Magnani's phonetically-learnt lines, gauche hesitations and hurried synchronicities. Indeed, throughout the film, the melodramatic excess of every speech and gesture foregrounds each actor's insubstantial and one-dimensional presence as an actor rather than a character. The film's signature refrain – "where does theatre end and life begin?" – is itself a melodramatic question rather than a transcendent one: *The Golden Coach* is concerned with the theatre of life rather than the relationship between theatre and life, or performance and identification. It is a "character-less" film in the sense that its characters are types, completely formulaic and authentic illusions. The opening credits separate the film's "players" into three groups: the "Italian Actors," the "Spanish Court," and "Others." The cast of *The Golden Coach* is comprised of actors who will play "actors," and the performances of the Viceroy (Duncan Lamont) and his courtiers are every bit as theatrical as that of Camilla and her *commedia* companions. There is no bridging of the gap between actor and character, artifice and reality. Camilla remains a performer acting the role of a performer who wants to be real. The impossibility of this desire – its complete artificiality – is the "inner truth" of Renoir's film.

At the "beginning" of *The Golden Coach*, there is a long shot of the stage and its closed curtain. The camera then tracks forward as the curtain opens to reveal the stage set. The tracking continues as various characters (courtiers and servants) rush to get a look at the coach as it is transported through the town. This scene is reversed at the end of the film, as the coach – now an instrument of charity – leaves the palace. However, this is not the end of the film. The camera tracks back and then stops as the curtain closes. Don Antonio appears from behind the curtain and brings proceedings to a close. Camilla is ushered on to the centre of stage and is congratulated by Don Antonio for her devotion to theatre and "those two little hours" when she "belongs to the audience." Finally, Don Antonio asks her whether or not she regrets sacrificing the attentions and temptations of her three suitors. Everything stops, the camera catches Camilla slightly askew as she intones: "A little." Camilla is forever Columbine and Columbine is forever Camilla, her "a little" is a nothing more or less than a *coup de théâtre*. *The Golden Coach* does not seek from the cinema a means of transforming fictions into reality, actors into characters. Its aim is much more ambitious than this; namely, to render into cinema that most inscrutable of questions: what is the true nature of the relationship between acting and being, art and life? This question is as real to Renoir's film as it is to the world of *commedia dell'arte*. So too is a refusal to answer it – only stories have endings.

In with-holding the inclination to contain the dissident shape – that spirit of the *immediate* – which is essential to the *commedia* experience, *The Golden Coach* succeeds in transforming the theatricality of *commedia dell'arte* into the language of cinema. In this respect, Renoir's film is not only unique in terms of its cinematic rendering of *commedia* concerns and conventions but it is also an invaluable reference point in critical debates about the formal relationship between theatre and film, theatrical adaptation and film *mise en scène*. There is also a much more important reason why this film deserves our attention. In the absurd outbursts of Vivaldi, in the riot of colour, the impulses of the camera, the perfect imperfections of the acting, Renoir's homage to *commedia dell'arte* becomes a challenge for the future of the cinema itself. Ultimately, if *The Golden Coach* teaches us anything, it is that there is always more to film-making than carefully crafted scripts, precision cinematography, invisible edits, and studious actors.[27]

Notes

[1] *Renoir on Renoir: Interviews, Essays, and Remarks*. Trans. Carol Volk. (Cambridge: Cambridge University Press, 1989), 243.
[2] André Bazin, *Jean Renoir*. Ed. François Truffaut. Trans. W. W. Halsey and William H. Simon (New York: Da Capo Press, 1992), 279. Throughout this essay I have rendered the film title in its English form despite the fact that – strictly speaking – *The Golden Coach* was a Franco-Italian co-production.

According to Raymond Durgnant, Renoir "[considered] the English version as the original, since Anna Magnani and most of the actors played in English." *Jean Renoir* (Berkeley: University of California Press, 1974), 286. On its release, the film was a commercial failure and all three versions (English, French and Italian) were subsequently re-cut. The film was restored by the Cinémathèque Française in 1991.

[3] Richard Boston, *Boudu Saved from Drowning* (London: BFI, 1994), 11.

[4] Some of best introductions to the spirit and techniques of *commedia* theatre are "handbooks" written primarily for performers and teachers. I found two texts very helpful in this regard: Barry Grantham, *Playing Commedia: A Training Guide to Commedia Techniques* (London: Nick Hern, 2000) and John Rudlin, *Commedia dell'arte: An Actor's Handbook* (London: Routlege, 1994.). An excellent introduction to a range of more complex issues and research questions can be found in the essays contained in a special issue of *Theatre Research International*, ed. Peg Katritzky, 23 February, 1998.

[5] Kenneth Richards and Laura Richards, *The Commedia dell'Arte: A Documentary History* (Oxford: Blackwell, 1998), 10.

[6] "When we strain for perfect clarity, what we finally achieve is perfectly banal." Orson Welles, "Jean Renoir: The Greatest of all Directors," *Los Angeles Times*, 18 February 1979, 6.

[7] Susan Harrow, "From Symbolism to Modernism: Appollinaire's Harlequin-Acrobat," in *Studies in Commedia dell'Arte*, ed. David J. George and Christopher J. Gossip (Cardiff: University of Wales Press, 1993), 199. More general surveys of the influence of *commedia dell'arte* on twentieth century theatre, literature, film and the visual arts are available in: Martin Green and John Swan, *The Triumph of Pierrot: The Commedia dell'Arte and the Modern Imagination*. Rev. ed. (Pennsylvania: Pennsylvania State University Press, 1993). James Fisher, *The Theatre of Yesterday and Tomorrow: Commedia dell'Arte on the Modern Stage* (Lampeter: Edwin Mellen, 1992). Lynne Lawner, *Harlequin on the Moon: Commedia dell'Arte and the Visual Arts* (New York: Harry N. Abrams. 1998).

[8] Christopher Faulkner, *The Social Cinema of Jean Renoir* (Princeton: Princeton University Press, 1986), 166.

[9] Kathleen Chamberlain, "The Three Stooges and the *Commedia dell'Arte*," in *The Film Comedy Reader*, ed. Gregg Rickman (New York: Limelight Editions, 2001), 53-59.

[10] Bazin, *Jean Renoir*, 217.

[11] One should also be careful here not to overlook the influence of the French comic tradition on both Renoir's work and French theatre and film, more generally: "American achievements have unjustly overshadowed the French Slapstick tradition. It can be traced directly from *commedia dell'arte* through

Debureau and the French music hall to the early film *cascadeurs* and Max
Linder, Chaplin's mentor. The line continues through René Clair, Fernandel,
Jacques Tati, and the freaky quirks of Louis de Funes [...] Renoir's physical
sensitivity owes a good deal to mime, being the link between acting and
dance, and this mode of sensitized knock-about and intricate comic plotting
[...] facilitates a flexible interaction between genres." Durgnant, *Renoir*, 56-
57.

[12] Sergei M. Eisenstein, "Theatre and Cinema (1934)," in *Selected Works:
Writings, 1934-1947*. Vol. 3, ed. Richard Taylor (London: BFI, 1996), 9.

[13] Sergie M. Eisenstein, "Excerpts from Eisenstein's Lectures at the Institute
of Cinematography (1934)," in Marie Seton, *Sergei M. Eisenstein: A
Biography*. Rev. ed. (London: Denis Dobson, 1978 (1952)), 489.

[14] Eisenstein, "Theatre and Cinema," 8. An excellent introductory treatment
of "typage" can be found in Jacques Aumont, *Montage Eisenstein*. Trans. Lee
Hildreth, Constance Pentley and Andrew Ross (London: BFI, 1987), 141-
144.

[15] W. Gareth Jones, "*Commedia dell'arte*: Blok and Meyerhold: 1904-1917,"
in *Studies in Commedia Dell'Arte*, ed. George and Gossip (Cardiff:
University of Wales Press, 1993), 196. See also, Douglas J. Clayton, *Pierrot
in Petrograd: Commedia dell'Arte/ Balagan in Twentieth-Century Russian
Theatre and Drama* (McGill Queen's University Press, 1994).

[16] Eisenstein, "The Montage of Film Attractions (1924)," in *Selected Works:
Writings, 1922-1934*. Vol. 1., ed. Richard Taylor (London: BFI, 1988), 46.

[17] In many respects, Jacques Rivette remains Renoir's only true successor and
– from films such as *L'Amour Fou* (1968) and *Celine et Julie vont en bateau*
(1974) to *Va* Savoir! (2001) – he has consistently explored the relationship
between theatre and life, performance and reality. *Va Savoir!* is interesting
because it pays homage to Renoir and *The Golden Coach* in particular: the
film opens and closes in a theatre and the main protagonist in Rivette's film
is called Camille.

[18] *Renoir on Renoir*, 237.

[19] *La Règle du Jeu* also takes its "dramatic device of a symmetrical grouping
of upper-class and lower-class characters, aristocratic masters and dependent
servants [from Marivaux] [...] who had his own roots in the Italian *commedia
dell'arte* and [who] wrote for an Italian company." Peter Wollen, *Paris
Hollywood: Writings on Film* (London: Verso, 2002),153.

[20] His first being *The River* (1951), which was itself the first Technicolor film
to be made in India.

[21] Although Renoir had been interested in a film project based on Mérimée's
story since 1939, the idea originally belonged to Visconti. See Jeanne-Marie
Clerc, "Du *Carrosse du St. Sacrement* au *Carrosse d'Or*: Intertextes et Texts

Culturels," in *Nouvelles Approches de L'Œuvres de Jean Renoir*, ed. Frank
Curot (Université Paul-Valéry Montpellier III, 1995), 63-74.
[22] Renoir, *My Life and My Films*, 266-67.
[23] Faulkner, *Social Cinema of Jean Renoir*, 190.
[24] Tony Richardson, "*The Golden Coach*," Rev. *Sight & Sound*, 23 April 4.
1954, 199.
[25] Durgnant, *Renoir*, 291.
[26] *My Life and My Films*, 267.
[27] An earlier and shorter version of this essay appeared in *Film and Film
Comment*, 3 (2004: Waterford Institute of Technology, Rep. of Ireland).

Bibliography

Aumont, Jacques. *Montage Eisenstein*. Translated by Lee Hildreth,
      Constance Pentley and Andrew Ross. London: BFI, 1987.
Bazin, André. "Theatre and Cinema." In *What is Cinema?* Vol. 1.,
      translated by Hugh Gray (76-124). Berkeley: University of
      California Press, 1967.
—. *Jean Renoir*. Edited by François Truffaut. Translated by W. W.
      Halsey and William H. Simon. New York: Da Capo Press, 1992.
      Boston, Richard. *Boudu Saved from Drowning*. London: BFI, 1994.
Chamberlain, Kathleen. "The Three Stooges and the *Commedia dell'Arte*."
      In *The Film Comedy Reader*, edited by Gregg Rickman (53-59).
      New York: Limelight Editions, 2001.
Clayton, Douglas J.. *Pierrot in Petrograd: Commedia dell'Arte/Balagan
      in Twentieth-Century Russian Theatre and Drama*. McGill Queen's
      University Press, 1994.
Clerc, Jeanne-Marie. "Du *Carrosse du St. Sacrement* au *Carrosse d'Or*:
      Intertextes et Texts Culturels," in *Nouvelles Approches de L'Œuvres
      de Jean Renoir*, edited by Frank Curot (63-74). Université Paul-
      Valéry Montpellier III, 1995.
Durgnant, Raymond. *Jean Renoir*. Berkeley: University of California
      Press, 1974.
Eisenstein. Sergei M.. "The Montage of Film Attractions (1924)." In
      Selected Works: Writings, 1922-1934. Vol. 1, edited by Ed. Richard
      Taylor (39-58). London: BFI, 1988.
—. "Theatre and Cinema (1934)." In *Selected Works: Writings, 1934-
      1947*. Vol. 3, edited by Richard Taylor (2-14). London: BFI,
      1996.
—. "Excerpts from Eisenstein's Lectures at the Institute of

Cinematography (1934)." In Seton, Marie. *Sergei M. Eisenstein: A Biography*. Rev. ed. London: Denis Dobson, 1978 (1952). 486-493.

Faulkner, Christopher. *Jean Renoir: A Guide to References and Resources*. Boston: Prentice-Hall, 1979.

—. *The Social Cinema of Jean Renoir*. Princeton: Princeton University Press, 1986.

Fisher, James. *The Theatre of Yesterday and Tomorrow: Commedia dell'Arte on the Modern Stage*. Lampeter: Edwin Mellen, 1992.

Grantham, Barry. *Playing Commedia: A Training Guide to Commedia Techniques*. London: Nick Hern, 2000.

Green, Martin and Swan, John. *The Triumph of Pierrot: The Commedia dell'Arte and the Modern Imagination*. Rev. ed. Pennsylvania: Pennsylvania State University Press, 1993.

Harrow, Susan. "From Symbolism to Modernism: Appollinaire's Harlequinn-Acrobat." In *Studies in Commedia dell'Arte*, edited by David J. George and Christopher J. Gossip (199-226). Cardiff: University of Wales Press, 1993.

Jones, Gareth W.. "*Commedia dell'arte*: Blok and Meyerhold: 1904-1917." In *Studies in Commedia dell'Arte*, edited by George and Gossip. 185-197.

Katritzky, M.A. Ed. *Theatre Research International: Special Issue*. 23.2. 1998.

Lawner, Lynne. *Harlequin on the Moon: Commedia dell'Arte and the Visual Arts*. New York: Harry N. Abrams. 1998.

Mitry, Jean. *The Aesthetics and Psychology of the Cinema*. Translated by Christopher King. Bloomington: Indiana University Press, 1997.

Renoir, Jean. *My Life and My Films*. Translated by Norman Denny. New York: Da Capo Press, 1974.

—. *Renoir on Renoir: Interviews, Essays, and Remarks*. Edited by. Ronald Bowers. Trans. Christopher Volk. Cambridge: Cambridge University Press, 1989.

Richards, Kenneth and Richards, Laura. *The Commedia dell'Arte: A Documentary History*. Oxford: Blackwell, 1998.

Richardson, Tony. "*The Golden Coach*." Rev. *Sight & Sound*. 23.4. 1954: 199.

Rudlin, John. *Commedia dell'arte: An Actor's Handbook*. London: Routlege, 1994.

Welles, Orson. "Jean Renoir: The Greatest of all Directors," *Los Angeles Times*. 18 February 1979, 6.

Wollen, Peter. *Paris Hollywood*. London: Verso, 2003.

From Nestroy to Wenzel & Mensching: carnivalesque revolutionaries in the German and Austrian theatrical tradition

David Robb

According to the Russian philosopher and literary theorist Mikhail Bakhtin "great changes [...] are always preceded by a certain carnival consciousness that paves the way."[1] One can see this, for example, in the explosion of satirical, literary pamphlets (*Flugblätter*) in the *Vormärz* period leading up to the 1848 revolution in Germany and Austria.[2] Often distributed and performed by the travelling craftsmen (*Gesellen*) in town market places, these texts mocked and laughed at the powers-at-be, and were an expression of the political will of the people which, albeit temporarily, toppled both German and Austrian systems in 1848. It was in this brief four-month period in Vienna where censorship was momentarily uplifted and Johann Nestroy wrote his famous revolutionary farce *Freiheit in Krähwinkel* (*Freedom Comes to Krähwinkel*)[3].

A carnival consciousness can also be posited in relation to the period of the GDR's peaceful "people's" revolution of autumn 1989. To illustrate this I would like to compare *Freedom Comes to Krähwinkel*, as an example of "clownesque" theatre, with Hans-Eckardt Wenzel and Steffen Mensching's *Letztes aus der Da Da eR* (*Last News from the Da Da eR*)[4]. This was the final part of a satirical clowns revue series that had began in 1982 and reached its climax in the winter of 1989/1990. Of course the two periods are not directly comparable. In the early 1980s *Da Da eR* was an oasis of carnivalesque mockery amidst a dearth of public political criticism due to the extent of censorship particularly in the aftermath of the expulsion of the singer/songwriter Wolf Biermann in 1976.[5] Nonetheless one can chart throughout the 1980s in the GDR – albeit in a subtler, more codified way than in the *Vormärz* – increasing dissent amongst political *Liedermacher*, which came to a head during the months of the so-called *Wende* of 1989. Artists such as Wenzel and Mensching, Gerhard Gundermann, Dieter Beckert and Jürgen Wolff had, for example, begun experimenting with theatrical forms pioneering a new GDR trend in *Liedertheater* (song-theatre). The carnivalesque *Hammer-Rehwü* of 1982, a collaboration between the groups Karls Enkel, Wacholder and Beckert & Schulz, set the critical standard.[6] This culminated seven years later in the unrestrained mockery of *Letztes aus der Da Da eR* which reflected a population's cathartic need to laugh their ageing, soon-to-be deposed leadership into their graves.

The word "clownesque" I use here in a general sense to relate to the parodic approach of a rogue, clown or fool figure in the carnival tradition as defined by Bakhtin.[7] In the course of this chapter it will be examined how such carnivalesque and clownesque traits display themselves in both pieces, particularly in the character Ultra from *Freiheit in Krähwinkel* and in the figures Weh and Meh from *Letztes aus der Da Da eR*. In this respect both pieces demonstrate a "clownesque" treatment of their respective revolutions. In terms of the comedy, both mock the powers at be in, at times, a remarkably similar way. But, over and above that, both pieces reveal a comical approach to the *whole* issue of revolution and *all* of its protagonists. Ultimately this ambivalence highlights the problems of reducing the carnivalesque aesthetic to the status of a weapon of the oppressed, reflecting the uneasy relationship between the carnivalesque and political subversion.

Before ascertaining further parallels, attention must be drawn firstly to the formal and structural differences between *Freiheit in Krähwinkel* and *Letztes aus der Da Da eR*. The former is a cross between popular Viennese farce (in the *Volkstheater* tradition) and modern political comedy in the style of Brecht or Horváth. *Da Da eR* on the other hand, as the play on words between Dada and the DDR suggests, is more of a cabaret revue consisting of satirical songs, clowns dialogue and slapstick. What both pieces have in common, however, as well as the trait of anti-illusionist artificiality, is the clownesque approach to the subject matter of revolution. Despite lying 140 years apart, one encounters distinct thematic parallels: particularly in the objects of parody: in the parody of the rulers, the secret police and their informers, the system of censorship, the turn-coats who try to capitalise out of the upheaval and, last but not least, the revolutionaries themselves, who, in both, are portrayed as being simply not up to the job.

Firstly, the powers at be in both are depicted as comically out of touch with unfolding events. For example, in *Krähwinkel*, the mayor pulls a blanket over his head in order not to hear the commotion of the rioters.[8] In a dialogue from *Da Da eR*, reminiscent in its form of the grotesque clowns scene from Brecht's *Baden Lesson of Consent* or Vladimir and Estragon's surreal exchanges in Beckett's *Waiting for Godot*, the clowns Weh and Meh ridicule the decrepit East German leadership who reminisce on the glory days of the 1950s, 60s and 70s, but are too senile to remember the 1980s.

> Weh: Do you remember the 1950s?
> Both remember passionately the good old days.
> Meh: Do you remember the 1960s?
> Meh and Weh snap their fingers to the rhythm of a long-forgotten hit.
> Weh: Do you remember the 1970s?
> *They laugh like two old lady-killers.*
> Meh: Do you remember the 1980s?
> *The laughter sticks in their throats.*

Weh: What was going on in the 1980s? Woodstock?
Meh: I don't think anything was going on in the 1980s
[...]⁹

The secret police are lampooned in both productions for having been made redundant by the revolutions. Because censorship had been lifted during the 1848 revolution in Vienna Nestroy was able to give the night watchman Klaus the lines: "Freedom has cost the job of not one single night-watchman, but it has that of a few thousand informers."[10] In the "Thank-you-chorus" of *Da Da eR* Wenzel and Mensching similarly mock the Stasi police informers. They thank them ironically for spying on their performances over the years, looking for criticisms in their texts: "Thanks to all the secret men/ so skilled in matters of the soul/ who in perpetual darkness/ write reports so punctually/ [...]/ who memorise in all our work/ every subordinate clause."[11] This song, first performed in the production *Altes aus der Da Da eR* (*Old News from the Da Da eR*)[12] in autumn 1988, one year before the peaceful revolution, is an illustration of the developing carnival consciousness towards the end of the GDR. Even in the mid-1980s such undisguised utterances referring to the Stasi would not yet have been dared in public.

In a version of the song written after the fall of the Wall, the clowns Weh and Meh thank the informers for changing their colours overnight "as if nothing had happened."[13] Later, the clowns transform into the roles of these Stasi turncoats singing gleefully: "Let's take all the discs and the German mark/ and burn all the secret files in the park/ hallelujah."[14] Likewise in *Krähwinkel* the turncoats and opportunists are exposed. The nobles are depicted as jumping on the bandwagon of freedom as reflected in the opportunism of the privy councillor who believes the political instability will increase the value of his shares[15], and not least in Sperling's ridiculous poem "An Ode to Freedom." In the original Austrian German dialect the vowels are played with – in clownesque hybridic fashion – to force a rhyme at the end of each line, thus emphasising the farcical element (see endnote).[16]

What comes over here very strongly is the idea of a people *playing* at revolution – in effect merely clowning around. This is underlined at the end when, in a carnivalesque transformation, members of the bourgeoisie and nobility dress up as revolutionary students.[17] By witness accounts, this was indeed a reflection of real-life events in Vienna at the time. Rudolf Münz writes about the farcical theatricalisation of the 1848 revolution in everyday life. Even the theatres themselves took part. At the height of the uprising, Carl, the director of Nestroy's theatre, had himself and his actors dressed up in costumes reminiscent of uniforms of the revolutionary National Garde and march through the streets.[18] As Münz remarks, such play-acting in public life is reminiscent of the inter-relationship between the theatrical and political stage which Heinrich Heine described in his famous metaphor from 1826. In this, god and the angels look down from their vantage point in heaven complaining at the poor standard of acting in public life.[19] Indeed *Krähwinkel* is a farcical reflection of the "play" of political reality: revolution is even once portrayed as a spectator sport. Pemperl says: "We're just off to watch a bit of revolution [...] who knows when there will be another one."[20] This was precisely the point. According to Münz, Nestroy's work reflected the insight that such theatricalisation of life hindered real action on the world stage; the four months of temporary change in 1848 in Germany and Austria – a *Jetztzeit* (time in the now) of revolution – was simply too short and light-weight to triumph over the millennia of history, and to cause any meaningful change.[21]

In the end the revolution reveals itself to have been a carnivalesque time-out. Wenzel and Mensching also realise this in 1989. They and many of their contemporaries had envisaged a rebellion along the lines of a Prague Spring, which would have brought about a more humane socialism within the GDR. But with the fall of the Wall and with peoples' demands for the Deutchmark and a quick reunification with the capitalist West, there is a sense of a restoration of the old pre-communist order. Indeed, after the initial uprising, the East Germans who *then* take to the streets in their hundreds of thousands, only after the danger of military intervention has passed, are similarly play-acting; revolutionary posturing hides their real motive which is to get hold of the Deutschmark. In this period of December 1989 and January 1990 Wenzel and Mensching revive a song from their *Die komische Tragödie des 18. Brumaire* (*Comical Tragedy of the 18th Brumaire*)[22] production about the 1848 revolution in Paris. Here they sing: "The people are as ever no match for the situation"[23]: the chance for a real revolution had, yet again, as in 1848, been missed. As the song depicts, people are too caught up with material concerns and comforts: boiling baby nappies and onion soup, waiting for the weather to improve, comparing the prices of cheese.[24]

In this respect, a clear line that connects *Krähwinkel* with *Da Da eR* is the theme of human fallibility, expressed via clownesque self-parody. In both cases this reflects the inability of people to grasp revolutionary opportunities, because of the constraints of human nature. This trait is reflected in the Krähwinkel activists of 1848. Having met up in the pub and declared the need for action, they decide their next stop will be the cafe, where they can continue to *talk about* revolution. Later, after the night watchman has had his teeth smashed by the reactionaries, he puns: "it doesn't matter. Now we'll get down to some real biting talk!"[25] Similarly Weh and Meh echo this lack of practicality in the "Revolution Scene" of *Da Da eR* where they play two conspirators who cannot agree on a date for revolution because of mundane considerations such as dentist appointments.

Thus in neither *Freiheit in Krähwinkel* nor *Letztes aus der Da Da eR* is it simply a question of one-sided, political satire. Both function, far more, as parodies of the shortcomings of society as a whole. This holistic approach can be examined in terms of the ambivalent carnivalesque tradition whereby, according to Bakhtin, the person laughing does not raise himself "above the object of his mockery", but laughs at "the wholeness of the world's comic aspect."[26] We see this trait in the harlequinesque protagonist Ultra in *Krähwinkel*. He mocks the reactionary forces, but simultaneously reveals himself in a comic light. For example, when he rises to address the mob in order to calm down their passions, he is comically out of his depth. In a typical harlequinesque transformation he simply switches tact, telling them what they want to hear instead: "Freedom, revolt, victory or death!"[27] In being willing to take on any role they demand of him, he reveals himself as a parody of the revolutionary hero.

In this part it is useful to mention Rudolf Münz's study of the *teatro dell'arte* in the German-speaking countries. This can show us how Ultra is specifically influenced by the figure of Harlequin from *commedia dell'arte*. Münz rejects Rommel's claim of a hostile competition in the eighteenth century between the down-to-earth German *Hans Wurst* theatre (represented by Stranitsky) and the stylised Italian and French *commedia*.[28] He also rejects the claim that the *commedia* had no significant influence in Germany and Austria before the end of the 1720s.[29] In fact, according to Münz, there were many points of contact between the two. As early as 1711 Stranitsky, the original Hanswurst, had put on *Fuchsmundi* which, with its "'indirect,' grotesque, ambivalent character [...] contained important elements of *commedia*."[30] This was evident in the masks and transformations of the figures, where, Fuchsmundi took on other roles such as Arlequin, Pierrot, Mezzetin and Columbine.[31] In 1742 Prehauser, Stranitsky's Hanswurst successor, shared the limelight with Bernardon, the Harlequin character played by the Austrian Kurz.[32] Münz states that at the start of the eighteenth century little differentiation was made at all between the names "Hanswurst" and "Harlekin."[33] A basic aspect in common was the fool's skill in demystifying the world by means of magic, and unmasking myth by means of parody. A further commonality lay in the comical inversions of reality. In this traumatic period of transition from feudal to bourgeois society these created a utopian realm in which people's longings for self-realisation could be expressed.[34]

Significantly for the development of Austrian *Volkstheater*, however, "Pickelhäring-Hanswurst" and "Harlekin-Bernardon" did go their separate ways in the course of the eighteenth century. Münz talks of the "indirect," parodic approach of Harlequin and his family members, who stemmed from medieval carnival culture. These "operate within the contours of their [...] unofficial, ambivalent, grotesque, chimerical world of laughter." This is set in opposition to "the 'other,' real, official world of seriousness." By comparison Hanswurst and his relatives operated "in the real world of seriousness itself. This they confront directly with their foolish laughter, which results in the particular mixture of seriousness and fun [which constitutes Hans Wurst theatre]." In short, Münz concludes, if Hanswurst is basically about the "idealistic, illusionary inversion of reality," Harlequin reflects "the real upside-down reality" itself.[35]

From this standpoint one can argue that significant remnants of carnivalesque influences reside in *Freiheit in Krähwinkel*. Here – despite structural and stylistic differences to *commedia* – Ultra can be seen as a harlequinesque figure in a *chronotope* (a Bakhtinian term meaning "time space")[36] that comes close to the late-Renaissance comedy. There is admittedly no magic – unlike in earlier Nestroy plays – but time, space and logic in *Krähwinkel* are not to be taken seriously. In this way the characters indeed belong to "the real upside-down reality."

Similarly in *Da Da eR* the clowns Weh and Meh belong to a grotesque world. The role transformations, robust use of the body, obscenities and bawdry humour all link Wenzel and Mensching to the profane tradition of the low comic genres. This feature, which they share with Nestroy, sets both apart from the more civilised Hanswurst tradition of clowning that developed in *Volkstheater* of the Enlightenment. A major aspect of this untamed approach, according to Münz, is the dialogicity of language (double meanings, parodic hybrids etc).[37] Bakhtin describes a hybrid as "the repulsion of the foreign-born sacred word."[38] A dialogic process takes place in that two styles meet in the same word, "the language being parodied [...] and the language that parodies."[39] Examples of this abound in *Krähwinkel*. For example, Ultra dialogicises the term "Privy Councillor", saying there is no longer a place for the secrets of "private council" in the new democratic climate of openness.[40] This can also be found in the nonsense speech. When Ultra deceives the mayor in his disguise as a Russian prince he simply speaks German with Russian word-endings. With the words "Verbrennski Proklamazki Constituzki" he pretends that he wants to burn the revolutionary constitution. In this way he procures the important parchment which the mayor is withholding from the Krähwinkel people.[41] When Ultra then comes back disguised as the European Commissioner for Freedom and Equality he parodies his own status as revolutionary hero by playing on the similarity of the words "Gleichheit" (freedom) and "Gleichgültigkeit" (indifference) and in this way proclaims the "Gleichgiltigkeit" of all classes[42], a nonsensical hybrid of the two words. Similarly on the theme of censorship Ultra uses a dialogic play on words: "A censor is a pencil turned person or a person turned pencil."[43] Further on the theme of censorship he says (playing on the fact that "pressure" is the identical word in German as "print" or "press"): "That damned white paper! This pressure in regard of the press is something pressing for the person."[44]

Word plays and speech hybrids play a frequent role also in *Da Da eR*. Such hybridisation is part of an old carnival tradition going back to the Latin *parodia sacra*. In this way official language is ridiculed and revealed as dead rhetoric. In the scene "It is a special honour for me", the parody of an official prize-giving ceremony, the term "Academy of Arts" transforms into the "Epidemy of Arts."[45] In "Do you remember the 1960s?" Weh and Meh say that all words in the 1980s that began with "pol" were forbidden with the exception of "police". This leads to the parodic hybrid of the well-known phrase: "These are the exceptions that make the rules, like politburo"[46] where the clowns allude to the undemocratic nature of the government.

The political aspect of parodic hybridisation is evident in Wenzel and Mensching's general aesthetic. As the portrayed phenomenon clashes together with its caricature the illogicality of the phenomenon is revealed. This is exemplified by the "Piko-railway scene," a slapstick number dealing with the virtual impossibility for GDR citizens to travel to the West. Here, the clowns attempt to construct a model railway with which they will travel to the West. In typical carnivalesque reversal of logic this object is denoted by something, which it is not: in this case a music stand.[47] This corresponds comically with the convoluted logic surrounding the subject matter itself – i.e. travel to the West – in GDR official public discourse.[48] When their building attempts fail, Meh blames gravity. In response Weh says: "Gravity is the last thing that holds us here"[49] alluding to the taboo theme of border fortifications.

Here is an example not of the overt political, but of the "indirect" harlequinesque approach which Münz writes about. This is what enabled Mensching and Wenzel, reminiscent of the *commedia* troupes in the Italian and French royal courts of the seventeenth century[50] to evade censorship and banishment, and earned them the tag "court jesters of the GDR" from their contemporaries.[51] Indeed, the figures of Weh and Meh as well as that of Ultra possess significant characteristics of the Harlequin. Ultra combines (as is usual with Harlequin) a rogue-like quality with intermittent foolishness, and has the typical parasitical attitude to life, evident above all in his opportunism. But the harlequinesque is most clearly expressed in the "multiplicity of personalities"[52] which Ultra adopts. This feature made it particularly difficult for critics to ascertain the exact political stance of Nestroy in 1848. But Ultra's transformability is in keeping with the carnivalesque aesthetic itself, according to which every dogma and ideology is necessarily relativised and shown to be impermanent. Such an ambivalence is confirmed by Ultra's opening utterances. In his first couplet he denounces the system of censorship and repression, only to mitigate this standpoint in his following speech by pointing out the relativity of the concept of freedom, doubting whether the Krähwinkel people will be happier with their new freedom "after their chains are broken."[53] It is also reflected in the opportunism of his disguises, which change to suit any situation he finds himself in. His statement in scene eight: "You can find me anywhere where people are prepared to give me their trust"[54] embodies his true essence, because Ultra is the epitome of harlequinesque transformability. One minute he is against all the trappings of bourgeois society including marriage, the next he falls in love with Lady von Frankenfrey whose hand he finally wins. This is however entirely consistent with his role as a rogue, which enables him to assume any disguise he wishes to achieve his aims, be they subversive or conformist. In this respect Ultra belongs to the mythical fool's tradition whereby according to Bakhtin, the rogue, clown and fool have no direct, but rather a metaphorical significance: "One cannot take them literally, because they are not what they seem [...] They are life's maskers; their being coincides with their role, and outside this role they simply do not exist."[55]

In their respective "clownesque" appearances, however, Weh and Meh are quite different from Ultra. Ultra is ultimately an identifiable character in a Volksstück who in the course of the play adopts various disguises. On the other hand Weh and Meh remain in their revue (on the surface) the same grotesque, masked figures. But these figures are never static. Mensching remembered in interview how at the start of the clowns' revue series in 1982 the Weh figure had linked into the tradition of the foolish Harlequin. At the same time it possessed aspects of the stupid, infantile August and the melancholy French Pierrot. The faster, more devilish Meh frequently gave the slower Weh a cuff on the ear. Mensching commented:

> These are the durable, archaic clown models. But gradually we deviated from these types because we learnt our own, more differentiating techniques of playing. And these figures increasingly blended into one another, taking on the other's characteristics [according to the situation].[56]

This polyvalent signification potential of the clown's mask is exploited in *Letztes aus der Da Da eR* as Weh and Meh slip in and out of the caricatured social roles. In this way one encounters a dialogic interplay between the various different political agendas of the period, be it that of the disgraced leadership, the turncoat Stasi informers, the disappointed liberal left-wingers, or the German nationalistic lynch mob. With this mask-play Mensching and Wenzel find a way to artistically deal with the contradictions of their own political position in the GDR. After the fall of the Wall the media seek scapegoats amongst the artists and intelligentsia, whom they accuse of having collaborated with the system. The clowns had already alluded to their own complicity by nicknaming themselves the "court jesters of the nation" in the "Thank-you chorus." In a twist, the scene "The clowns deserve to be shot" was added to the new finale, in which they ironically offer themselves up to the audience for execution, presenting a view from the perspective of a revengeful public, singing: "They conned us/ Now we stand there looking stupid/ Amidst the falling-down scenery/ As if in delirium/ Surrounded by the bosses/ The clowns deserve to be shot."[57] In doing so, they acknowledge their ambiguous relationship to the GDR state. In 1998 Wenzel stated in interview he believed that this relationship characterised the vast majority of people; that it was unrealistic to divide people into clear-cut categories of rebels and opportunists.[58] Seen in this light, the ambivalent clownesque aesthetic was particularly applicable in relation to Weh and Meh's parodies of everyday social behaviour in the *Da Da eR* productions throughout the 1980s.

Although it is not clear from this scene what political standpoint the authors Mensching and Wenzel are endorsing, this constitutes nonetheless a serious altercation with the political reality, one that could not have taken place within the comical form of a Nestroy farce. It is perhaps partly due to this that his political stance towards the 1848 revolution is so disputed. *Freiheit in Krähwinkel* sheds no more light on this. Herein lies the main common aspect of both pieces. Despite its aforementioned serious, if ironic, conclusion *Letztes aus der Da Da eR* is first and foremost a comical as opposed to a political revue. Spectators who wish to take home an unambiguous political message can only be disappointed. Nestroy and Wenzel and Mensching are all authors in their own respective rational, enlightened periods. But in their relationship to the raw, undiluted comic traditions of the *commedia dell'arte* they are conjuring up the spirit of carnival, which ultimately laughs at any rational discourse, be it authoritarian or oppositional, that becomes dogmatic or set in stone. This philosophy is reflected in the transformations and mistaken identities, in the nonsensical word plays, hybrids and aphorisms and in the expressions of the grotesque body. Here they connect with what Münz describes (with regard to Nestroy) as the mythical consciousness of the pre-rationalistic tradition of the "Harlequin principle."[59] This had its home in a *Volkstheater* that was a-moral, a-causal, a-rational and a-historic[60], and contrasted with the more civilising, rational and moralising tendencies of the newer Austrian folk comedy. This folk theatre "rejected the taming process by standardised exclusion. Figures such as Zanni, Pulcinella, Arlecchino, Harlekin, Bernardon, Kasperle who originated in folk mythology were a symbol of "otherness" merely by virtue of their appearance."[61] In *Krähwinkel*, for example, we can see that Ultra still possess the mythical, even at times devilish aspect of a Harlequin. His character transformations, whether into Father Ignatius or Metternich, are simply otherworldly set against the rational philosophy of his time. Such clown figures inhabit their own mythical *chronotope*, as Bakhtin would say: their own relationship to time and space.

Nor are they bound by ideological constraints. Wenzel and Mensching, too, have found a sanctuary in this "other" world, where they can enact an otherness that would be impossible in socialist, every day life because of its taboos and dogmas.

If these carnivalesque elements make it difficult to ascertain Nestroy's actual political persuasion, the plot at least unfolds in a recognisable milieu. The revolutionary events of Vienna are simply transported to Krähwinkel, a well-known, mythical place in the Austrian comical tradition. The political jokes are more direct, too: there was no need for allusion since the play was performed during the period in 1848 when censorship was not in force. By comparison the grotesque clowns world of Wenzel and Mensching is a step further away from realism. With perfect awareness of its chronotope that corresponds only to their abstract fool's world, the play glides through the scenes. The movements, gestures and use of space are all an inseparable part of their performance. Only seldom does the narrative leave the grotesque time and space coordinates of the clown's world. Any references to the political reality are seen only from the viewpoint of the clown. Personalities (such as the Stasi chief Mielke in "Do you remember the 1980s") are only hinted at in a grotesque manner. In this way the performance avoids sinking into provincial cabaret and assumes a more universal dimension as the clowns link into what Bakhtin terms "the big time."[62] Although the "small time" of the GDR is left behind, the political contradictions of this land continue to be dealt with on this greater, more abstract level. According to Heiner Maaß "the clown moves into a world of timelessness."[63] He creates for himself a greater and simultaneously grotesque environment in which he can develop his fool's freedom and ultimately represent any standpoint he likes. From this grotesque perspective the clowns reflect the daily changing political agenda of a GDR state in its last throes.

The constructing of such a chronotope was to a certain extent necessary on account of the strict censorship in the GDR, above all in the period from 1982 to 1988 when the forerunner clowns series *Neues aus der Da Da eR* (*Latest from the Da Da eR*) was being developed. Although they allowed themselves much more direct criticism in the next stage *Altes aus der Da Da eR* in autumn 1988, this was still couched within their highly developed aesthetic of clownesque abstraction. This contributed greatly to their artistic success as well as to their avoidance of censorship.

Both Nestroy's *Freiheit in Krähwinkel* and Mensching and Wenzel's *Letztes aus der Da Da eR* reflect the "carnival consciousness" of a people in the midst of a popular revolution. In their parodic treatment of revolution the figures of Ultra, Weh and Meh all draw on the grotesque characteristics of the pre-Enlightenment Harlequin. But above all, both show the uncomfortable partnership between politics and the ambivalent carnivalesque. In the twentieth century artists such as Brecht and Chaplin[64] combined motifs from the clown tradition with politics, but this served to promote ambiguity (or to illustrate a dialectic in the case of Brecht) rather than an unambiguous political statement. As the cases of Ultra and Weh and Meh show, the carnival fool belongs to himself and can never be completely appropriated by any political or ideological agenda. This contributed to at one and the same time the aesthetic success of the production as well as its survival from censorship. The carnivalesque fool belongs, as ever, only to himself and can never be totally appropriated for a political cause.

Wenzel and Mensching © Dietmar Korth, Berlin.

Notes

[1] Mikhail Bakhtin, *Rabelais and his World* (Bloomington: University of Indiana Press, 1984), 49.

[2] See Barbara James and Walter Moßmann, *1848. Flugblätterlieder und Dokumente einer zerbrochenen Revolution* (Darmstadt: Luchterhand, 1983).

[3] Johann Nestroy, *Freiheit in Krähwinkel*, in *Stücke 26/1, Historische-kritische Ausgabe*, ed. John R. P. McKenzie (Vienna: Jugend und Volk, 1995), 11.

[4] Steffen Mensching and Hans-Eckardt Wenzel, *Allerletztes aus der Da Da eR/Hundekomödie*, ed. Andrea Doberenz (Halle and Leipzig: Mitteldeutscher Verlag, 1991).
[5] Wolf Biermann was a singer/songwriter who was banned from performing or publishing in the GDR between 1965 and 1976. In 1976 he was allowed out to West Germany to do a tour and, after a concert in Cologne, was stripped of his GDR citizenship and not allowed to return.
[6] See David Robb, *Zwei Clowns im Lande des verlorenen Lachens. Das Liedertheater Wenzel & Mensching* (Berlin: Ch. Links, 1998), 51-70.
[7] Mikhail Bakhtin, *The Dialogic Imagination* (Austin: University of Texas Press, 1981), 158-167.
[8] Nestroy, 36.
[9] Mensching & Wenzel, 29. This and all subsequent English translations from the German by David Robb.
Weh: Weißt du noch die 50er Jahre?
Beide erinnern sich mit glühenden Augen der guten alten Zeit.
Meh: Weißt du noch die 60er Jahre?
Meh und Weh schnipsen den Takt eines längst vergessenen Hits.
Weh: Weißt du noch die 70er Jahre?
Sie lachen wie zwei alte Schwerenöter.
Meh: Weißt du noch die 80er Jahre?
Beiden bleibt das Lachen im Halse stecken.
Weh: Was war denn eigentlich los in den 80er Jahren? Woodstock?
Meh: Ich glaube, in den 80er Jahren war nichts los [...]
[10] Nestroy, 11. English translation by David Robb: "Die Freiheit hat noch keinen einzigen Nachtwächter, wohl aber schon a paar tausend Spitzeln brotlos g'macht."
[11] Mensching & Wenzel, 55-56: "Dank all den geheimen Männern/ Jenen guten Seelen-Kennern/ die im steten Dunkel bleiben/ Pünktlich die Berichte schreiben/ [...]/ Die aus allen unsr'n Werken/ Jeden Nebensatz sich merken."
[12] Mensching & Wenzel, *Altes aus der Da Da eR*, unpublished manuscript and video (Berlin: Liedzentrum der Akademie der Künste der DDR, 1989).
[13] Mensching & Wenzel, 20: "Vorneweg mit neuen Thesen/ So als wäre nichts gewesen."
[14] Ibid, 32: "Nimm die Disketten und die deutsche Mark/ Komm laß uns die Akten verbrennen im Park."
[15] Nestroy, 58.
[16] Ibid, 54: "Ey! Ey!/ Wie sind wir so frey!/ Das ist uns so neu,/ Sonst nur Sclaverey,/ Jetzt Freypresserey/ Volksregiererey!/ D'rum Jubelgeschrey,/ Wie sind wir so frey!/ Ey ey! Ey ey!"
[17] Ibid, 72.

[18] Rudolf Münz, "Nestroy und die Tradition des Volkstheaters," in *Impulse. Aufsätze, Quellen, Berichte zur deutschen Klassik und Romantik*, ed. Werner Schubert and Reiner Schlichting (Berlin and Weimar: Aufbau Verlag, 1988), 211-212.

[19] Heinrich Heine, *Das Buch le Grand, XI*, in *Reisebilder* (Munich: Goldmann, 1982), 262.

[20] Nestroy, 48-49: "a bisserl Revolution anschaun [...] Wer weiß, wann wieder a Revolution is!"

[21] See Münz, "Nestroy", 208-209.

[22] Karls Enkel, *Die komische Tragödie des 18. Brumaire nach Karl Marx, oder Ohrfeigen sind schlimmer als Dolchstöße*, unpublished manuscript and video (Berlin: Liedzentrum der Akademie der Künste der DDR, 1983).

[23] Mensching & Wenzel, 51: "Aber das Volk ist wie immer der Lage nicht gewachsen."

[24] Ibid, 51.

[25] Nestroy, 50: "das nutzt nix, jetzt wird erst recht bissig g'redt."

[26] Bakhtin, *Rabelais*, 12.

[27] Nestroy, 22. "Auf also! Freiheit, Umsturz! Sieg oder Tod!"

[28] Rudolf Münz, *Das 'andere' Theater. Studien über ein duetschsprachiges teatro dell'arte der Lessingzeit* (Berlin: Henschel Verlag, 1979), 114.

[29] O. Rommel, *Die Alt-Wiener Volkskomödie. Ihre Geschichte vom barocken Welttheater bis zum Tode Nestroys* (Wien, 1952), 177. Quoted in Münz, *Das 'andere' Theater*, 115.

[30] Münz, *Das 'andere' Theater*, 113.

[31] Ibid.

[32] Ibid, 160-162.

[33] Ibid, 119.

[34] Ibid, 120.

[35] Ibid, 120-121.

[36] See Bakhtin, *The Dialogical Imagination*, 84.

[37] Münz, "Nestroy", 233.

[38] Bakhtin, *The Dialogic Imagination*, 77.

[39] Ibid, 75.

[40] Nestroy, 56. "Und dann is, Gott sey Danck, die Zeit vorbey, wo das 'Geheimer Rath' eine Auszeichnung war. Ein guter ehrlicher Rath darf jetzt nicht geheim seyn, 's ganze Volck muß ihn hören können." See also Joel Schechter and Jack Zipes: "Slave Language Comes to Krähwinkel. Notes on Nestroy's Political Satire," in *Theater*, Spring, 1981, 72-75.

[41] Nestroy, 42-44.

[42] Ibid, 52.

[43] Ibid, 26: "Ein Censor is ein Menschgewordener Bleistift oder ein Bleistift gewordener Mensch."

[44] Ibid, 20: "Das verdammte weiße Papir! Dieser Druck in Rücksicht des Drucks is was Drückendes für einen Menschen."

[45] Mensching & Wenzel, 40.

[46] Ibid, 30: "Das sind die Ausnahmen, die die Regeln bestätigen, wie Politbüro."

[47] This is what Bakhtin calls a "time-space negation" where "carnival objects [...] are, so to speak turned inside out, utilized in the wrong way, contrary to common use" in *Rabelais*, 411.

[48] Wenzel stated in an essay on the similarly masked production the *Hammer-Rehwü*: "The land that defined itself as historically progressive was in the process of reinterpreting reality by means of an illogical historical 'dualectic.' And it seemed that everything was masked just like the actors on the old video [of the *Hammer-Rehwü*]." Wenzel, "Die Unschärfe alter Aufnahmen," in *Hammer-Rehwü 82 Dokumentation*, (Potsdam: Brandenburgische Landeszentrale für politische Bildung, 1993), unpaged.

[49] *Da Da eR*, 47: "Die Schwerkraft ist das letzte, was uns hier hält."

[50] Margot Berthold writes of an incident in Paris in 1697 where a commedia group was banished from the court of Louis XIV for making fun of the king's wife, Madame de Maintenon, in a manner that was not sufficiently disguised. "Altersloses Theater: commedia dell' arte – gestern und heute" in *Gaukler, Clowns und Komödianten. Tragikomödie im Film. Von Chaplin bis Fellini*, ed. Walter Stock (Gerolzhofen: Bundesarbeits-gemeinschaft für Jugendfilmarbeit und Medienerziehung e.V, 1988), 24.

[51] See Reinholdt Ständer, "Wenzel und Mensching. Die Kult-Clowns aus der Da Da eR," in *Folk-Michel* 4, 1997, 24-26.

[52] Münz, "Nestroy," 233.

[53] Nestroy, 19.

[54] Ibid.

[55] Bakhtin, *The Dialogic Imagination*, 159.

[56] Personal interview with Mensching, 21 February, 1994.

[57] Mensching & Wenzel, 53.

[58] "Es ist ja so, daß heute die Geschichte so betrachtet wird, als ob es eine klare Trennung in Dissidenten und Doktrinäre gegeben hätte. Und so war es nicht. Der Riß ging durch die Leute durch." Hans-Eckart Wenzel in interview with Jens Rosbach, on "Zwei Clowns," Deutschland-Radio, 15 March, 1998.

[59] Münz, "Nestroy," 222.

[60] Ibid, 221.

[61] Ibid, 222.

[62] Bakhtin, *Die Ästhetik des Wortes* (Frankfurt am Main: Suhrkamp, 1981), 347. The German translation of this is "die große Zeit."
[63] Heiner Maaß, "Das Irrwitzige im Vermächtnis der Clowns" in Mensching & Wenzel, 155.
[64] *See David Robb, "Carnivalesque meets Modernity in the Films of Charlie Chaplin and Karl Valentin" in Song Hwee Lim and Stephanie Dennison (eds):* Remapping World Cinemas. Identity Culture and Politics in Film *(London and New York: Wallflower, 2005 in print)*

Bibliography

Bakhtin, Mikhail. *Rabelais and his World*. Bloomington: University of
    Indiana Press, 1984.
—. *Die Ästhetik des Wortes*. Frankfurt am Main: Suhrkamp, 1981.
—. *The Dialogic Imagination*. Austin: University of Texas Press,
    1981.
Berthold, Margot. "Altersloses Theater: commedia dell' arte – gestern und
    heute." In *Gaukler, Clowns und Komödianten. Tragikomödie im
    Film. Von Chaplin bis Fellini*, edited by Walter Stock, 11-27.
    Gerolzhofen: Bundesarbeitsgemeinschaft für Jugendfilmarbeit und
    Medienerziehung e.V, 1988.
Heine, Heinrich. *Das Buch le Grand, XI*. In *Reisebilder* (229-286).
    Munich: Goldmann, 1982.
James, Barbara and Walter Moßmann. *1848. Flugblätterlieder und
    Dokumente einer zerbrochenen Revolution*. Darmstadt:
    Luchterhand, 1983.
Karls Enkel, *Die komische Tragödie des 18. Brumaire nach Karl Marx,
    oder Ohrfeigen sind schlimmer als Dolchstöße*. Unpublished
    manuscript and video. Berlin: Liedzentrum der Akademie der
    Künste der DDR, 1983.
Mensching, Steffen and Hans-Eckardt Wenzel. *Allerletztes aus der Da
    Da eR/Hundekomödie*. Edited by Andrea Doberenz. Halle and
    Leipzig: Mitteldeutscher Verlag, 1991.
Mensching & Wenzel, *Altes aus der Da Da eR*, unpublished manuscript
    and video (Berlin: Liedzentrum der Akademie der Künste der DDR,
    1989).
Münz, Rudolf. *Das 'andere' Theater. Studien über ein duetschsprachiges
    teatro dell'arte der Lessingzeit*. Berlin: Henschel Verlag, 1979.
—. "Nestroy und die Tradition des Volkstheaters." In *Impulse.
    Aufsätze, Quellen, Berichte zur deutschen Klassik und Romantik,*

edited by Werner Schubert and Reiner Schlichting (192-254). Berlin
and Weimar: Aufbau Verlag, 1988.

Nestroy, Johann. *Freiheit in Krähwinkel*. In *Stücke 26/1, Historische-
kritische Ausgabe,* edited by John R. P. McKenzie (7-77). Vienna:
Jugend und Volk, 1995.

Robb, David. *Zwei Clowns im Lande des verlorenen Lachens. Das
Liedertheater Wenzel & Mensching.* Berlin: Ch. Links, 1998.

—. "Wenzel & Mensching: "A Carnivalesque Clowns' Act Spanning
the GDR and United Germany," German Studies Revue 23, 1
(2000): 53-68.

—. "Carnivalesque meets Modernity in the Films of Charlie Chaplin
and Karl Valentin." In *Remapping World Cinemas. Identity Culture
and Politics in Film,* edited by Song Hwee Lim and Stephanie
Dennison (London and New York: Wallflower, 2006.

Schechter, Joel and Jack Zipes. "Slave Language Comes to Krähwinkel.
Notes on Nestroy's Political Satire," *Theater,* Spring (1981): 72-75.

Ständer, Reinhard. "Wenzel und Mensching. Die Kult-Clowns aus der
Da Da eR," *Folk-Michel* 4, 1997, 24-26.

Wenzel et al, *Hammer-Rehwü 82 Dokumentation,* (Potsdam:
Brandenburgische Landeszentrale für politische Bildung, 1993).

Karolos Koun, Karaghiozis and *The Birds*:
Aristophanes as Popular Theatre

Marina Kotzamani

Aristophanes and the Greek Shadow Puppet theatre Karaghiozis have been connected in a variety of interesting ways. Karaghiozis is a popular theatrical genre that was flourishing the first half of the 20th century in Greece. It has stock characters, traditionally made of leather or cardboard, who are animated behind an illuminated white screen. The shadow puppet theatre's hero is Karaghiozis, a grotesque figure who is always hungry. The improvised plots typically evolve around Karaghiozis' comic efforts to find something to eat. Humour is earthy, farcical and grotesque. The soul of the shadow puppet theatre is the animator who improvises the action, moves the puppets on the screen, sings and does the voices of all the characters.

Scholars have noted similarities between Karaghiozis and the heroes of Aristophanes. Moreover, they have pointed out the existence of structural resemblances between the scenarios of the shadow puppet theatre and Attic comedy.[1] Other studies have focused on establishing links between the two genres, tracing the origin of both to ancient Greek festivities and rituals.[2] A hitherto almost unexplored field of research concerns the relationship of Karaghiozis to the performance of Attic comedy in modern Greece. Just like Karaghiozis, Attic comedy has been interpreted as popular theatre on the Greek stage since the early 1900s. Characteristically, translators would not hesitate to render the original into demotic Greek, the low variety of the language used in colloquial situations.[3] This is of course also the language of Karaghiozis. In the early part of the century performance of both genres was strongly associated with low class popular entertainment.[4] There is also evidence that the revue, another extremely popular theatrical genre at that time was a common source of inspiration in shaping both the translations of Aristophanes and the scenarios of Karaghiozis.[5] In the second part of the 20th century Greek artists have perhaps explored the connection between Karaghiozis and Aristophanes in a more direct way. For example, the Karaghiozis animator G. Michopoulos did an adaptation of Aristophanes' *Birds* for the shadow puppet theatre in 1984.[6] The composer Dionysis Savvopoulos created a highly original performance piece based on *The Acharnians*, freely mixing immediately recognisable elements from Karaghiozis in his work.[7] Perhaps the initial inspiration for this project came from a production of *The Acharnians* presented by Karolos Koun in 1976, in which the director emphasised a close parallel between the Aristophanic hero

Dikaiopolis and Karaghiozis.[8]

In all the instances I mentioned, Greek artists have approached Attic comedy as popular theatre. It is this association that invites the connection to the shadow puppet theatre. In an article published in 1963, the painter Yannis Tsarouchis explains that he has drawn a common lesson from Aristophanes and Karaghiozis:

> The voice of the majestic Dedousaros (a major shadow puppet player) in the night, the voice of Pan and the Satyrs, of Zeus and of Aristophanes, was haunting me all my life, [...] compelling me to scorn with the harshness of youth everything "philological," "civilized," "artistic."[9]

Tsarouchis was a major collaborator in a landmark production of Aristophanes' *Birds*, directed by Karolos Koun in 1959. Koun (1908-1987), probably the most significant director of the 20th century in Greece, is also a key figure in the modern stage history of Attic comedy; he directed most of Aristophanes' extant plays, fully articulating in his work a sophisticated popular aesthetic drawn from the Greek folk culture. Far from being picturesque, folk influence is well assimilated and refined in his work to produce a powerful modern interpretation of Attic comedy as ritual. At the same time Koun was sensitive to the political nature of Aristophanes' plays and was successful in recasting their relevance in a contemporary context.

Karaghiozis has been a major folk source of inspiration for Koun in developing his popular approach to Attic comedy. Influence from Karaghiozis is easy to detect in Koun's later productions of Attic comedy, such as *The Acharnians* (1976) and *Peace* (1977), in which the Oriental aesthetic of the *mise en scene* directly evokes the shadow puppet theatre. In this article I focus on *The Birds* and argue that, even though more subtle and indirect, influence from Karaghiozis is already present in the earlier production and has inspired Koun to develop a highly original and imaginative interpretation of the play. His work deserves to be acknowledged, along with the French director Charles Dullin's better known production of *The Birds* of 1928, as one of the two most significant productions of the play in the twentieth century.

The Birds is one of Aristophanes' wildest fantasy plays. At the opening of the comedy, two Athenians, Pisthetairos and Evelpides are searching for the land of the birds, as they hope to live there a life free of the decadence and demagogy of political life which suffocated them in their native city. The birds are initially hostile to the strangers but welcome them after Pisthetairos persuades them that they are older and more powerful than the humans and the gods, and can successfully reclaim their ancient supremacy. They accept him as their leader and he sets out to build in their paradisian land a fortified sovereign state not unlike Athens. Various opportunists arrive from the earth, such as the priest, the sycophant and the law-maker, hoping to make profits from offering services to the new state. Pisthetairos and the birds chase them away. Finally the gods arrive, hungry and angry because the birds have not been letting the animal sacrifices of the humans pass through their land. Pisthetairos negotiates peace with them and to seal the agreement, he asks for the ultimate power status symbol: to marry Ms. Universe. The gods agree and the play ends happily with the marriage. The ending however appears to be ambivalent or ironic as Pisthetairos seems to have become a paternalistic and authoritarian ruler.

Indeed, in his interpretation, Charles Dullin emphasised a political reading of *The Birds*, focusing on the theme of the corrosive effects of leadership.[10] In Bernard Zimmer's adaptation for the French production, Pisthetairos is unambiguously cast as a cynical liberal who becomes an absolute monarch. For example, he dismisses the priest declaring: "I've had enough of thinkers [...] I govern, therefore I prohibit thinking. I will be Pope; that's all [...] I will silence the dissatisfied."[11] At the end of the play Evelpides, disillusioned, complains that only six months ago Pisthetairos was shouting "long live the revolution." The birds beat him with their wings to silence him and sing a hymn for the power and glory of their state while Pisthetairos and his bride – in an ironic ending – engage in a long embrace, as in Hollywood films. Dullin's political interpretation of the play also did full justice to the play's fantastical elements, in a *mise en scene* inspired by the circus and popular entertainments.

Similarly to Dullin, Koun was fascinated by the political import of Aristophanes' satire, as well as by its playfulness. I will show that he too presented a political reading of *The Birds,* which, however, contrasts sharply to Dullin's in presenting Pisthetairos as an earnest and honest leader who does not betray the birds. Koun's *Birds* premiered at the Athens Theatre Festival in 1959. It was shown again in revised form in Athens in 1962 and had major revivals in 1975 and 1997. Moreover, it was taken on extensive touring in Eastern and Western Europe in the 60s and 70s, to enthusiastic international critical acclaim. Besides Tsarouchis, who did the set and costumes for the *Birds*, the director collaborated on this project with another foremost artist in Greece's modern cultural history, the composer Chadzidakis, who wrote the music.[12] A translation of the original was employed in production, prepared by Vassilis Rotas.[13] His work occasionally paraphrases the Aristophanic text.

Koun regarded Aristophanes as a revolutionary author, who ridiculed power figures and exposed abuse of authority in his plays.[14] In discussing *Birds*, the director found that the first visitors to Cloudcuckooland from the earth would be immediately recognisable by a modern audience as representatives of imperialism. Koun wished to stage Aristophanes as living, contemporary theatre, respecting, however, the original form of the plays, that is, the ceremonial and ritualistic elements of classical drama. For a Greek artist, according to Koun, this involves finding points of contact between the ancient ceremonial context of the comedies and the remnants of rituals and festivities that have survived in the Modern Greek popular tradition, which are of both Eastern and Western origin.[15] Koun's emphasis on the ritualistic elements of Greek drama led him to assign primary importance to the chorus. Indeed, he regarded it as "the principal component in ancient drama."[16] Through sound, music and movement the chorus illuminates the heroes and creates the mood or spirit of the play, which it communicates to the audience.

The chorus of birds in Koun's production constitute the people. These are the underprivileged Greeks, the victims of the ruling classes. Rulers and exploiters live in Athens. There are many references to socio-political aspects of modern Greece in this interpretation. Thus, the ancient city has become a place where all mountains have been turned into building plots and islands into airports (implying foreign military bases).[17] At the beginning of the play, Pisthetairos and Evelpides are on a quest for a place where the official state of the right at that time could not repress them: "[...] we are looking for a place without politicians, courts of law, slandering, critics, police [...]"[18] In an interpolated passage, the birds lament that they have lost the glory of their ancestors and refer to their own land as "psorokostaina."[19] This is a slang term that Greeks use between themselves humorously to refer to the misery, poverty and destitution of the modern country. It literally means, the land of Kostas (a common Greek name) that is full of scab. The inhabitants of the Cloudcuckooland then are the suffering classes, excluded from leadership.

The painter Tsarouchis brilliantly represented their land, using the poorest of means. When the production was presented at the theatre of Epidaurus almost all of the action was set at the orchestra. The only addition to the natural setting was a raised, unadorned wooden platform at the background, composed of three planks on different levels.[20] The structure was framed by wooden posts at the back, most of which were dressed with canvas. The set appears to have been inspired by the improvised stages of itinerant performers in popular festivals. The use of canvas and wood also evokes the stage of the shadow puppet theatre and the derelict dwelling of its proletarian hero, Karaghiozis.

Tsarouchis's set also does justice to the ingenious theatrical instinct of Aristophanes. The Attic dramatist wisely refuses to give any stage directions that would aid in conceptualising Cloudcuckooland. Pisthetairos and Evelpides can only find it using birds as guides. It is unclear, though, where the birds take them. The land of the birds is simply and tautologically the space in which birds live. For the reader, the space is inseparable from its inhabitants. The inhabitants are the space. The abstract quality of Tsarouchis's design allows the set to assume multiple functions in production. Also, it allows for acting to be centrally prominent.

The chorus has a protagonistic part in the performance. Koun and Tsarouchis resolutely moved away from realism and from stereotyping in the representation of the birds. Interestingly, the costumes of the chorus created an effect of sexlessness, or of sexual ambiguity, as if in the land of the birds even gender roles are open to redefinition. Actors wore terra-cotta body suits that gave an impression of nudity, especially as nipples were accentuated with brown circles.[21] They wore half masks and elaborate feather headdresses. Feathers were also attached to their back and to their arms. The chorus was in continuous mobility, singing, dancing and moving about in bird-like fashion. Some birds were grotesque and humorous, others had grace and beauty. Koun celebrated the people in his production, paying a loving tribute to their humour, resourcefulness, innocence, beauty and heroism. Their presence on stage conveyed a vivid sense of joy and exultation to the audience, accentuated by Manos Chadzidakis' music.[22] Some of the chorals, however, were distinctly perceived as bittersweet.[23] Indeed, there is also a feeling of empathy in the production for the people's suffering. The critic of the *Daily Mail* wrote an inspired review about the rich gamut of moods and feelings that the presence of the birds inspires to the audience:

> wingless humans and masked gods seem poor creatures to be pitied [...] for their inferiority to the flying elite. [...] Birds are ludicrous and touching and somehow beautiful, sensual without being fleshy, active without being irritating. They are all lovingly entwined regardless of sex.[24]

Far from being an opportunist and a manipulator, Pisthetairos in Koun's interpretation is firmly on the side of the people. To begin with, his positioning on stage is indicative of his attitude towards power. Pisthetairos does not seek to reinforce his public image by addressing the birds from the raised platform. Except for the final scene of his marriage, the only occasion when he does appear on the platform is at the outset, when he explains his plan about Cloudcuckooland to the birds. However, in that scene, he appears on the platform in the position of the accused, wishing to defend himself. His space is the orchestra, which he shares with the birds. For the most part he is surrounded by the chorus and is frequently hard to pick out when the birds are dancing. When he faces the visitors to the Cloudcuckooland birds are frequently behind him and chase the visitor off the stage with him. This character then is spatially in a very intimate relation to the chorus. He appears to be a chorus leader, or as a reviewer aptly describes him, a master of ceremonies.[25]

Pisthetairos' appearance directly evokes the hero of the Greek shadow puppet theatre, Karaghiozis. The protagonist in Koun's production is a grotesque comic character, wearing a short Grecian tunic that leaves his hairy legs exposed. He is bald and wears a half mask that accentuates in black his eyes and eyebrows. He has a moustache and a beard. Karaghiozis is also bald, and has facial hair and dark, pronounced features. His tattered costume leaves his limbs exposed. Pisthetairos is not as grotesque as Karaghiozis, lacking his big nose and hyper extended arm. However, in Koun's production the hero is frequently carrying a stick, which forces him to gesticulate with one arm.

The similarities between Pisthetairos and Karaghiozis go beyond physical appearance. Typically, the plots of Karaghiozis explore relations of power. The most common type of set in this theatre presents two dwellings, facing each other on either side of the stage: the palace of the Pasha who rules the land and the hut of Karaghiozis, his poorest subject, who is always hungry. Characters are clearly differentiated into high and low. In the improvised plots, Karaghiozis is summoned from the palace to fulfil a need or desire of its inhabitants, or to do a job. Karaghiozis is extremely resourceful and witty, outsmarting all other characters on stage. However, he is possessed by a farcical, anarchic spirit that leads him to mess up every job he undertakes. In the end, he is invariably beaten up by the authorities and returns to his hut. The audience knows that each performance of the shadows ends in a circular way with Karaghiozis going back to the point where he began. A firm convention of the Greek shadow puppet theatre is that the status quo is permanent.

Karaghiozis frequently appears to subvert the power of the Pasha by repeating his utterances, substituting nonsense words, tautologies or puns that render them absurd. However, this behaviour is never really construed as a serious confrontation with authority. The Pasha appears not to notice and

Karaghiozis never takes his challenge to the extreme of claiming authority for himself even though he is clearly superior to the ruler in wit. The hero's stance has baffled commentators, who have presented widely divergent interpretations of his behaviour ranging from servility towards the authorities to heroism. In a perceptive essay, Tsarouchis presents the plays of the shadows as dramas of occupation and likens Karaghiozis' stance towards the status quo to that of Antigone. Both are anti-heroes who resist the authorities by absolutely refusing to make plans of personal advancement in the repressive situations they find themselves in.[26]

The leadership of Pisthetairos appears to owe its anti-authoritarian streak to Karaghiozis. Like all the visitors to Cloudcuckooland, human and divine, the priest who volunteers to inaugurate the new state is unambiguously construed as a high character in Koun's production. His inauguration ceremony directly evokes a modern Greek priest, as he is chanting in the style of the orthodox liturgy. When Pisthetairos dismisses the priest and undertakes to perform the ceremony himself he is not hereby asserting his authority over the church, as he clearly does in Dullin's interpretation. Rather, in chanting he is assuming the role of the priest in play. It is noteworthy that he ousts the priest in a language strongly reminiscent of Karaghiozis. Indeed, he even uses Karaghiozis's favourite invective, calling the priest "grousouzis" (a hoopoe).[27] In the production of *The Birds*, the irony of Pisthetairos' chanting is subtler than in Karaghiozis. On a similar occasion, the hero of the shadows would bluntly parody the priest with his exaggerated nasalised voice and grotesque gestures. Pisthetairos is more earnest. He is chanting in a half serious, half mocking tone, allowing the audience to see him as a leader aware of the dangers of abusing authority. The priest incident is a typical example of how Pisthetairos carries himself in the Greek production. He is a leader with a sense of measure, directing irony towards his own power figure.

In this interpretation his resemblance to Karaghiozis also highlights his strong affinity to the chorus of the underprivileged. He is one of the people himself. In stressing his intimacy to the birds, Koun ingeniously expands on the apparatus of the shadow puppet theatre, adding to it a prominent element of Greek drama: the chorus. Like Karaghiozis, Pisthetairos is faithful to his class. His strong identification to it makes him impermeable to change. Karaghiozis's lack of interest in climbing the social ladder gives his character fixity and stability: he does not develop in the course of the action. Similarly, in Koun's production there is no perceptible difference in Pisthetairos between the first and the second part of the play, where we see him exercise his power.

Pisthetairos strongly evokes Karaghiozis in his reactions not only to the priest but generally to all the profiteers who visit the new state. Indeed, this series of repetitive episodes in the comedy, in which one after the other the visitors get rejected by Pisthetairos, is a structural feature also encountered in Karaghiozis. In the scenarios of the shadow puppet theatre there is invariably a repetitive series of individual encounters between Karaghiozis and the other characters, who all come to him with the same plea. In Rotas' translation, Pisthetairos derides the characters in a way strongly reminiscent of Karaghiozis. For example, the poet and the soothsayer talk in katharevousa, the high form of Greek, historically used by the literate on official situations. Thus the poet says: "We are all masters,/ industrious servants of the muses/ as Homer says."[28] The word the poet uses for industrious is "otreros." In his response, Pisthetairos paraphrases "otreros" with "tripa," which means "hole." This is a word of demotike, the low, colloquial variety of Greek, historically used by the people. Feigning innocence, in the manner of Karaghiozis, Pisthetairos says to the poet: "Oh! that's why your shirt is otrere (industrious), that is, is full of holes."[29] He continues in a manner typical of Karaghiozis, mixing katharevousa and demotike and appearing simultaneously inviting and threatening: "So my dear poet, what bad wind has brought you here?"[30] Just like Karaghiozis, Pisthetairos drives away the visitors with slaps and kicks, a method of which Aristophanes also approves. Again, in these passages, the translation appears to paraphrase the shadow puppet lingo. For example, Pisthetairos beats the Inspector up, telling him sarcastically that he is giving him "his salary" and his "diplomatic passport": "Then take your salary, here it is, there and there! [...] And here's the diplomatic passport."[31]

In performance, the evocations of Karaghiozis become clearer. The actor Thymios Karakatsanis who played Pisthetairos in the 1997 revival nasalised his voice occasionally, in the manner of Karaghiozis. The visitors to Cloudcuckooland – and especially Poseidon – also occasionally adopted the characteristic "high" voices of the Ottoman authority figures in Karaghiozis. These characters were played in a highly exaggerated, grotesque style, which made them appear like enormous caricatures. For the most part, the visitors are not modelled after particular figures in the shadow puppet theatre. Yet, they create an unrealistic, two dimensional effect that evokes these puppets, as well as the giant, grotesque figures of another popular genre, the carnival. Each has a characteristic way of talking and walking. For example, the Lawmaker swayed from side to side, as he moved by raising his legs very high. This made his limbs appear to be detachable from his body, just like the limbs of most characters in the shadow puppet theatre. Iris was an impressive apparition with an enormous white cardboard head, who could not stop swaying her whole body back and forth as she talked. Perhaps the initial inspiration for this character comes from the Jew, or Visola-Visola in Karaghiozis, who gives the impression of being totally unscrewed as he walks. The character of the Sycophant, played by Mimis Kouyoumtzis in the 1975 revival, is evidently modelled after Stavrakas, a character who pretends to be tough but is really cowardly. Kouyoumtzis talked in the tough street style of Stavrakas and was dressed exactly like him: he wore a three piece suit, a hat and carried worry beads. Moreover, he had a similar way of posing, with one leg bent in front of the other.

The ending of *The Birds* in Koun's interpretation is melancholy and laden with irony. After successfully negotiating with the gods, Pisthetairos leaves to fetch his bride. The birds prepare for the feast, adorning the wooden stage with palm leaves and strings of multicoloured light bulbs and flags, strongly reminiscent of the decoration employed for churches or festivals on the occasion of religious holidays in Greece. The entire final scene is set as theatre within theatre, on the wooden stage. First the messenger appears on the platform, announcing the arrival of the bridal procession. Then the procession appears and they all stand on the stage, while the birds are at the orchestra, watching, as guests to the wedding. They also form an on-stage audience, drawing attention to the wedding as artifice, or play. This effect is intensified by Chadzidakis' music which is distinctly melancholy, clashing in tone with the festivity of the occasion. Church bells ring solemnly, and the music is reminiscent of religious funerary tunes. Indeed, the marriage looks more like the funeral ceremony on Good Friday in Greece, when the bier of Christ is carried in procession around the church. Koun's production ends with the bridal couple and the guests marching solemnly in semicircular procession off the stage.

Apparently, the happiness in Cloudcuckooland is over. It does not seem though as if Pisthetairos has sold out to the gods. The only clue to a change in this character occurs in the scene of the negotiation with the gods. In this the chorus is for the first time absent from the stage and Pisthetairos, as specified in the original, is busy with the barbecue of the birds who rebelled against his authority. It is noteworthy, though, that the barbecue is presented more as a trick to get the hungry gods to consent to the popular leader's terms for peace. The exploitation of the birds is downplayed. Unlike Dullin, Koun does not interpret the play as a popular leader's betrayal of the people. In the final scene, Pisthetairos shares the solemnity of the chorus. The marriage is not a personal triumph for the hero. His final celebratory address to the chorus in the original is delivered in a sad tone and is drowned by the mournful music. His voice becomes inaudible in the end. Indeed, Pisthetairos appears to be presented as a loser, just like the birds.

The meta-theatrical setting of the final scene renders the interpretation of the play clear. In the revival of 1975 there also seems to have been an on-stage audience of two Athenians watching the action. Their presence further supports a reading of the production as meta-theatre. The people's victories against authority in *Birds* are presented as play; Cloudcuckooland, the state where the people rule, is a pleasant fantasy that holds true only in the theatre. No matter how resourceful the people, those in power will always repress them. This is in fact also the circular, bitter ending reserved for Karaghiozis, whose fortunes can never pick up. The hero knows this well, as he invites the audience at the beginning of each performance to join him in satiating their hunger, by eating and drinking richly. This is of course an imaginary banquet, that occurs in play. The birds can certainly identify with Karaghiozis. Koun brought them together in his production, giving Karaghiozis a chorus. I can envisage them all singing Karaghiozis' famous aphorism: "we will drink, we will eat and we will go to bed on an empty stomach."

So far, my interpretation of Koun's *Birds* has solely been based on analysis of the production. I am assuming that the central axis of conflict in the Greek production is between Pisthetairos and the birds on one side versus the human and divine visitors who represent authoritarian power figures on the other. A consideration of the socio-political circumstances in Greece in the late fifties lends support to my interpretation. When Koun's production premiered, in 1959, Greece was still suffering the after-effects of the bloody civil war (1946-1949) between the right and the communist left, in which the former had prevailed. Throughout the fifties there had been a succession of authoritarian right wing governments in power, which spent enormous resources on containing "the enemy within," that is, citizens with communist sympathies, real or imagined. The security police had files on the political views of citizens and kept close watch on left wing sympathisers. The government held firm political control through the requirement of state clearance for state employment or even for the issuing of a passport. Manipulation of the electoral law before elections by the right wing governments ensured the continued rule of the right. Furthermore, the right had on its side other oppressive powers, namely the church, the palace and the US. which scandalously intervened in domestic policy. A member of NATO since 1952, Greece had been firmly harnessed to the Western defence system during the Cold War.

In 1959, the political situation looked a little more optimistic for non right-wing citizens. In the general elections earlier that year the United Democratic Front, a cover for the communist party, had emerged as a significant power with a quarter of the vote. The confidence of non right-wing citizens would be strengthened in the early sixties with the rising power of the left and especially of the centre, which succeeded in becoming the governing party in 1964, under the leadership of George Papandreou. Papandreou's agenda of political, economic and social reforms led to a clash with the US, as well as with domestic powers and especially the army, who was at the time the self appointed guardian of nationalist values. Increasing political unrest led to the military coup of 1967 which ushered in the seven year dictatorship of Giorgos Papadopoulos.

Koun's production accurately reflects the political climate of the 1950s from the point of view of non right-wing citizens, and even appears, in retrospect, to presage the rise of progressive powers in the sixties and their final demise in 1967 by authoritarianism. The strengthening of progressive parties, already apparent in the late fifties made it possible for Koun to envisage in his production Pisthetairos as a popular leader, genuinely sympathetic to the people. Since the left had never been in power after the end of the civil war, it was irrelevant for Koun to focus on the corruptive impact of leadership on the protagonist. The central problem for any progressive leader, as political history of the early 1960s showed, was how to contain the stifling powers threatening democratic government. No wonder then that Koun emphasized in his interpretation Pisthetairos' confrontation with the status quo. The production's mournful ending conveys a pessimistic message about the capacity of a new progressive state to hold against the adversity of threatening powers. No explanation is given for why Pisthetairos' marriage is not genuinely celebratory and for how the gods, after being contained by Pisthetairos seem to have prevailed again. In the political climate of the fifties in Greece, just as in Karaghiozis, authoritarian rule seemed like the natural law. In this context, leadership of the left could not be viewed as anything other than a utopia, or a parenthesis to right wing domination.

Indeed, just as art had imitated life in Koun's *Birds*, life hastened to imitate art. A day after its premiere, on August 29 1959, the production was banned by K. Tsatsos, a minister of Karamanlis's right-wing government. What provoked this drastic action was the comical episode between Pisthetairos and the priest which Tsatsos regarded as offensive to the religious sensibility of the Greek people. Clearly, as the left wing newspaper *Avgi* was quick to point out, Aristophanes was perceived as a threat to the established order for ridiculing "the precinct of the Helleno-Christian civilization." "How can a regime that is based on sycophancies, police forces and petty politicians," wrote Tsouparopoulos, tolerate Aristophanes' sarcasm? "So, get out Mr. Aristophanes! We ain't dumb birds!"[32]

Avgi, as well as the progressive literary journal *Epitheorisi Technis*, took the theatre critics to task for lending justification to the government ban of Koun's production by exaggerating its weaknesses. This criticism, which I believe is justified, unveils yet another abuse of authority testifying to the effectiveness of Koun's production as powerful social commentary. In contrast to the enthusiastic foreign press, domestic critics were initially annoyed by the low-brow, popular spirit of the production, especially as this was presented at a venue of high culture, the Odeion Herodes Atticus, in the context of the official Athens Festival. Thus they dismissed Tsarouchis's superb work of poor theatre precisely for its unassuming, humble character. The well-known novelist Angelos Terzakis found it distasteful that the set had been deliberately cast in the style of a hut. The word he uses is "paranga," which directly evokes for the Greeks the dwelling of Karaghiozis. Similarly, Vassos Varikas noted disapprovingly that "the set was reminiscent of a refugee camp undergoing demolition [...] and the costumes lacked the dazzle to transport us to the fairy tale land of the birds."[33]

Koun's production of *Birds* was important in firmly entrenching in the modern Greek postwar theatre an interpretation of Aristophanes as a popular playwright and as a partisan of progressive politics. In a successful pun, hinging on the similarity between the words "aristos" (best) and "aristeros" (left or leftist), Voula Damianakou in *Avgi* renamed Aristophanes "Aristerophanes," that is, one who reveals himself as leftist, noting that the poet had plenty of unpatriotic qualities, such as his support of the folk spirit and of the popular language.[34] Indeed, it must have been Aristophanes' notoriety as a communist that led the junta in the late sixties to put a ban on production of his plays in Greece.[35] However, in the long run, it would be the partisans of progressive politics who would have the last laugh. In a celebratory revival of Koun's *Birds* a year after the fall of the junta, in 1975, Pisthetairos and Evelpides set out for yet another search of Cloudcuckooland, claiming they were looking for a place without juntas. By that time, Karaghiozis, Pisthetairos and his chorus had become fully legitimised and Koun's interpretation of *Birds* was already a classic.

Notes

[1] See for example, Cedric H. Whitman, "Karaghiozes and Aristophanic Comedy," Appendix in *Aristophanes and the Comic Hero* (Cambridge, Mass: Harvard University Press, 1964), 281-293; Phanis J. Kakridis, "Karagiozis und Aristophanes. Gedanken zur Form griechischer Volkskomodien," *Hellenica* I (1972), 18-20; Linda Suny Myrsiades, "Aristophanic Comedy and the Modern Greek Karagkiozis Performance," in *Classical and Modern Literature*, 2 (1987): 99-110.

[2] See for example, K. Biris, *O Karaghiozis. Elleniko Laiko Theatro*, Athens and "Ellenikos o Karaghiozis" *Theatro* 10 (1963): 9-19; Thanassis Fotiades, "Elleniko Theatro Skion," *Anthropos* 2, 1 (1975): 46-67.

[3] See for example Georgios Souris, trans., Aristophanes *Nefele* (Athens: Ekdotike Eteria 1910); Polyvios Demetrakopoulos a famous writer of revue sketches at the beginning of last century translated into demotic Greek *The Clouds, Lysistrata, Women at the Thesmophoria Festival, Women in the Assembly, The Frogs* and *The Birds*. These were all published by Fexis in 1910; he also translated *Peace*, which was published by Fexis in 1919.

[4] See Gonda Van Steen, *Venom in Verse: Aristophanes in Modern Greece* (Princeton, NJ: Princeton University Press, 2000).

[5] See Thodoros Chatzipantazis, "Esagogi sten Athenaike Epitheorisi" in Thodoros Chatzipantazis and Lila Maraka, *E Athenaike Epitheorisi* Vol. 1 (Athens: Ermes, 1977), 7-216.

[6] See Gonda Van Steen, "Aristophanes on the modern Greek Stage," *Dialogos*, 2 (1995), 71-90.

[7] Dionysis Savopoulos, *O Aristophanes pou gyrise apo ta thymarakia. Acharnes*. (Athens, 1977) Record.

[8] See Gonda Van Steen, "Aristophanes on the modern Greek Stage."

[9] Yannis Tsarouchis, "Mathema Aletheias" in *Agathon to Eksomologeisthe* (Athens: Kastaniotis, 1986), 61, my translation.

[10] Monique Surel-Tupin, "Les Oiseaux d'Aristophane Chez Monsieur Dullin," in *Aristophane-Dullin*, ed. J. L. Barrault and M. C. Pasquier (Paris: Galimard, Cahiers Renaud Barrault, 1985), 91-111.

[11] Bernard Zimmer, *Les Oiseaux* (Paris: Gallimard, 1928), 56.

[12] Manos Chatzidakis, *Ornithes tou Aristophane* (Athens: Polygram, 1960; 1994). Audiorecording.

[13] Vassilis Rotas, translator and editor, *Aristophanes, Ornithes* (Athens: Epikeroteta, 1996).

[14] Karolos Koun, "The Director and Ancient Drama Today," unidentified source and translator, in file on Karolos Koun, Archive of the Theater Museum, Athens.

[15] Ibid. See also, Karolos Koun, "To Archaio Theatro" and "E Ornithes sto Theatro Ethnon" in *Kanoume Theatro gia ten Psyche Mas*. (Athens: Kastaniotis, 1987), 33-36 and 40-42 respectively.

[16] Quoted in Michael Maggiar, "Karolos Koun and the Theatro Technis," Doctoral Dissertation, The City University of New York, 1990, 226.

[17] Rotas, 62.

[18] Ibid, 57.

[19] Ibid, 80.

[20] My analysis of Koun's production is based on my recollections of seeing the revival of 1997, as well as on the following visual sources: videotapes of Koun's revivals of the *Birds*, in 1975 and 1997; photographs of the original production and its revivals, in the File on the *Birds*, deposited in the Archive of *Theatro Technis*, in Athens, Greece. Some of these photographs have been published in the collection *Theatro Technis 1942-1972*, ed. S. Zarambouka-Sare (Athens: Ellenike Eteria Theatrou Technis, 1972).

[21] Some English reviewers found the birds to be sexy. For example, Colin Frame, the critic of the *Evening News* writes that the costuming of the chorus must be "the sexiest concoction of overdressed nudity in London;" David Pryce-Jones in *The Spectator*, describes the birds as "sensual." Both of these reviews refer to the production of Koun's *Birds* that was seen in London, in May of 1964 and are deposited in the File on the *Birds*, in the Archive of Theatro Technes in Athens, Greece.

[22] For example, Harold Hobson in *The Sunday Times* (17 May 1964), writes: "I had expected to have to treat the *Birds* with respect [...] What I had not reckoned on is the spontaneous enjoyment, the exhilaration, and the swift pleasure which this entertainment gives;" similarly, Ronald Bryden in "Rite of Spring" in the *New Statesman* mentions that the total effect of the production "[...] is to make you feel you've witnessed not a classic of a dead literature, but a boisterous small society exploding in holiday;" File on the *Birds*, Archive of Theatro Technes in Athens, Greece.

[23] John Rosselli in "Greek Art Theater Company at the Aldwych," in the *Guardian* mentions that the birds have "the bitter-sweet Mediterranean heart;" similarly, Bamber Gascoigne in "Old birds in new feathers" in *The Observer* writes: "[...] when the chorus sings there is, even in happy passages, that sweet sadness mainly familiar in Russian songs;" file on the *Birds*, Archive of Theatro Technes in Athens, Greece.

[24] Bernard Levin, "A Gentle Comedy of Cuckoo Land," in *Daily Mail,* File on the *Birds*, Archive of Theatro Technes in Athens, Greece.

[25] Mentioned in Richard Buckle, "The dancing *Birds*," in *The Sunday Times* 24 May 1964, File on the *Birds*, Archive of Theatro Technes in Athens, Greece.

[26] Rotas, 60.

[27] Yannis Tsarouchis, "Skorpies Skepseis gia ton Karaghiozi" in *Agathon to Exomologeisthe* (Athens: Kastaniotis, 1986), 45-53.

[28] Ibid, 97.

[29] Ibid.

[30] Ibid.

[31] Ibid, 102-103.

[32] Cited in Gonda Van Steen, *Venom in Verse* ... , 126-127. In the chapter "Koun's *Birds* of 1959: Paravase of Right-Wing Politics," the author discusses insightfully the reception of *The Birds*. The present article complements her work by emphasizing production analysis. For a critique of Van Steen's of interpretation of Koun's aesthetics see my review: "Gonda Van Steen, *Venom in Verse*. Princeton, NJ: Princeton University Press, 2000," *Journal of Modern Greek Studies* 18 (2000): 453-455.

[33] See Angelos Terzakis, "Ornithes" in *To Vema*, 31 May 1960;Vassos Varikas, "E Ornithes tou Aristophane," *Ta Nea*, 4 June 1960.

[34] See Gonda Van Steen, *Venom in Verse*, 131.

[35] Mentioned in Costa-Gavras' film *Z* (1969).

Bibliography

Biris, K. "Ellenikos o Karaghiozis." *Theatro* 10 (1963): 9-19.

Chatzidakis, Manos. *Ornithes tou Aristophane.* Athens, Greece:Polygram, 1960; 1994. Audio recording.

Chatzipantazis, Thodoros and Lila Maraka. *E Athenaike Epitheorisi* Vol. 1 (Athens: Ermes, 1977).

Damianakou, Voula. "E Mache tou Orniakou" and "To Praxikopema ke e Kritike" in *Aristophanes Ornithes*, edited and translated by Vassilis Rotas, 22-24 and 26-36 respectively. Athens: Epiairoteta, 1996.

Fotiadis, Thanassis. "Elleniko Theatro Skion," *Anthropos* Vol. II, 1, (1975): 46-67.

Kakridis, Phanis J. "Karaghiozis und Aristophanes. Gedanken zur Form Giechischer Volkskomodien." *Hellenica* I (1972): 18-20.

Kokori, Patricia. "O Rolos tou Karolou Koun ste Diamorfose tes Ellenikes Ekdoches tou Theatrikou Modernismou." *Ekkyklema* 21 (1989): 34-40.

Kotzamani, Marina. "Lysistrata Joins the Soviet Revolution:Aristophanes as

Engaged Theater." In *Rebel Women*, edited by John Dillon and Stephen Wilmer. London: Methuen 2005.

—. "Gonda Van Steen. *Venom in Verse*." *Journal of Modern Greek Studies*, 18, No. 2 (October 2000): 453-455.

Koun, Karolos. *The Birds*. Video recordings of Koun's production, as revived in 1975 and 1997. Athens, Greece: Archive of the Theatro Technes.

—. *Kanoume Theatro gia ten Psyche Mas*. Athens: Kastaniotis, 1987.

Maggiar, Michael. "Karolos Koun and the Theatro Technis." Doctoral Dissertation, The City University of New York, 1990.

Myrsiades, Linda Suny. "Aristophanic Comedy and the Modern Greek Karaghiozis Performance." *Classical and Modern Literature*, 2 (1987): 99-110.

—. "Oral Composition and the Karaghiozis Performance." *Theatre Research International* V, No. 2 (Spring 1980): 107-121.

—. "The Karaghiozis Performance in Nineteenth-Century Greece." *Byzantine and Modern Greek Studies* 2 (1976): 83-97.

Rotas, Vassilis, translator and editor. *Aristophanes Ornithes*. Athens: Epikairoteta, 1996.

Savopoulos, Dionysis. *O Aristophanes pou gyrise apo ta thymarakia*. *Acharnes*. Athens, Greece:Lyra, 1977. Audio recording.

Surel-Tupin, Monique. "Les Oiseaux d'Aristophane Chez Monsieur Dullin." *Cahiers Renaud Barrault* (1985): 91-111.

Tsarouchis, Yannis. *Agathon to Eksomologeisthe*. Athens: Kastaniotis, 1986.

Van Steen, Gonda. *Venom in Verse: Aristophanes in Modern Greece*. Princeton, NJ: Princeton University Press, 2000.

—. "Aristophanes on the Modern Greek Stage." *Dialogos*, 2 (1995): 71-90.

Stothard, Peter. "Greek Art Theatre." *Plays and Players* 24, No. 10 (July 1977): 24-25.

Surel-Tupin, Monique. "Les Oiseaux d'Aristophane Chez Monsieur Dullin." In *Aristophane-Dullin*, edited by J. L. Barrault and M. C. Pasquier, 91-111. Paris: Galimard, Cahiers Renaud Barrault, 1985.

Tsirimocos, Elisabeth. "La Place d'Aristophane dans le Théatre Grec Contemporain." Doctoral Dissertation, Université de Paris I, Sorbonne, 1977.

Whitman, Cedric H. *Aristophanes and the Comic Hero*. Cambridge, Mass: Harvard University Press, 1964.

Zarambouka-Sare, S, ed. *Theatro Technis 1942-1972*. Athens: Ellenike Eteria Theatrou Technis, 1972.

Zimmer, Bernard. *Les Oiseaux*. Paris: Gallimard, 1928.

The Clown as Social Critic: Kerouac's Vision

Stephen Llano

Jack Kerouac occupies a strange position in American literary studies. His books have been described as "thinly-veiled" novelisations of his personal experiences of living on the road during cross country trips during the 1940s.[1] Many works have explored Kerouac's novels and why they continue to draw a large audience and still hover outside the realm of being considered great works of literature. One possible explanation is that the novels Kerouac wrote delve deep into what makes novels so great as a genre. Mikhail Bakhtin's theories on language could be productive in offering an understanding of how Kerouac's novels may offer something more to readers than just a good story. In this chapter, I examine two of Kerouac's protagonists in his novels against Bakhtin's theories of the clown in the novel. I argue that through these characterisations, Kerouac's clown figures offer a social criticism to the reader, and encourage the reader to question their own epistemology. Each character's use of language offers a different view of the world and creates a space for reconsideration of dominant meaning. After an initial discussion of some of Bakhtin's theoretical assumptions and how these will be adopted into the following analysis, I will explore two of Kerouac's characters through this framework: Slim in *Pic* and Dean Moriarty from *On the Road.* Through this new lens a deeper understanding of Kerouac's novels and the role of the clown in literature will become possible.

1. Bakhtin, Language and the Clown

For Mikhail Bakhtin, the figure of the clown in the novel has the ability to comment on society by being outside of social norms while also being located inside those norms. The clown is a blending of the fool and the rogue into one being who then can serve as "life's unmasker," people who uphold "the right to be other in this world, the right not to make common cause with any single one of the existing categories that life makes available; none of these categories suits them."[2] In this short essay I do not have the space to explain Bakhtin's theories as clearly and in depth as they deserve. But to understand the role of the clown in the novel it is key to understand two of Bakhtin's more global concepts: Heteroglossia, and dialogised heteroglossia.

The novel, for Bakhtin, is a site where the different ways language becomes used, understood and appropriated is explored. This exploration occurs through characters conversing with one another, describing each other to the reader or other characters, or narrating the events of the story. Bakhtin assumes that this multiple voiced language combination in the novel will

always push toward the limits of non-understanding between two or more
characters:

> Thus double-voicedness in the novel, as distinct from
> double-voicedness in rhetorical or other forms, always
> tends toward a double-*languagedness* as its own outside
> limit. Therefore, novelistic double-voicedness cannot be
> unfolded into logical contradictions or into purely dramatic
> contrasts. It is this quality that determines the
> distinctiveness of novelistic dialogues, which push to the
> limit the mutual non-understanding represented by people
> *who speak in different languages.*[3]

The different languages that Bakhtin mentions are not different
languages in the sense that Spanish and German are distinct. The distinction
Bakhtin argues for is one of meaning – that is, each character will in their
own way use language and description to legitimise their view of the world.
These combinations of world views are thereby set along side each other in
the text. In the novel, there emerges the figure of the clown, who, as a
blending of a fool and a rogue, is able to challenge the dominant hierarchy.
This challenge is offered through language, a language that points out the
contradictions and inability to have meaning between these various world
views:

> Between the rogue and the fool there emerges, as a unique
> coupling of the two, the image of the *clown.* He is a rogue
> who dons the mask of a fool in order to motivate distortions
> and shufflings of languages and labels, thus unmasking
> them by not understanding them [...] [T]he clown is the
> one who has the right to speak in otherwise unacceptable
> languages and the right to maliciously distort languages that
> *are* acceptable.[4]

The clown serves as "life's unmasker" through mis-understanding of
the language offered by the other characters. What is considered normal to
some the clown might reject. Through this rejection comes the possibility of
a unique social criticism for the reader, who is party and observer of these
conflicts through words. The reader may assign a winner or a loser, but most
definitely the reader must assign meaning to the statements, or utterances, of
the various characters.

Not only is the language of the characters important for determining
possible meanings in a text, but the reader brings a certain filter of meaning
to the text during the process of reading it. Bakhtin offers a compelling

argument that the path words must take in a reader's own vocabulary seem to prevent a unified and objectively true reading for all readers. Lived experience with words is the ultimate filter, and each reader has his or her own:

> The linguistic significance of a given utterance is understood against the background of language, while its actual meaning is understood against the background of other concrete utterances on the same theme, a background made up of contradictory opinions, points of view and value judgments – that is, precisely that background that, as we see, complicates the path of any word towards is present to the speaker not in the object, but rather in the consciousness of the listener, as his perceptive background, pregnant with responses and objections.[5]

The reader's own understanding of the values, conflicts and meanings swimming in the novel's progression is another meaning that is folded in with the meanings of the author and the characters. This makes a unified reading of the meaning of a novel impossible for Bakhtin, and in practice the reader will experience the novel to have one clear meaning based on their own linguistic and semantic history with words as well as the characters' deployment of language. This reader-contributed "background" to the discourse is different for every reader and adds a "new and unique influence on its style" every time the book is read.[6] Therefore identifying reader heteroglossia and claiming final meaning from it would be the equivalent of assembling a biography of a person from a few photographs – we can get a sense of meaning, but never a total and final meaning from that reader. Likewise, since the languages and word choices of the characters and the novels can only be experienced though reading their discourse, our own heteroglossia will alter interpretation upon each reading. At first glance this might be a limitation to analysis, but it also allows the social critique room to manoeuvre. Since some of the meanings of the reader can be asserted to a point by the author, there is an additional concept besides heteroglossia that allows for more developed double meanings to occur.

Dialogised heteroglossia, where the speaker chooses an inappropriate or improper "language" in which to address a particular audience, relies on the double voice that the author and the characters share. Bakhtin's notion of heteroglossia is never explicitly defined in his work, but he does give a few examples that help to explain the concept. The most telling example of heteroglossia is the peasant who may choose to use the language he prays in to address the agents of state power and control[7]. It is the creator of the novel, the author, who creates fictional characters from different roles of society and makes them interact. When characters from different facets of society interact in dialogue – use their unique languages at and with each other – a value conflict occurs. As I argued earlier, these meanings can never be completely understood in totality. They do not persuade the reader to adopt them uncritically. Instead, they expose the reader to many different stances against and within reality. We can then begin to understand novels as epistemological frameworks that can poke holes in, dismantle or interrupt the normal understanding of the reader. Although the reader will not always accept the new epistemology, the challenge has been made, and the reader has experienced it through the powerful and unforgettable conflicts in the language of the novel.

The implications of this theory conclude in the role of the clown as a character in the novel. Clown figures, as a blending of what is acceptable and unacceptable, of non-understanding with a position of being beyond the society of the other characters, offer comments that are dialogised. Clown figures, through their implicit inability or refusal to understand the society they interact with, therefore perform an individualised and particular resistance to the norms of the other characters. The clown, therefore, is the performative enactment of a dialogised social criticism that is rooted in assumptions about the correct and incorrect use of language. This is not lost on Kerouac's character development in his novels. The examples I have chosen are to merely offer the beginnings of a criticism that seeks out variations of Bakhtin's clown theory. Through these examples perhaps a clearer identity for clown characters in the novel and their possibility could arise. I examine the physical clowning of Slim from *Pic,* and Dean Moriarty from *On the Road.* Each is unique in the sort of social critique offered to the reader, and powerful through the use of the clown.

2.   *Pic* and the physical clowning of Slim

Pic is a short novel written by Jack Kerouac that tells the story of a young southern African-American boy named Pictorial Review Jackson, or "Pic" for short. Pic lives with his grandfather in North Carolina. The death of his grandfather prompts conflict over how and with whom Pic should be raised. Slim, Pic's older brother from New York City, convinces Pic to run away from home and come with him on a trip back to New York, and their journeys constitute the bulk of the novel. In this section, I will argue that Slim serves as a clown in this novel, offering a physical or performed resistance to the social norms of 1950s and 1960s American Society. This is established through the language not just said by Pic or Slim, but also through the language used to describe Slim's physical appearance and actions.

Pic's brother Slim arrives early in the book to take Pic to New York with him, but is rejected by the family due to his appearance and his residence. Slim returns secretly to take Pic with him. After sneaking out, Pic and Slim head for town:

> "Po little boy," he say, and give a sigh, and hitch me up higher on his back. "I guess you're as much scared of ever'thing like a grown man is. It's like the man say in the Bible – A fugitive and a vagabond shalt thou be in the earth. You ain't scarce eleven years old and already knowed that, I don't guess you didn't. Well, I come and made a vagabond out of you proper," and we walk along and come to see the lights of town up ahead, and he don't say nothing. Then here we go step on the road.[8]

Slim's quotation from the Bible to Pic is almost Bakhtin's specific example of the dialogised heteroglossia, where the language used for God is used for the commoner, or *vice versa*. In this case, it seems Slim talks to Pic his brother in a religious "language" as opposed to the straightforward way he talked to his family and Mr. Otis earlier on in the novel. Slim's goal is obviously to make Pic fulfil his destiny and he explains to him a story involving their father's fierce fight with the other family members years ago that blinded one of the members. Because of this, Pic would never be treated as an equal, so Slim decided to come get Pic to live with him. Slim describes why their lot must be cast together by explaining the disappearance of their father:

> "Where'd he go?" I ax my brother, and try to remember my father's face, but it wasn't no use. "Nobody know," my brother say, and he walk along glum, and he say "Little man, your father was a *wild man* and a *bad man* and that's all he was, or is, and whether he's alive or dead and where-EVER he's at tonight. Your mother's long dead, poor soul, and nobody blamed *her* for becomin' crazy and dyin like she done. Boy," my brother say to me, and turn his head to look at me, "you and me come from the *dark*." He said that, and said it jess as glum.[9]

This discussion sets up the exact value premises of the book that Slim and Pic – as descendents of slaves and sons of a father who wandered off are somehow outside of all the institutions and people they encounter. Whatever *is* America, as they encounter it, is something other than what they are. Slim is a rogue and it's Pic's destiny to be one as well. They represent

what is outside, or *not*. As Bakhtin indicates, this very distinction between
characters in novels is at the heart of heteroglossia, and how novels offer
meaning:

> As we have said above, the narrator's story or the story of
> the posited author is structured against the background of
> normal literary language, the expected literary horizon.
> Every moment of the story has a conscious relationship
> with this normal language and its belief system, is in fact
> set against them, and set against them *dialogically:* one
> point of view opposed to another, one evaluation opposed
> to another, one accent opposed to another.[10]

The heteroglossia in this important scene is the two brothers
discussing family with the "language" of religious metaphor or quest behind
it. The dialogism enters in when Slim, who just recently alluded their
existence as vagabonds to a greater Biblical goal or vision, refers to the both
of them as "dark" or clearly, outside of society. Nevertheless, Slim is clearly
of American society with his foolish behaviour, attire and love for his
brother. This contradiction is what sets Slim as the rogue, outside of society
but clearly from it – the position of Bakhtin's clown.

The best example of Slim's social critique is using Pic's
inexperience to challenge the laws of society through language and
contradiction. The brothers cross into Maryland via bus, and Slim tells Pic
that they can sit in the front of the bus now. Pic does not understand why, and
Slim begins an explanation of segregation in dialogised heteroglossic terms.
Slim uses the discourse of the "official" to highlight the ridiculousness of
segregation laws:

> [...] when I axed him who Jim Crow was, he said "That's
> you, boy." "I ain't no Jim Crow anyhow," I told him, "case
> you know my name is Pictorial Jackson." "Oh," says Slim,
> "is that so? Well, I never knowed that, uh-huh. Looky-here,
> Jim," he said, "don't you know about the law that says you
> can't sit in the front of the bus when the bus runs below the
> Mason Dixie line?" "What for you call me Jim?' 'Now
> Jim!," he says, and cluck-cluck at me solemn. "You mean
> to tell me you don't know about that line?" "What line?" I
> say. "I ain't seed no such a line." "What?" he say. "Why,
> we just crossed it back there in Maryland. Didn't you see
> Mason and Dixie holdin that line across the road?"[11]

This façade of non-understanding is double-voiced in that it is a clear understanding but refusal of any of Pic's statements of ignorance about the Jim Crow laws. It confuses through hybrid explanation the Jim Crow laws, even the name of which Pic confuses, allowing Slim, to point out how the official use of language is to group all blacks similarly when they very much consider themselves individuals.

Slim continues the discussion after arguing with Pic about the existence of the Mason-Dixon line as a tangible visible line:

> "But there *is* such a line, only thing is, it ain't on the *ground* and it ain't in the air neither, it's jess in the head of Mason and Dixie, jess like all other lines, border lines, state lines, parallel thirty-eight lines and iron Europe curtain lines is all jess 'maginary lines in people's heads and don't have nothin' to do with the ground." Grandpa, Slim said that jess as quiet, and didn't call me Jim no more, and said to hisself, "Yes sir, that's all it is."[12]

Here the social critique is expanded from just racist law to the idea of the border as nothing but a fantasy. Due to Pic's age, we realize possible misunderstanding with the allusions to the Cold War. These comments could be interpreted by the reader as a moment of self-persuasion by Slim. But we also receive the utterance and the rejection of borders and racism, as imaginary and fantasy with no objective value. This dialogism of Kerouac's critique, Slim's critique and Pic's interpretation sets up a powerful critique of societal borders and racist law. Readers see the critique through the eyes of Pic, and the innocence of a young boy who doesn't understand what his brother means. This intersection allows for an appreciation of innocence and a conceptualisation of the insidiousness of segregation, displaying the power of clown figures to offer new perspectives through language to critique.

3.   **Dean Moriarty: Clowning the American Dream**

On the Road is of course Kerouac's most famous and most examined book. Almost overnight since its publication, Kerouac and the Beatniks gained almost instant fame and recognition. Omar Swartz argues that *On the Road* represents, "a rhetorical document with persuasive significance in helping people to restructure their lives."[13] Swartz believes Kerouac to be a "cultural rhetorician" who offers the character of Dean Moriarty as "the burning antidote to everything that is ill in civilisation; the madman convict who infuses life into both Kerouac and, by Kerouac's influence, a larger body in American culture; the single embodiment of a new vision for America."[14] I agree with Swartz that *On the Road* is a powerful rhetorical artefact that offers a persuasive epistemology. I believe not that

Dean is the solution to American social ills at the time, as Swartz claims, but that he is rather a clowning embodiment of those societal values. Dean, through his desire to fully enact American values, tries to push them beyond their own logical extreme. Dean is trying to be too American and in doing so he becomes a clown and presents a powerful critique of capitalist society.

Dean Moriarty and Sal Paradise are the main characters of the novel. Through the course of the book, they travel from California and New York and back again four times. They interact with numerous characters who are sometimes stereotypes of the regions of America.

Early on, Dean is established as a figure outside of mainstream American society since, "he actually was born on the road when his parents were passing through Salt Lake City in 1926, in a jalopy, on their way to Los Angeles."[15] Sal and his friend hear stories about Dean and wonder if they "would ever meet the strange Dean Moriarty," described as "a young jailkid shrouded in mystery."[16] Dean is a character that from the beginning of the novel is outside of society, a rogue. Dean's family background comes out, described by Sal when he first arrives in Denver looking for Dean:

> Dean was the son of a wino, one of the most tottering bums of Larimer Street, and Dean had in fact been brought up generally on Larimer Street, and thereabouts. He used to plead in court at the age of six to have his father set free. He used to beg in front of Larimer alleys and sneak the money back to his father, who waited among the broken bottles with an old buddy. Then when Dean grew up he began hanging around the Glenarm poolhalls; he set a Denver record for stealing cars and went to the reformatory. From the age of eleven to seventeen he was usually in reform school. His specialty was stealing cars, gunning for girls coming out of high school in the afternoon, driving them out to the mountains, making them, and coming back to sleep in any available hotel bathtub in town.[17]

Dean is clearly established as a rogue through thievery, unscrupulous behaviour with young women and as a type of con-artist, working as a beggar for his father. Sal, attempting to get Dean and his wife back together, observes Dean, "blissful and blabbering and frantically rocking," when reunited with his wife. Sal observes, "Only a guy who's spent five years in jail can go to such maniacal helpless extremes."[18] Dean's clown characteristics are evident partially through his establishment as a rogue. Others in the novel mark Dean as a fool or clown right away. Sal's aunt, "took one look at Dean and decided that he was a madman."[19] Sal describes Dean as, "simply a youth tremendously excited with life, and though he was a con-man, he was only conning because he wanted so much to live and to get involved with people who would otherwise pay no attention to him."[20] Dean described his ideas "so torrentially that people in buses looked around to see the 'overexcited nut.'"[21] In Denver, one of Sal's friends interrogates Dean as to whether he is involved with three women at the same time. "Dean shuffled on the rug and said, 'Oh yes, oh yes, that's the way it goes,' and looked at his watch, and Major snuffed down his nose [...] Major insisted he was a moron and a fool."[22] These quotations show that Dean's behaviour, from the perspective of the other characters, is the behaviour of the fool. Both elements of the clown have been established.

The critique Dean offers is through dialogism: his own and Sal's. Dean's manner revealed his obsessiveness with time – "He had become absolutely mad in his movements; he seemed to be doing everything at the same time."[23] Perhaps one of the most direct descriptions of Dean as a fool comes when Sal describes Dean at work as a parking lot attendant:

> The most fantastic parking-lot attendant in the world, he can back a car forty miles an hour into a tight squeeze and stop at the wall, jump out, race among fenders, leap into another car, circle it fifty miles an hour in a narrow space, back swiftly into tight spot, *hump*, snap the car with the emergency so that you see it bounce as he flies out; then clear to the ticket shack, sprinting like a track star, hand a ticket, leap into a newly arrived car before the owner's half out, leap literally under him as he steps out, start the car with the door flapping, and roar off to the next available spot, arc, pop in, break, out, run; working like that without pause eight hours a night, evening rush hours and after-theater rush hours, in greasy wino pants with a frayed fur-lined jacket and beat shoes that flap.[24]

Sal's description, which mentions Dean's floppy shoes, gives the impression of a circus performance. Dean's dedication to doing this job is evident, yet he performs it with a foolish passion. Sal describes him like a "track star" running with energy to deliver the next ticket. It is a comedy routine performed in all seriousness by someone who steals cars regularly. The ridiculousness of the manner in which this job is performed by Dean is part of a critique of a society that is continuously demanding complete dedication to one's occupation. Dean's passion eclipses the scale of the task at hand with an overflowing recklessness.

The critique also occurs in Dean's language, a dialogised form of the language of what I call "business vernacular." One example is when Dean first arrives in New York to meet Sal with his wife MaryLou:

They got off the Greyhound bus at 50th street and cut
around the corner looking for a place to eat and went right
in Hector's, and since then Hector's cafeteria has always
been a big symbol of New York for Dean. . .[a]ll this time
Dean was telling MaryLou things like this: "Now darling,
here we are in New York and although I haven't quite told
you everything that I was thinking about when we crossed
Missouri and especially at the point when we passed the
Boonville reformatory which reminded me of my jail
problem, it is absolutely necessary now to postpone all
those leftover things concerning our personal lovethings
and at once begin thinking of specific worklife plans
[...]"[25]

Dean is also seen as somewhat foolish in his immediate desire to
place his "lovethings" to the side to work on "worklife plans" – terms that are
unusual and have ambivalent meaning. They sound like combinations of
values held in American society. In addition, Dean is making very specific
plans that will happen at very specific times. Dean's focus on values of work
and family and making clear plans after just arriving is typical behaviour for
him, and displays foolishness in his "professional" manner of communicating
his desire.

Consider the following scene when Sal meets up with Dean for the
first time in Denver. Dean immediately insists "it's absolutely necessary for
me to take him out and fix him up with a girl."[26] Dean then lays out the plan
to his girlfriend of the time, Camille:

"It is now" (looking at his watch) "exactly one-fourteen. I
shall be back at exactly *three*-fourteen, for our hour of
reverie together, real sweet reverie darling, and then, as you
know, as I told you and as we agreed, I have to go and see
the one-legged lawyer about those papers – in the middle of
the night, strange as it seems and as I tho-roly explained."
[...] "So now in this exact minute I must dress, put on my
pants, go back to life, that is to outside life, streets and what
not, as we agreed, it is now one-*fifteen* and time's running,
running -- "
"Well all right Dean but please be sure and be back at
three."
"Just as I said, darling, and remember not three but three-
fourteen. Are we straight in the deepest and most wonderful
depths of our souls, dear darling?" And he went over and

kissed her several times [...] I was amazed. Everything was so crazy."[27]

This scene presents the ridiculous nature of Dean's obsession with the value of time. Commodified and increasing in importance to Americans especially in the post-war years, this is ridiculed through the obsession and foolishness of Dean, who becomes upset that his discussion of the plan took away two minutes of time. Dean's use of standard negotiation phrases, such as "as we agreed" and "are we straight" perhaps suggest a foolish use of a "language" more suited to a more businesslike forum. This is a dialogism of "professionalism" used in conversation with a romantic partner, and allows the reader to see how the value of saving time can be ridiculous.

Sal reveals to Dean that he wants to get married and settle down so that he can "go someplace and find something" and stop the "franticness and jumping around." Dean replies to Sal, "I've been digging you for years about the *home* and the marriage and all those fine wonderful things about your soul"[28] Yet even the value of settling down and having a family is pushed to extremes by Dean: he has three women in three different places and children from two. This brings up how Dean views relationships: "[T]o him sex was the one and only important thing in life, although he had to sweat and curse to make a living and so on."[29] After a while this catches up with Dean and earns him the anger and disrespect of people who used to celebrate him. Dean, excommunicated from the homes of his various women decides to travel with Sal back to New York and is chastised by an old friend:

> "You have absolutely no regard for anybody buy yourself and your damned kicks. All you think about is what's hanging between your legs and how much money or fun you can get out of people and then you just throw them aside. Not only that but you're silly about it. It never occurs to you that life is serious and there are people trying to make something decent out of it instead of just goofing all the time."
> That's what Dean was, the HOLY GOOF.[30]

Sal displays the contradiction clearly: Dean values everything society values, making him holy, but embodies the values to the point of lunacy. Dean injured his thumb and hardly ever changed the bandage, adding more to his clowning appearance:

> [T]hey all sat around looking at Dean with lowered and hating eyes, and he stood on the carpet in the middle of them and giggled – he just giggled. He made a little dance. His bandage was getting dirtier all the time; it began to flop

and unroll. I suddenly realized that Dean, by virtue of his enormous series of sins, was becoming the Idiot, the Imbecile, the Saint of the lot.[31]

Although his former friends are angry at him for leaving his wife and daughter for another trip, Dean fails to understand why this would be a problem. Through this failed understanding, the mask of the arbitrariness of the preferred values becomes more visible: Sal realizes this by indicating Dean's "sins" – his disavowal of what is obviously important through attempting to enact the importance at its highest level as the image of the "holy goof."

There is one place in particular where Dean's use of language offers the critique clearly Sal and Dean in this scene are sharing a ride to Denver with a couple and are in the back seat watching them drive the car:

> "Oh, man! Man! Man!" moaned Dean. "And it's not even the beginning of it – and now here we are at last going east together, we've never gone east together, Sal, think of it, we'll dig Denver together and see what everybody's doing although that matters little to us, the point being that we know what IT is and we know TIME and we know that everything is really FINE." Then he whispered, clutching my sleeve, sweating, "Now you just dig them in front. They have worries, they're counting the miles, they're thinking about where to sleep tonight, how much money for gas, the weather, how they'll get there – and all the time they'll get there anyway, you see. But they need to worry and betray time with urgencies false and otherwise, purely anxious and whiny, their souls really won't be at peace unless they can latch on to an established and proven worry and having once found it they assume facial expressions to fit and go with it, which is, you see, unhappiness and all the time it all flies by them and they know it and that *too* worries them no end."[32]

Dean seems to be contradicting his earlier action critiquing these people for having concerns that he shares. Dean's argument could be seen as a criticism of the actualisation of worry. Dean doesn't understand why people don't celebrate life in the time they are given instead of waiting for a future time to arrive for their happiness. Dean also believes he has discovered the root of all unhappiness: that there is a time and place for everything to work out on its own. This sort of belief is something that directly contradicts with some traditional American epistemologies – that individuals have the right to predict and control their futures and the consequences of their life choices. Dean here seems to be arguing that such a perspective is a cycle that can only lead to unhappiness. The only alternative is to abandon such concerns, to embrace "IT" – which is deliberately left open and undefined. The reader is invited to define "IT" in an attempt to understand the meaning of the novel, and that would involve creating some alternative to the values brought up previously and pushed to their limits by Dean's actions.

Sal eventually has to say goodbye to Dean after he settles down in New York. Sal sits on a pier overlooking New Jersey and the horizon thinking about Dean and how "nobody knows what's going to happen to anybody besides the forlorn rags of growing old."[33] Sal cannot completely accept Dean's worldview and hence, Dean's critique of society is elevated (perhaps reduced) to something spiritual, saintly, or a way of being that is only reserved for Dean. The language suggests that this action can only be embraced by the chosen few, of which the reader might become. Sal is placed in a position outside of Dean's politics, but shows great reverence for them. This appreciation is added to the readers' understanding, and must be considered by them as they try to construct meaning from the book.

4.   Conclusions

This very short study of Kerouac's clowns reveals the contribution of these figures to the complex possibilities of meaning in novels. In offering some conclusions to this analysis, I keep at the forefront of my mind Bakhtin's concept of unfinalisability – the idea that nothing "final" or absolute can be said when dialogue is at stake. "[T]he world is not only a messy place, but is also an open place"[34] I take this concept to mean that critics of novels and their meaning should frame their discoveries in terms of possibility rather than correctness of interpretation. Criticism of texts can perhaps therefore move past notions of the proper interpretation to a discussion of the depth of possibilities offered to the interpreter.

This chapter represents only a beginning of a larger inquiry of the possibilities of the clown in novels, so there are many questions remaining. For example, what are the possibilities for the human subject in the discourse of the clown? In these examples we see potential for political agency and perhaps the tools for rhetorically reconstructing the subject in a way to use that agency. Perhaps the clown figure offers the possibility of dialogue where these tools can be offered to the reader. Secondly, there is the question of similarity and difference between clown figures and the other characters in a novel. I have argued above that some characters make the clown figures' arguments more palatable to the reader. Is there a rhetoric to this? Is it something that is directly influenced in stylistic ways by the author or the reception of specific readers? Perhaps the similarities and differences in clown figures are intrinsic to the environment or "sphere" in which that discourse occurs. All of these questions would be interesting points of departure for future investigation

Jack Kerouac's work will continue to spark interest and ideas among scholars and general readers alike. Focusing on the power of the clown as a social critic is one new way to perhaps see the power through the possibility offered by the complexity of language in the novel.

Notes

[1] Omar Swartz, *The View from the Road: The rhetorical vision of Jack Kerouac* (Carbondale, Il: Southern Illinois Press, 1999).

[2] Mikhail Bakhtin, *The Dialogic Imagination*, ed. Michael Holquist, trans. Caryl Emerson and Michael Holquist (Austin: University of Texas, 1981), 159.

[3] Ibid, 336.

[4] Ibid, 405.

[5] Ibid, 281.

[6] Ibid.

[7] Ibid, 295-296.

[8] Jack Kerouac, *Satori in Paris & Pic* (New York: Penguin Books, 1971), 158.

[9] Ibid, 160.

[10] Bakhtin, 314.

[11] Kerouac, 172.

[12] Ibid.

[13] Swartz, xi.

[14] Ibid, 90.

[15] Jack Kerouac, *On the Road* (New York: Penguin, 1957), 1.

[16] Ibid, 2.

[17] Ibid, 37.

[18] Ibid, 132.

[19] Ibid, 3.

[20] Ibid, 4.

[21] Ibid, 5.

[22] Ibid, 46.

[23] Ibid, 114.

[24] Ibid, 6.

[25] Ibid, 2.

[26] Ibid, 43.

[27] Ibid.

[28] Ibid, 117.

[29] Ibid, 2.
[30] Ibid, 194.
[31] Ibid.
[32] Ibid, 210.
[33] Ibid, 307.
[34] Gary Morson and Caryl Emerson, *Mikhail Bakhtin: Creation of a Prosaics* (Stanford, California: Stanford University Press, 1990), 36.

Bibliography

Bakhtin, Mikhail. *The Dialogic Imagination.* Translated by Caryl Emerson and Michael Holquist. Edited by Michael Holquist. Austin: University Of Texas Press, 1981.

Kerouac, Jack. *The Dharma Bums.* New York: Penguin Books, 1958.

—. *On the Road.* New York: Penguin Books, 1957.

—. *Satori in Paris & Pic.* New York: Penguin Books, 1971.

Morson, Gary and Caryl Emerson. *Mikhail Bakhtin: Creation of a Prosaics* Stanford, California: Stanford University Press, 1990.

Swartz, Omar. *The View from On the Road: The rhetorical vision of Jack Kerouac.* Carbondale, IL: Southern Illinois University Press, 1999.

Picaresque Narratology:
Lazarillo de Tormes and Edgar Hilsenrath's *Der Nazi und der Friseur*

Bernhard Malkmus

1.   The picaresque hero and modernity

The picaresque hero embodies both the victim of social circumstances and the potential of human beings to survive the severest hardships by virtue of their ingenuity. He represents the extreme form of the Aristotelian *zõon politikón* by showing both dependence on society, and how this dependence turns into a kind of depravity from which he can only be disentangled by dissociating himself from society while simultaneously playing the sycophant at the core of society. Alan Sillitoe has captured this ambivalence in his reflections on the mentality of the picaresque hero with admirable precision:

> He [the pícaro] finds his way out of any labyrinth because he is God's plaything, but he never knows the grace of God. God is for those who believe in the superiority of the spirit, the necessity of ethics, the comfort of morals. While they pray, he preys on them, without whom he would have no existence. He is the devil on two sticks, the spirit of anarchy which resides in everyone.[1]

This triggers a Janus-faced quality with both an individual and a social dimension. By staging different characters, by wearing masks, by pretending and by faking roles, the pícaro unveils society as *theatrum mundi*. The pícaro can observe the forces at work behind the stage, which make people behave the way they do, because he is forced to or chooses to succumb to the histrionic character of social life to an even greater extent than anyone else. For him playing a wide range of different roles is often a question of survival. This predestines him to become a virtuoso faker *sui generis* who implicitly debunks the very notion of authenticity and calls into doubt one of the tenets of post-Enlightenment and bourgeois culture, namely the consistency and organic development of character. From the pícaro's point of view every walk of life appears as a second-hand derivative rather than a fully-fledged and individual biography. Even the classic role of the convert in Christian confession literature is not granted the quality of authenticity, since conversion is nothing but yet another role-play in the *mundus inversus* of picaresque adventures.

The peculiar position of the pícaro can be described as both engaged and yet disengaging, detached and yet dependent. This awkward position of someone who is ostracised and at the same time chooses to turn this marginalisation into a role as a 'sitter on the fence' has been described as "half outsider"[2] by the critic Claudio Guillén. According to him, the pícaro can neither be part of society nor refuse to get involved in the social sphere, he is caught up in the "confrontation between the individual and his environment which is also a conflict between inwardness and experience."[3] In this paradoxical overdetermination he embodies the paradigmatic literary role-player and at the same time the actual indispensability of role-playing in social life. This makes the pícaro, who is often blatantly non-political, a paramount commentator of politics and power structures.

In his essay "Homo Sociologicus" the sociologist Ralf Dahrendorf calls society "eine ärgerliche Tatsache [.], der wir uns nicht ungestraft entziehen können"[4] – irritating in the sense that humans have no ways of escaping the conflicting role models society is constantly imposing on them. The model of the "homo sociologicus" abstains from the rationalistic and individualistic notion of free will and operates on the assumption that the role player is necessarily heteronomous. Role theory also assumes that most role players are exchangeable with regard to most of their social acts.[5] Irrespective of whether a role position is an ascribed or a voluntarily adopted one, it inevitably involves a process of internalisation of external role patterns and finally what Dahrendorf termed the de-personalisation ("Entpersönlichung"[6]) of individuality. In that sense, the picaresque hero and in particular his modern successor in the form of confidence men and tricksters[7] epitomises and enacts this anthropological category of "depersonalisation" as the quintessential "hollow man" who does not give away his hollowness, but rather clings to it as the source of his identity fiction.

The modern pícaro is depersonalised in the sense that he is capable of representing a completely flexible concept of individuality. While his depersonalisation might grant him success in a world of acceleration and social mobility, there is always an uncanny undercurrent: He is aware of the fact that he is a hollow man, that he is not grounded anywhere apart from in the dynamics of his shape-shifting. His home is the evanescence of social structures.

A. The Spanish pícaro

A majority of modern picaresque fiction is loosely but clearly modelled on the Spanish picaresque novel or tale of the *Siglo de Oro* by virtue of its contradictory and oscillating narrative perspectives. These works can often be read as a form of *apologia* addressed to an audience which is not clearly defined. This character of a written defence statement is a trademark of the classical Spanish pícaro craze triggered by *Lazarillo de Tormes y sus Fortunas y Adversidades* (1554). In the chapter "Tractado Séptimo. Como Lázaro se asentó con un alguacil, y de lo que le acaesció con él" of *Lazarillo*, the narrator establishes an ambiguity regarding the narrative frame by rendering the addressee of the whole book opaque. It ends with the use of the highly ambiguous formula "Vuestra Merced." The range of possible meanings of this term includes a benefactor who has commissioned this work – a very different context from that of private introspection. The seventh chapter is contradictory in so far as it offers two different perspectives from which the whole autobiography could have been written. On the one hand, the narrator Lazarillo superimposes a teleology on his life story, which makes his position as low civil servant appear well-deserved and legitimate; he portrays himself both as victim and survivor talent:

> [A]t this present, I live in mine office, and exercise it to God's service and yours. Sir, it is so that I have the charge to cry the wines that are sold in this city, and to make inquirance, with open cry, for things that have been lost, and when any suffer persecution by justice, I do accompany them, declaring with loud voice their offence. I am (in plain language) a common crier.[8]

On the other hand, he has to defend his wife against accusations of adultery and himself against social envy due to his secure position in Toledo as "pregonero," city crier and bailiff, in view of his amoral and criminal record. The ambiguity lies in Lazarillo's double bind: if he downplays his hardship, he cannot expect mercy with regard to his criminal past; if he exaggerates his struggle, his credibility as to whether he has really changed his life will be undermined. The socio-political background of this double-bind is the *homo novus*, the social climber, as opposed to the impoverished *hidalgo* class of Renaissance Spain: he has to legitimise his position, which he did not inherit, by proving his moral values and virtues.

The reference to "Vuestra Merced" remains relatively obscure. It could refer to an official of the royal administration, to a member of the clergy, or as mentioned above to someone who commissioned the novel. In this context Christian W. Thomsen points out that the word *confessiones*, which was often taken as an inversion and travesty of the Augustinian concept of introspection, has a double meaning in church Latin, the second one being *panegyricon*, "praise."[9] Lazarillo translates his double-bind into a double narrative vacillating between the perspective of a youngster, who tries to make ends meet and shows off his versatility, on the one hand, and a mature retrospective narrator on the other hand. These two perspectives combine to create the unique picaresque mode which is rooted in the perpetual oscillation between self-praise and self-debunking. It is this structural feature that defines the genre's affinity to the issues of social communication and confidence.

Lazarillo de Tormes is told simultaneously *ab initio* by a naïve narrative voice and from the end by a mature narrative voice. Both voices are present at the same time throughout the entire novel, either complementing or undercutting each other. The co-existence of these two perspectives can be studied in the famous beginning of the novel, where Lazarillo ruminates about his childhood:

> And after the time I came to the age of eight years, there was laid to my father's charge that he had shamefully cut the seams of men's sacks that came thither to grind, wherefore he was taken and imprisoned, and being tormented he confessed the whole matter, denying nothing wherefore he was persecuted. I trust in God that he is now in paradise, seeing that the Gospel doth say, that blessed are such as confess their faults.[10]

On the surface this passage is a simple statement of the difficult situation of his family and their infringement of the law. It is only the reference to the gospel according to St. John in the phrase "persecución por justicia" which sheds an ironical and ambiguous light on the whole passage, turning the value system upside down and introducing the idea of appraisal for the shrewdness and versatility of the pícaro.

The following section analyses these traces in one of the most extreme post-war picaresque novels, extreme both in terms of structure and imagery.

B. Edgar Hilsenrath's *Der Nazi und der Friseur*

Edgar Hilsenrath's successful and acclaimed bestseller *Der Nazi und der Friseur* (1977) tells the story of a Jewish and a German child, Itzig Finkelstein and Max Schulz, who grow up in the same petit bourgeois quarter of the small German town Wieshalle. Itzig is the son of a successful barber; he is a talented student at school and looks extremely Aryan. Max grows up in a dysfunctional family; he is reliant on Itzig's help at school and looks like one of the racist caricatures of Jews in Nazi propaganda. He becomes intimately acquainted with Jewish life, religion and culture. Later he ends up killing Itzig and his whole family in a death camp in Eastern Europe. After the war he makes a living as a black marketeer in Berlin and then decides to change identities, take on the name "Itzig Finkelstein," convert to Zionism and emigrate to Palestine. There he sets up a successful barbershop and gets involved in Zionist political activism. Towards the end of his life, he confesses his sins as a mass murderer to a lawyer acquaintance. They fail to find an appropriate retribution for his guilt, before he dies. The structure is, however, more complex than this summary would indicate.

Although completely different in its internal communicative set-up, Hilsenrath's novel employs the general narrative situation of the Spanish prototype, in particular the characteristic techniques of pseudo-autobiography and a para-encyclopaedic approach to society.[11] It remains unclear from what point of retrospection the narrator approaches his own walk of life and to what degree he manipulates it in order to justify himself in the light of accusations not known to the reader. Max/Itzig is the perfect picaresque Janus character of simulation and dissimulation. He plays with his identity and involves others in this play. Frau Holle, his mistress in post-war Berlin, asks him about his wish to adopt a new identity:

> "What's that – a different identity?"
> "When somebody changes shape", said Max Schulz.
> "Like a magician", said Frau Holle.
> "Yes, quite", said Max Schulz.[12]

Max/Itzig is the epitome of the picaresque pretender and debunker: Every attempt by the reader to obtain a clear and unequivocal notion of the intentions of the narrator and the motivations of each narrative move is undercut and rendered vain. In *Der Nazi und der Friseur* the reader is at the mercy of a mass murderer's *apologia*. It remains opaque until the end, why Max/Itzig is making his public confession, i.e. publishing his biography and apparently revealing his identity as a German mass murderer, at that moment. The reader – like in most classic picaresque novels – is not kept informed about the psychological incentives and motives behind the confessions.

In the sparse secondary literature on the novel there is no hint at the fact that the whole novel could be read as the story of the traumatic loss of personality of a Jewish survivor of the Shoah, who is obsessed with his German past, one who identifies himself to an extreme degree with German culture and ends up suffering from schizophrenia during and after the deportations. His obsessions after the war could be read as symptomatic evidence of either a deep-rooted trauma or survivor guilt or both. One of the clearest signs of a schizophrenic split of personality can be found in chapter four. The new Itzig Finkelstein addresses the dead one:

> It's a pity you never knew the Jewish black marketeer Itzig Finkelstein in Berlin. Itzig Finkelstein [...] his black Mercedes ... he was quite a guy, let me tell you. Right out of the *Stürmer*. And who cut him out of the paper? The old Nazis.[13]

Earlier on the reader is faced with the disturbing and highly ambiguous phrase stating that he, Max Schulz, had actually died in Poland in 1945. Interpretations can range from his actual physical death and Itzig's schizophrenic adoption of Max's identity as his 'Mr Hyde' to the conventional one which sees a continuation in behaviour and strategy between Max, the murderer, and Itzig as Max's post-war role. Another interesting issue is the fact that Hilsenrath deleted the ending in the final authoritative German version which was published six years after its English translation due to the extreme caution of German publishers in view of this highly controversial rendition of the Shoah topic. The English ending takes place in heaven, where God condemns Max/Itzig, and then is asked accusatory questions about the reasons for his absence on earth. Finally God is accused of passivity:

> "[...] where were you? [...]"
> And the One and Only says: "I watched!" [...]
> "Then your guilt is greater than mine!" I say. "If that is true
> [...] then you cannot be my judge!" [...]
> And the One and Only climbed down from his seat of
> judgment and placed himself next to me at my side."[14]

The fact that Hilsenrath still uses the leitmotifs of theodicy and *deus absconditus*[15] in the final version but drops the idea of a final divine verdict, keeps the identity problem of the protagonist open to the kind of diverse and disparate interpretations adumbrated above.

An interpretation centring around the psychopath Itzig with his "Dachschaden" (deranged mind) rather than on Max, the mass murderer, is not necessarily the most obvious reading, but it is a possible one, and marks the extreme opposite of the interpretation of Max as a shrewd pícaro, who changes his identity and thrives on post-war philo-Semitism. The text allows the Max/Itzig story to be read both ways and thereby exploits the full potential of the classic picaresque narrative structure. Hilsenrath incorporates the characteristic ambiguity of the narrative voice of the picaresque novel in his book and thereby manages to strike a balance between an analytical approach to the Shoah and a rendition of the traumatic loss of tradition, society, culture and individuality during the extermination warfare in Central and Eastern Europe. [16] The two extreme readings of the novel are like two pictures inherent in an optical illusion, each only being visible one at a time. The observer, however, is always fully aware of the fact that there is a second way of looking at the picture. The two versions coexist without blending into each other. Hilsenrath's art blurs boundaries, he is an iconoclast and appropriates excessive polysemies in order to create an arena of non-discourses about the Shoah.

C. The pícaro as stranger and adventurer – a modernist genealogy

In a systemic sense, the modern pícaro exemplifies the principle of mediation as a form of totalisation which only works as a histrionic enactment of absolute transparency and adaptability. He elucidates the double effect of disguise and revelation of the fragmentation by means of enacting roles as totalising interpretations of individuality and society. That shows the degree to which history consists of histories as a multiplicity of conflicting genealogies which are only working as a coherent principle within the set frame of a role. The pícaro shows that it is only frames without pictures that make up the gallery of modern life.

The modern brother of the classic pícaro is afloat on top of the social situation because he is capable of adopting different registers. He is a parasite of the fertile soil of intersection between different social circles, although he is not fully participating in any of them. One of his main preoccupations is to divert social and material energy and resources for himself. By appropriating the two extreme forms of modern experience, individualism and anonymity, the modern pícaro exemplifies its paradoxical foundation.

The prominence of the picaresque protagonist and anti-hero in fiction dealing with the specific situation of late nineteenth and early twentieth century Western societies and their national and colonial disasters is inextricably intertwined with the particular ambivalence and communication situation mentioned above. The pícaro stages himself as a victim of these circumstances and at the same time ransacks them in his own interest.

The modern pícaro embodies in many respects both Simmel's "Fremder"[17] and "Abenteurer."[18] The stranger, as Simmel famously puts it, "nicht als der Wandernde, der heute kommt und morgen geht, sondern als der, der heute kommt und morgen bleibt"[19] is not part of the environment within which he moves and works; he is potentially always on the move, but stays for the time being and has social claims to make. Paradoxically the "stranger" is part of the common daily routine within the host society, but he is always potentially sidetracking the whole system – and it is exactly this quality that shapes the way he is perceived by the majority of people. It is his "objectivity" which frightens his environment, a quality which potentially calls whole social systems into doubt.

The adventurer as the second prototype of modernity reminiscent of the picaresque experience is marked by the paradoxical approach to life with which he establishes a relation of "Notwendigkeit" (necessity) between coincidence (the product of fragmentisation) and anonymity (the product of acceleration). It is his art of incorporating coincidences into the context of his particular situation as "necessary," i.e. driven by an internal logic not accessible to the public, that makes him appear uncanny and eccentric. By doing so he masters the unexpected as something that appears expectable, yet never is, and transcends mere idiosyncrasy. This reinstates the original meaning of the German word "not-wendig"[20]:

> When the professional adventurer makes a system of life out of his life's lack of system, when out of his inner necessity he seeks the naked, external accidents and builds them into that necessity, he only, so to speak, makes macroscopically visible that which is the essential form of every adventure', even that of the non-adventurous person. For by adventure we always mean a third something, neither the sheer, abrupt event whose meaning – a mere given – simply remains outside us nor the consistent sequence of life in which every element supplements every other toward an inclusively integrated meaning.[21]

Simmel's concept of the "adventure" describes a quintessentially modern experience in an environment of acceleration, rapid social change and the dictate of fashion. It neither represents the absolutely exceptional and unexpected event nor is it an integral part of the daily routine; it rather constitutes a third configuration outside this binary context, a configuration which is dependent on the perpetuation of the disintegration and recreation of the very binarity it undercuts. Modernity creates its own type of events, and the adventurer is the one who assembles them in a tentative order that is coherent with a system which seems to be a natural part of his identity, yet is only part of his art of adjustment to society.

The modern pícaro as adventurer in Simmel's sense exposes himself to an unconditional presence of reality by imposing his own conditions onto it. He both totalises a perspective and marks this perspective as insufficient and tentative, in order to lay certain claims on the society. In the way the grotesque body is imagined and used in Edgar Hilsenrath's work, one can observe a similar vacillation of singularisation and totalisation. In Hilsenrath, the elements of the grotesque and the comic transcend the protagonists' affinity to the epistemological position of Simmel's categories. Insofar as Hilsenrath is indebted to the epistemological setting Simmel analyses, he pitches it against the experience of the Shoah as both a continuation of certain features of modernisation processes[22] and absolute failure and reversal of civilisation.

2. The neopicaresque and the grotesque
A. The grotesque as a category of reception

The blasphemous attempt of Hilsenrath to conflate the ghastly barbarism of the Shoah with what many Westerners embrace as their genuine tradition, the self-made man, adaptable to rapidly and radically changing circumstances, is reflected in the incompatibility of the terrible historical backdrop and the ease with which the protagonist manoeuvres through his picaresque adventures, the casualness of the narrative tone and the vastness of the grotesque imagery. It is exactly this grotesque ulcer of imagination that inhabits the paradoxical interface between horror and the psychological triviality of survival strategies. It undercuts the notion of a possible distinction between order and non-order, between the orderly, obedient life of an average citizen and the crimes of the genocide. The grotesque is, however, not a way out of the predicament of having to live and cope with and tentatively even reconcile the "evil" and readily available concepts of "normality." It is not a monstrous exaggeration which pastes everything over with the label of nausea and world-weariness by establishing a new mode of communicability between radical opposites, but rather establishes a new dialectic within a field hitherto regarded as too disparate to allow for any kind of dialectical fathoming. This mode of communication between implied narrator, fictitious narrator and a multiplicity of implied readers introduces the notion of the grotesque as an art of creating specific modes of reader response and drawing on certain scopes of expectation and deliberately disappointing them:

> The grotesque is not concerned with fear of death but with fear of life. Part of the structure of the grotesque is the failure of our categories of orientation within the world [...] demons break into our daily lives. As soon as we can name these powers and ascribe a place within the cosmic order to them, the grotesque would lose part of his nature.[23]

The grotesque is not predominantly defined as a literary or rhetorical device but as a form of experiencing and structuring the world. Not only is it not a rendition of what the world looks like once deprived of all its disguises and deluding veils, it also does not provide a unifying principle for reconciling the poles of horror and the ease with which humans lead their lives. That is to say, the grotesque is not a hermetically sealed realm of mannerist imagination but a mode of continuous refusal of epistemological reconciliation. It does not establish a coherent fictitious world, but rather a perpetual incentive to engage in questioning the modes of representation of this very world. Pietzker defined the grotesque as a "structure of how we perceive things consciously."[24]

The grotesque in literature is an art of exposure to the uncanny by juxtaposing the horrors of human history and human psyche and its triviality, and thereby rooting the two in one another. The readers are perpetually disappointed in their interpretative anticipations of the narrative and its epistemological foundation. The excess of the grotesque and its semiosis dispels the spell reality casts over the horror. The readers' confrontation with this excessive semiosis and its embeddedness in the constant inversion of the narrative structure explicated above create an unbridgeable gap between reality and imagination which makes an anticipatory reader response impossible. The effect is a growing sense of the unbearable character of reality. The topography the characters of Hilsenrath are passing through is Europe as a huge "Grove of the Six Million," as the Shoah memorial which Max/Itzig helps initiate in Israel is aptly called.

All grotesque traditions are based on the fundamental principles of distortion and alienation through mingling disparate and heterogeneous parts, for example organic with anorganic, animal with human, mechanical with living. They are fundamentally marked by the fact that the unexpected preys on what is conventionalised as reality and is not perceived as something completely alien although it has an alienating, if not destructive impact on that very reality. Its main characteristic is the *mundus inversus* topic. The grotesque turns the ghastly into the ridiculous, and the ridiculous into the ghastly and thereby develops its potential to the full. The reader response is automatically ambiguous, even contradictory; it vacillates between fascination and revulsion. Grotesqueness is defined as the intrusion upon a realm of normative reality without causing a phenomenological clash. In *Lazarillo*, for example, the intrusion of the grotesque is not perceived as a clash of realms of reality, yet it is also not a mere rhetorical strategy of hyperbole. Ambiguity in *Lazarillo* is due to the position of the narrator and his ludistic approach to finding rhetorical analogies for his past. Thomsen[25] considers this rhetoric and the contrast it creates with the dismal depravity of the social situation as "grotesque." But the use of rhetoric as such does not suffice to term it "grotesque," it is the type of implied reader created by this kind of rhetoric and how this role is moulded to fit into the reality of the grotesque which establishes the grotesque as an artistic device.

As opposed to the fantastic, the grotesque is not a specific situation but the human condition itself. The fantastic is the intruder of something alien into a narrative realm and forms an antagonism. The grotesque is an alien intruder, too, but it does not cause surprise in the fictitious characters affected. It is inextricably intertwined with the category of the abject. Anne Fuchs has shown that the abject as a "space of anxiety" is a paradigmatic coordinate in German-Jewish literature in the 20th century from Freud's "drama of abjection"[26] *Der Mann Moses und die monotheistische Religion* to Hilsenrath, whose protagonists often drift through "a space of anxiety where their alienation from the outer world is matched by a sense of self-abjection."[27] Hilsenrath's grotesque and obsessive rendition of the abject finds a particular outlet in the grotesque imagery of the female as either a fat monster or a witch-like ugly old hag,[28] both of whom seduce and threaten male identity. The mutual interdependence of virility and castration-fear throughout the novel and its grotesque rendition in the form of phobic fantasies is tied in with the grotesque imagery of the human body on the battlefields and in the camps as abject, dismembered and disjoint from any kind of organic coherence or structure of growth.

B. The grotesque as the political unconscious

Hilsenrath pushes the picaresque genre and its ingenuity with regard to political imagination to its extremes by turning the topic of Jewish assimilation with German culture into Max Schulz's mimicry of a model Jew.[29] The picaresque double perspective is transformed into the double narrative of the perverse self-assertion of the perpetrator of mass murders and the victim's voice by virtue of the grotesque imagery of self-debasement. The voice of the grotesque undermines Max-Itzig's mimicry of identification and illusion of absolute shape-shifting. Fuchs states:

> Whereas, after Freud, identification usurps the place of identity, in Hilsenrath's post-Shoah world, camouflage replaces both identity and identification. Hilsenrath's novel is thus the modern version of another fairy-tale: that of the wolf in sheep's clothing.[30]

Leslie Fiedler has asserted that "[g]rotesque art presents us not with the world as we know it to be, but with the world as we fear it might be."[31] The evil becomes banal, since the reader realises that it is at the heart of many deep-rooted psychological, social and political "realities." The subversion of reason this art of the grotesque evokes in the readers is based on the all-encompassing consistency of grotesque imagination within the novel. In *Der Nazi und der Friseur* Max/Itzig points at this technique of coalescing concepts of the real and the grotesque in an aside addressed to the reader:

> I know what you're saying, "Max Schulz is going off his rocker! A nightmare! Nothing but a nightmare!"
> But why do you insist on that? Is it not true that God invented innocence in order to have it trampled in the mud [...] here on earth? And is it not true that the weak and defenceless are always trodden upon by the strong, clubbed to the ground, raped, despised, buggered? And at times in certain periods simply done away with? Is that not so? And if it is so [...] why is it that you maintain that Max Schulz is going off his rocker?[32]

Apart from an indirect defence of the literary grotesque this passage also offers a doubleness of perspectives reminiscent of *Lazarillo*. Hilsenrath plays with the perspective of the young innocent Max and his naïve view of human society. Apart from the typically neo-picaresque topic of the exchangeability of world and lunatic asylum, this passage also shows a submerged voice which demonstrates the uncanny innocence of the grotesque. The sentence "Zu gewissen Zeiten sogar einfach beseitigt?" fits perfectly well into the naïve tone of the whole passage, but it also renders the infiltration of language by what Victor Klemperer derisively called "Lingua Tertii Imperii" (LTI): "beseitigen," "to remove," stands euphemistically for "to exterminate" and was a typical Nazi term. As the quote from the Sermon on the Mount silently crept into Lazarillo's account of his childhood, this linguistic splinter turns the naïve perspective upside down without invalidating it. Concurrently these two voices orchestrate the art of the grotesque in Hilsenrath's novel.[33]

By reduplicating the horror in an implied reader who is oscillating between sympathising with and despising the protagonist, between terror and complicity with the day-to-day-life shrewdness of Max-Itzig, between tentative models of explanation and total dismissal of any form of interpretation, the novel manages to create an implied reader who cannot come to grips with the past, who does not pretend to indulge in "Vergangenheitsbewältigung." One example has to suffice to illustrate this:

> I was convinced my mother was right and Germany's future would not in any event be brown, and would be black. And so I too chose black. A few weeks after the liquidation of the great brown bear, I, Itzig Finkelstein, at that time still Max Schulz, decided to have myself transferred to the SS. I also gave up my membership in the Association for the Prevention of Cruelty to Animals. I, Itzig Finkelstein, at that time still Max Schulz, had made a choice.
> My former teacher Siegfried von Salzstange said to me once: "Max Schulz. Everybody who can fart can get into the brown SA. But not into the SS!"
> Because the SS, that was the union of the "Black Puritans," the elite of the new Germany. For mice like Max Schulz, who did not look like superman, but like the inferior mortals [...] yes, that's what they looked like, really, no joking [...] who looked as though they would not be able to understand the ethics of genocide [...] never understand it [...] for them admission to the SS was anything but easy.[34]

Even a passage like this one, which is not particularly marked by the otherwise typical excess of physical monstrosity, is a collation of different dimensions of grotesque transgressions: the grotesque of the identity swap of murderer and victim, the monstrosity of petit bourgeois fear of life, the perversity of the fact that Max-Itzig's career path is just yet another example of Hannah Arendt's "banality of evil." Hilsenrath made his novel an extensive footnote to Arendt's controversial reflections on the psychology of Nazi Germany in general and SS crimes in particular.

3.   **Conclusion: The grotesque as an interface between the Real and the Ideal – the notion of humour**

The grotesque is always based on some degree of plausibility when it comes to creating a fictitious reality. It does not draw on the notion of a latent, subconscious reality, it works in radical changes, in shifts between the poles of idiosyncratic mimetic detail reconstruction and deliberate distortion. It always takes its plausibility of presenting reality for granted, which makes the grotesque narrative a particularly appropriate example of the extreme violation which the Aristotelian *dýnaton* (the apt, the probable) can tolerate without completely abandoning the notion of 'reality'. The uncommented juxtaposition and inextricable interweaving of petit bourgeois milieu and mentality and national socialist mind-set incites contradictory reactions within the reader; from time to time the reader is wooed into a kind of complicity.

Yielding autonomy to the grotesque realms of imagination is a means of ludistic imagination which both postpones the inexplicability of the horror and simultaneously pokes fun at the vain attempts to find an appropriate narrative frame for telling the terror. At this point Hilsenrath meets with Tabori in the way they refer to German romantic notions of "Humor." Jean Paul's notion of "Humor" as the "umgekehrte Erhabene" (the inverted sublime) can be treated as one of the first modern concepts of the grotesque. It revolves around the idea that humorous contempt for life enables humans to overcome their "mechanical determinism" and triggers laughter in ever more rapid changes of perspectives. For Jean Paul, the encounter between the fragmentary Real and the holistic Ideal leads to mutual deconstruction:

> Humour, as the inverted sublime, does not destroy the individual but the finite thing by contrasting it with the idea. Humour does not know foolish acts or fools; it only knows foolishness and the world as a foolish entity. It does not focus on and single out little foolish acts but humiliates the "great." However, he does this – unlike parody – in

order to juxtapose it with the "small," and he lifts up the
"small" – unlike irony – in order to juxtapose the "small"
and the "great." The overall effect is the destruction of
both, since nothing can last in the face of infinity. [35]

For Tabori and Hilsenrath, too, the fragmentary Real makes the
Ideal splinter into ideologies. As Tabori put it:

> Humour   is   no   laughing   matter.   [...]   Genuine
> commemoration [of the past] is only possible as a sensual
> commemoration [...] It is impossible to come to grips with
> the past without re-experiencing it with our skin, tongue,
> nose, feet, belly.[36]

In the course of the secularisation of the supernatural, the grotesque
as form and epistemological category becomes paradigmatic for the subject-
object rift in modernity. As a means of communication between implied
author and *lector in fabula* it creates an uncanny translatability and
commensurability of grotesque linguistic devices, grotesque imagination and
grotesque forms of dissociation: subject vs. object, simulation vs.
dissimulation, narrated vs. narrating Ego. This dissociation is most manifest
in Hilsenrath's novel in the fourth chapter. The new Itzig is writing letters to
the old Itzig and tells anew the story with which the reader is already
familiar:

> Can you hear me, Itzig? And can you see me? Come! Play
> with me! Look for me! Where am I? Where did I hide
> myself?[37]

"Play with me!" – that is the characteristic trait of the lunatic
communication of Itzig/Max with himself and his dead *doppelgänger*. It is no
laughing matter, but it creates both complicit and critical readers who
inadvertently discover themselves entangled in the grotesque yarn of the
pícaro. This in turn reminds us of the inevitability of contradictions in how
humans remember and commemorate the past.

Notes

[1] Alan Sillitoe. *The mentality of the picaresque hero*. London: Turret Bookshop, 1993, 5.

[2] Claudio Guillén. *Literature as System: Essays toward the theory of literary history*. Princeton: Princeton University Press, 1971, 79.

[3] Guillén 1971, 78.

[4] Dahrendorf, Ralf. "Homo Sociologicus. Ein Versuch zur Geschichte, Bedeutung und Kritik der Kategorie der sozialen Rolle." In: *Kölner Zeitschrift für Soziologie und Sozialpsychologie*, part 1 in 10/2, 1958, 188-208: 194.

[5] Ralf Dahrendorf. "Homo Sociologicus. Ein Versuch zur Geschichte, Bedeutung und Kritik der Kategorie der sozialen Rolle." In: *Kölner Zeitschrift für Soziologie und Sozialpsychologie*, part 2 in 10/3, 1958, 345-350: 346.

[6] Dahrendorf 1958, 348.

[7] E.g. Melville, Mann; Grass, Hilsenrath, Barth, Bellow, Heller, Pynchon, Kosinski, Sigal, Matthews.

[8] Anon. *The Life of Lazarillo de Tormes*. English translation by David Rowland. Warminster: Aris & Phillips, 2000, 161. "En el cual el día de hoy vivo y resido a servicio de Dios y de Vuestra Merced. Y es que tengo cargo de pregonar los vins que en esta ciudad se venden, y en almonedas, y cosas perdidas, acompañar los que padecen persecuciones por justicia y declarar a voces sus delictos : pregonero, hablando en buen romance." Anon. [Alfonso de Valdéz] *Lazarillo de Tormes*. Ed. by Francisco Rico. Madrid: Catedra, 1987, 129.

[9] Cf. Christian W. Thomsen. "Aspekte des Grotesken im *Lazarillo de Tormes*," in: *Das Groteske in der Dichtung*, edited by Otto F. Best. 179-95. Darmstadt: Wissenschaftliche Buchgesellschaft, 1980, 183.

[10] *Lazarillo* 2000, 57. "Pues siendo yo niño de ocho años, achacaron a mi padre ciertas sangrías mal hechas en los costales de los que allí a moler venían, por lo cual fue preso, y confesó y no negó, y padeció persecución por justicia. Espero en Dios que está en la gloria, pues el Evangelio los llama bienaventurados." *Lazarillo* 1987, 14.

[11] Cf. Matthias Bauer. *Der Schelmenroman*. Stuttgart: Metzler, 1994, chapter 1.

[12] Translation B.M. "Was ist das – eine andere Identität?" "Wenn sich einer verwandelt", sagte Max Schulz. "So wie ein Zauberkünstler", sagte Frau Holle. "So ähnlich", sagte Max Schulz. Edgar Hilsenrath. *Der Nazi und der Friseur*. Munich: Piper, 1990, 83. The English version is different and not in

dialogue form, cf. Edgar Hilsenrath. *The Nazi and the Barber*. London: WH Allen, 1975, 81.

[13] Hilsenrath 1975, 162. "Schade, dass Du den jüdischen Schwarzhändler nie kennengelernt hast! Itzig Finkelstein in Berlin. Itzig Finkelstein [...] der mit dem schwarzen Mercedes. Das war ne Type sag ich Dir. Den haben sie aus dem Stürmer ausgeschnitten." Hilsenrath 1990, 176.

[14] Hilsenrath 1975, 302.

[15] Cf. Peter Stenberg. "'Ich habe Dich einen kleinen Augenblick verlassen.' Edgar Hilsenrath und der abwesende Gott." In: *Edgar Hilsenrath. Das Unsichtbare erzählen*, edited by Thomas Kraft. 178-90. Munich – Zurich: Piper, 1996, 185-7.

[16] The topic of madness is also an interesting comment on what has been aptly labelled Jewish self-hatred in Western culture. The claim of "the pseudoscience of nineteenth- and early twentieth-century racist biology" (Sander L. Gilman. *Jewish Self-Hatred. Anti-Semitism and the Hidden Language of the Jews*. Baltimore: Johns Hopkins University Press, 1986, 361) that Jews were more prone to neurasthenia and "madness" is inverted in Hilsenrath into a story oscillating between the narrative possibilities of either the epitome of an Aryan German gone mad or a Jew turned mad by the deportations. The complexity of the narrative perspective picks up on the collective stereotype equating madness and Jewish self-hatred in German Anti-Semitism (ibid., 290-1, 368). Max-Itzig can also be read as a grotesque rendition of Jewish self-hatred gone mad or as an extreme form of seeking atonement from the survivor guilt by acting out the fantasies of bad conscience of the perpetrators. Both of these interpretations would illustrate Gilman's thesis of Jewish self-hatred as a "double-bind model of identification and projection" (ibid., 392).

[17] Georg Simmel. *Gesammelte Werke Band 11: Soziologie. Untersuchungen über die Formen der Vergesellschaftung*, edited by Otthein Rammstedt. Frankfurt/Main: Suhrkamp, 1992, 764-71.

[18] Georg Simmel. *Philosophische Kultur*. Leipzig: Kröner, 1919, 7-24. Cf. also *Gesamtausgabe* vol. 14. Edited by Rüdiger Kramme and Otthein Rammstedt. 168-86. Frankfurt: Suhrkamp 1996.

[19] Simmel 1992, 764.

[20] 'capable of changing hardship', 'beneficial'

[21] Georg Simmel. *Simmel on Culture. Selected Writings*, edited by David Frisby & Mike Featherstone. London: Sage, 1997, 224-5. Cf. the original in Simmel 1919, 11.

[22] Cf. Zygmunt Bauman. *Modernity and the Holocaust*. Cambridge: Polity, 1989; Zygmunt Bauman. *Modernity and Ambivalence*. Cambridge: Polity, 1991, chapters 4+5

²³ Wolfgang Kayser. *Das Groteske*. Oldenburg: Stalling, 1957, 135f. (translation B.M.)
²⁴ Carl Pietzker. "Das Groteske." In: *Das Groteske in der Dichtung*, edited by Otto F. Best. 85-102. Darmstadt: Wissenschaftliche Buchgesellschaft, 1980, 88 ("Struktur eines Bewusstseinsaktes").
²⁵ Cf. Thomsen 1980.
²⁶ Anne Fuchs. *A Space of Anxiety. Dislocation and Abjection in Modern German-Jewish Literature*. Amsterdam: Rodopi, 1999, 177.
²⁷ Fuchs 1999, 178.
²⁸ On the history of the 'ugly old woman' in Latin and German aesthetic theory cf. Winfried Menninghaus. *Ekel. Theorie und Geschichte einer starken Empfindung*. Frankfurt/Main: Suhrkamp, 1999, 132-43.
²⁹ Cf. Fuchs 1999, 170, with reference to Homi Bhabha. *Locations of Culture*. London: Routledge, 1994, 85-92.
³⁰ Fuchs 1999, 171.
³¹ Fiedler, Leslie. *Freaks: myths and images of the secret self*. Harmondworth: Penguin, 1981, 11.
³² Hilsenrath 1975, 19. "Ich weiß, was Sie sagen: 'Max Schulz spinnt! Ein Alptraum! Nichts weiter!' Aber warum behaupten Sie das? Hat der liebe Gott nicht die Unschuld erfunden, damit sie zertreten wird [...] hier auf Erden? Und werden die Schwachen und Wehrlosen nicht von den Starken überrumpelt, niedergeknüppelt, vergewaltigt, verhöhnt, in den Arsch gefickt? Zu gewissen Zeiten sogar einfach beseitigt? Ist es nicht so? Und wenn es so ist [...] warum behaupten Sie dann, dass Max Schulz spinnt?" Hilsenrath 1990, 19.
³³ This hidden quote of Nazi language in Max/Itzig's monologue is a subtle inversion of the alleged hidden language of the Jews which had developed into an obsession in German-speaking societies by the 19th century and was closely associated either with Yiddish or mauscheln, i.e. speaking German with a Yiddish intonation. Hilsenrath turns this around and plays with the idea of language as an indicator of identity, be it racial or psychological. Cf. Gilman, *Jewish Self-Hatred*, 76f.
³⁴ Hilsenrath 1975, 48. "Ich war überzeugt, dass meine Mutter recht behalten und dass Deutschlands Zukunft auf keinen Fall braun, sondern Schwarz sein würde. Ich wählte also Schwarz. Einige Wochen nach der Liquidierung des "Großen Braunen" beschloss ich, Itzig Finkelstein, damals noch Max Schulz, mich zur SS versetzen zu lassen. Ich trat auch aus dem Tierschutzverein aus. Ich, Itzig Finkelstein, damals noch Max Schulz, hatte gewählt. Mein ehemaliger Deutschlehrer Siegfried von Salzstange, hatte einmal zu mir gesagt: "Max Schulz. In der braunen SA findet jeder Platz, der richtig furzen kann. Aber nicht in der SS!" – Denn die SS, das war der Verband der

schwarzen Puritaner, die Elite des Neuen Deutschland. Für Mäuschen wie den Max Schulz, die nicht wie Herrenmenschen aussahen, sondern wie Untermenschen [...] genau so und nicht anders [...] eben so aussahen, als ob sie die Ethik des Völkermordes nicht kapieren würden [...] gar nicht kapieren [...] für die war der Eintritt in die SS alles andere als leicht." Hilsenrath 1990, 58f.

[35] Cf. Jean Paul. *Vorschule der Ästhetik. Levana oder Erziehlehre*. Munich: Hanser, 1973, § 32 "Humoristische Totalität" (translation B.M.) "Der Humor, als das umgekehrte Erhabene, vernichtet nicht das Einzelne, sondern das Endliche durch den Kontrast mit der Idee. Es gibt für ihn keine einzelne Torheit, keine Toren, sondern nur Torheit und eine tolle Welt; er hebt [...] keine einzelne Narrheit heraus, sondern er erniedrigt das Große, aber – ungleich der Parodie – um ihm das Kleine, und erhöhet das Kleine, aber – ungleich der Ironie – um ihm das Große an die Seite zu setzen und so beide zu vernichten, weil vor der Unendlichkeit alles gleich ist und nichts."

[36] Cf. Georg Tabori. *Unterammergau oder Die Guten Deutschen*. Frankfurt/Main: Suhrkamp,1981, 202.

[37] Hilsenrath 1975, 158. "Kannst Du mich hören, Itzig? Und kannst Du mich sehen? Komm! Spiel mit mir! Wo bin ich? Wo hab ich mich versteckt?" Hilsenrath 1990, 173.

Bibliography

Anon. [Alfonso de Valdéz] *Lazarillo de Tormes*. Ed. by Francisco Rico. Madrid: Catedra, 1987.

—. *The Life of Lazarillo de Tormes*. English translation by David Rowland. Warminster: Aris & Phillips, 2000.

Hilsenrath, Edgar. *The Nazi and the Barber*. London: WH Allen, 1975.

—. *Der Nazi und der Friseur*. Munich: Piper, 1990.

Paul, Jean. *Vorschule der Ästhetik. Levana oder Erziehlehre*. Munich: Hanser, 1973.

Bauer, Matthias. *Der Schelmenroman*. Stuttgart: Metzler, 1994.

Bauman, Zygmunt. *Modernity and the Holocaust*. Cambridge: Polity, 1989.

—. *Modernity and Ambivalence*. Cambridge: Polity, 1991.

Bhabha, Homi. *Locations of Culture*. London: Routledge, 1994.

Dahrendorf, Ralf. "Homo Sociologicus. Ein Versuch zur Geschichte, Bedeutung und Kritik der Kategorie der sozialen Rolle." *Kölner Zeitschrift für Soziologie und Sozialpsychologie*, part 1 in 10/2 (1958): 188-208, part 2 in 10/3 (1958): 345-350

Fiedler, Leslie. *Freaks: myths and images of the secret self*. Harmondworth:

Penguin, 1981.

Fuchs, Anne. *A Space of Anxiety. Dislocation and Abjection in Modern German-Jewish Literature.* Amsterdam: Rodopi, 1999.

Gilman, Sander L. *Jewish Self-Hatred. Anti-Semitism and the Hidden Language of the Jews.* Baltimore: Johns Hopkins University Press, 1986.

Goffman, Erving: *The Presentation of Self in Everyday Life.* London: Allen Lane, 1969.

Guillén, Claudio. *Literature as System: Essays toward the theory of literary history.* Princeton: Princeton University Press, 1971.

Kayser, Wolfgang. *Das Groteske.* Oldenburg: Stalling, 1957.

Kraft, Thomas (ed.). *Edgar Hilsenrath. Das Unsichtbare erzählen.* Munich: Piper, 1996.

Menninghaus, Winfried. *Ekel. Theorie und Geschichte einer starken Empfindung.* Frankfurt/Main: Suhrkamp, 1999.

Pietzker, Carl. "Das Groteske." In: *Das Groteske in der Dichtung*, edited by Otto F. Best, 85-102. Darmstadt: Wissenschaftliche Buchgesellschaft, 1980.

Preisendanz, Wolfgang. "Humor als Rolle." In *Identität*, edited by Odo Marquard and Karlheinz Stierle, 423-34. Munich: Fink, 1979.

Sillitoe, Alan. *The mentality of the picaresque hero.* London: Turret Bookshop, 1993.

Simmel, Georg. *Philosophische Kultur.* Leipzig: Kröner, 1919.

---. *Gesammelte Werke Band 11: Soziologie. Untersuchungen über die Formen der Vergesellschaftung*, edited by Otthein Rammstedt. Frankfurt am Main: Suhrkamp, 1992.

Simmel, Georg: *Simmel on Culture. Selected Writings*, edited by David Frisby and Mike Featherstone. London: Sage, 1997.

Stenberg, Peter. "'Ich habe Dich einen kleinen Augenblick verlassen.' Edgar Hilsenrath und der abwesende Gott." In *Edgar Hilsenrath. Das Unsichtbare erzählen*, edited by Thomas Kraft, 178-90. Munich and Zurich: Piper, 1996.

Tabori, Georg. *Unterammergau oder Die Guten Deutschen.* Frankfurt am Main: Suhrkamp, 1981.

Thomsen, Christian W. "Aspekte des Grotesken im *Lazarillo de Tormes*." In *Das Groteske in der Dichtung*, edited by Otto F. Best, 179-95. Darmstadt: Wissenschaftliche Buchgesellschaft, 1980.

Notes on Contributors

David Robb is a Senior Lecturer in the School of Languages, Literatures and Performing Arts at the Queen's University of Belfast. He developed an interest in theatrical clowning while researching his PhD on the East Berlin cabaret duo Wenzel & Mensching, who integrated aspects of *commedia dell'arte* into their political song act. David Robb's book *Zwei Clowns im Lande des verlorenen Lachens: Das Liedertheater Wenzel & Mensching* was published in 1998. He is a specialist in German political song and has recently published the book *Protest Song in East and West Germany since the 1960s*. He is also an experienced songwriter and performing musician.

Robert Cheesmond graduated in Drama in 1969, and began a career as a professional theatre director and designer. He joined the Drama Department at the University of Hull in 1974, initially as Stage Director, now Lecturer in Drama. He has directed, designed and acted in many professional and University productions, including eight classic operas. His principal research interests are English Pantomime and Scenography. He was a founder member and sometime convenor of the Scenography Working Group of the International Federation for Theatre Research, and has organised conferences and given papers in Prague, Moscow, Krakow, Canterbury and Puebla, Mexico.

Dr Faye Ran is a Professor of Literature, Media and Cultural Studies, and an art curator. She has a PhD from Columbia University in English and Comparative Literature, and a PhD in Media Ecology: Culture & Communications from New York University. Dr Ran, a former Fulbright Scholar in Theatre, AFI Screenwriting Fellow, and Goodman Award winner has as producer/writer/director produced over 100 plays, films/videos, and multimedia productions on Off-Off Broadway and at international festivals. She has also curated over 150 art exhibitions. Her book, *The Tragicomic Passion*, is a history and analysis of tragicomedy and tragicomic characterisation in drama, film and literature.

Ashley Tobias is a specialist in Theatre and Theatre-in-Education. He did his PhD on *The Postmodern Theatre Clown* in theatre studies at Tel Aviv University. He is a Lecturer and theatre-teacher trainer in the School for Education at the Hebrew University, Jerusalem. He runs drama workshops and lectures at the David Yellin College, Jerusalem; Kerem Institute for Teacher Training, Jerusalem and the Kibbutzim College of Education in Tel Aviv. Dr.

Tobias is Head of Theatre Studies at the Nissui High School, Jerusalem. He is also a director of youth theatre and an actor trainer.

Rüdiger Görner is Professor of German and Founding Director of the Centre for Anglo-German Cultural Relations at Queen Mary College, University of London. From 1991-2004 he was Reader and Professor of German at Aston University in Birmingham. From 1999-2004 he was Director of the Institute of Germanic Studies, University of London. His recent publications include *Ecce Opus. Nietzsche-Revisionen im 20. Jahrhundert*, edited with Duncan Large (2003); *Rainer Maria Rilke. Im Herzwerk der Sprache* (2004) and *Thomas Mann. Der Zauber des Letzten* (2005)

Maxim Weintraub is a doctoral candidate and Whiting Foundation Fellow at Bryn Mawr College in the department of History of Art, and is currently completing his dissertation on the art of Bruce Nauman. Max currently lives and works in New York City.

Barbara Lewis, Associate Professor, is the Director of the William Monroe Trotter Institute for the Study of Black Culture at the University of Massachusetts-Boston, where she holds a joint appointment in the Department of Africana Studies and English. As a theatre historian, she has published on lynching and performance, minstrelsy, and the black arts movement of the sixties. As a playwright, her work has been presented at festivals and on professional stages in New York, New Jersey, and Toronto, Canada. As a Francophone scholar, she co-translated Faulkner, Mississippi by Edouard Glissant, which was published by Farrar, Straus & Giroux (1999).

Kayode Kofoworola is an editor, poet, critic and teacher. He holds BA and MA degrees in English Literature and Literature from Ahmadu Bello University, Zaria. His areas of interest include Translation Studies, Pyschoanalytic literature, African and Carribean Literature, Madness in Literature, Comedy, Cultural Studies and African-American literature. He is a member of some professional bodies and has some publications to his credit. In addition, he has attended and presented papers at some international conferences. He is presently a Lecturer at the Lagos City Polytechnic, Ikeja Lagos.

Ron Jenkins specialises in cross cultural investigations of comic traditions. The translator and director of numerous plays by Dario Fo, Jenkins is the author of *Artful Laughter: Dario Fo & Franca Rame* (Aperture, 2001). He holds a doctorate from Harvard University and a master's degree in buffoonery from the Ringling Brothers Clown College. His research has been supported by Fellowships from the Watson Foundation, the Danforth Foundation, the Asian Cultural Council, and the Guggenheim Foundation. Special support for this article came from the Nordic Institute for Asian Studies in Copenhagen.

Dr Stephen Knapper is a Lecturer in Drama at Kingston University. A co-founder of a small scale touring theatre company, The Red Noses, he trained with Jacques Lecoq in Paris and performed in cabaret, on television and the streets of Naples. He has written three articles on Complicite and is currently preparing his doctoral study on the mask of Scaramouche for publication.

Des O'Rawe holds a Ph.D. in English from Queen's University where he currently lectures in Film Studies. He is interested in the relations between cinema and theatre, particularly within the context of modernism. Recent essays have appeared in Literature/Film Quarterly, Screen, Screening the Past, and he has also published on Irish literary, visual and political culture.

Marina Kotzamani is an Assistant Professor in the Theater Department of the University of the Peloponnese, in Greece. She has published articles on modern productions of classical Greek drama, as well as on modern Greek theater and film. Other recent work on Aristophanes includes "Lysistrata Joins the Soviet Revolution: Aristophanes as Engaged Theater," in *Rebel Women. Staging Ancient Greek Drama Today* (2005); "Citizen artists on the web: the Lysistrata Project Theater" (March 06) and "Lysistrata on the Arab Stage PAJ" (May 06). Dr. Kotzamani has also collaborated as a dramaturg and translator with professional companies in New York City, including CSC and LaMama.

Stephen M. Llano is a Doctoral student in the Department of Communication, University of Pittsburgh. He has an MA in Communication and Rhetorical Studies from Syracuse University. He is working on a dissertation project examining the writings of the Beat Generation and their rhetorical definition of American identity. He wishes to thank Dr. James Janack of Syracuse University for advice and critique on the included chapter.

Bernhard F. Malkmus studied modern languages, English and social sciences at the Universities of Würzburg, Cambridge and Konstanz. He has held teaching and research fellowships at the Charles University, Prague and at Harvard University. He is currently Lektor and Director of Studies for German and supervisor for English literature at Pembroke College, Cambridge. He is also a PhD student at Cambridge University, working on a project on modern picaresque fiction.

Printed in the United Kingdom
by Lightning Source UK Ltd.
125632UK00001B/5/A